BOX OFFICE POISON

HOLLYWOOD'S STORY
IN A CENTURY OF FLOPS

BOX
OFFICE
POISON

TIM ROBEY

faber

First published in 2024
by Faber & Faber Limited
The Bindery, 51 Hatton Garden
London EC1N 8HN

Typeset by Typo•glyphix, Burton-on-Trent, DE14 3HE
Printed and bound by CPI Group (UK) Ltd, Croydon, CR0 4YY

A CIP record for this book
is available from the British Library

ISBN 978–0–571–38120–3

MIX
Paper | Supporting
responsible forestry
FSC® C171272

Printed and bound in the UK on FSC® certified paper in line with our continuing
commitment to ethical business practices, sustainability and the environment.
For further information see faber.co.uk/environmental-policy

2 4 6 8 10 9 7 5 3

For Michael Comber

CONTENTS

Preface 1

Intolerance (1916) 7
Queen Kelly (1929) 17
Freaks (1932) 27
Sylvia Scarlett (1935) 39
The Magnificent Ambersons (1942) 49
Land of the Pharaohs (1955) 59
Doctor Dolittle (1967) 69
Sorcerer (1977) 81
Dune (1984) 93
The Adventures of Baron Munchausen (1988) 107
Nothing But Trouble (1991) 119
The Hudsucker Proxy (1994) 131
Cutthroat Island (1995) 141
Speed 2: Cruise Control (1997) 153
Babe: Pig in the City (1998) 163
Supernova (2000) 175
Rollerball (2002) 185
The Adventures of Pluto Nash (2002) 197
Gigli (2003) 207
Catwoman (2004) 219
Alexander (2004) 229
A Sound of Thunder (2005) 241
Speed Racer (2008) 251
Synecdoche, New York (2008) 261

Pan (2015)   271

Cats (2019)   283

Afterword   295

Acknowledgements   299

Bibliography   301

Notes   305

Image credits   317

Index   321

PREFACE

Histories of studio film-making have a habit of skimming over the disasters – those moments of doomed expenditure that pull the curtain back on what the culture was thinking. As in: what the hell were they *thinking?*

Failure fascinates, though, for all the reasons that sure-fire success is a drag. Merely log the highest-grossing films of a given decade, the Best Picture winners, and so forth, and you're telling only a flattering fraction of the Hollywood story. You could also argue that the only genuinely interesting financial successes, in the world of cinema, are the ones no one saw coming.

James Cameron's *Titanic* (1997) was widely tipped to be a fiasco, and left every box office record in its wake. *The Blair Witch Project* (1999) was made for peanuts by a bunch of film students no one had ever heard of. Those are extreme cases – arguably the two most extreme – of beating the odds. The vast majority of hits, in an industry notoriously averse to betting on anything other than proven certainties, fall into neither category.

Films that flop exorbitantly are the flipside to that norm, and thereby reveal a lot. Before their downfall, they were often dreamed up erroneously as sure things, by some backstage calculus derived from everything box office is meant to teach us – in terms of popular taste, demographic reach, star power, genre favouritism.

Harshly exposing the flaws in that business model, the saga of an archetypal flop has everything. Escalating budgets. Clashing egos. Acts of God. It's far more compelling to read the story of an out-of-control *Gigli* (2003) than a machine-tooled megahit like *Avengers:*

Infinity War (2018). This isn't just because the prospect of a block-buster crashing and burning attracts our instincts for rubbernecking, but because flops themselves can be such durably interesting artefacts.

They're the medium's weirdos, outcasts, misfits, freaks. They can be reappropriated after the event as camp treats; they can linger, Ozymandias-like, as monuments to studio hubris, hobbled and crumbling; or they can electrify decades later for reasons of genuine artistry, as misunderstood, radical, ahead of their time.

All of these categories will be explored here, case by case. In nearly a quarter-century (yikes) of reviewing professionally, I've had to deal in print with all manner of eye-watering abominations – some of these among the more recent debacles that have made the cut. But there's a century of cinema to turn over, and I'm fascinated by what the bygone era can tell us with its turkeys.

The silent age, when film-makers were testing the boundaries of what this fledgling medium could achieve, saw the first monumental battles between art and commerce waged on screen, with directors, studios and stars hacking at each other in the fray. I've chosen two examples here that lost a fortune, and are among the most fascinating films of their day, not just for everything that went wrong, but for the creative ambition that survives in both pictures as we now have them.

Several other films in this book are near masterpieces. Their stark financial failure will be tackled, but so will their risky flexes and unorthodox brilliance. Each was deeply costly to the careers of those film-makers, who were sent to directors' jail for having soaraway visions no one managed to sell. The least they deserve is retrospective appreciation for what they got on screen, however painfully unrewarded it went at the time.

Another subset of what's included are what we might opt to call 'disasterpieces' – films with wild, commercially fatal problems but a peculiar integrity. There are some uniquely messy enterprises we can behold with the benefit of hindsight and not really imagine, or even want, fixed. There's an aura to such behemoths I've always found alluring: they might have defeated their makers, but somehow they live on, not least as test cases for how not to spend a studio's millions.

The chosen films are a jumbled, motley crew – but that's kind of the idea. Without knowing it, they all say something about the circumstances that saw them produced. And while plenty of them should be fed to the wolves head first, others can be held up as magnificent. Quality's meant to be all over the map.

Instead, two main criteria govern what's in. The production on each film has to have been epic or crackers, a comedy of errors, or in some way freshly entertaining to recount. (A few old warhorses are discussed only in passing, simply because they've been flogged to death.) On top of that, their commercial fortunes need to have been genuinely atrocious. Nothing here broke even, or nearly did. Nothing that was savagely panned by critics but crawled home with a modest profit (John Boorman's berserk *Exorcist II* (1977), for instance) counts as enough of a bomb.

Waterworld (1995) needs a mention. It's an instructive case of an at-the-time infamous bellyflop that actually wasn't one, despite being a summer blockbuster released amid damning media coverage of hubris and overspend. It's also not terrible, and that's what saved it, differentiating it from Kevin Costner's subsequent post-apocalyptic clunker, *The Postman* (1997). *Waterworld* cost Universal around $175m, an unprecedented sum at the time, but recouped $264.2m at the global box office. With the added expense of prints and marketing, this still left it marginally in the red; a few years later, thanks to ancillary revenues from home entertainment, it would have crossed the line.

—————

It's hard to say exactly when mainstream reporting began weighing in so avidly, and more often correctly, to predict flops. Industry bibles such as *Variety* have been totting up grosses and sussing out budgets since day one. Somewhere along the line, this tipped over into weekly sport across America's breakfast tables.

News pages started trumpeting the victory laps of *Star Wars* (1977) at the same time as flaunting, with often gleeful *Schadenfreude*, the ballooning costs and seemingly ruinous delays of *Apocalypse Now* (1979) – or 'Apocalypse Later', as it was snarkily dubbed while production in the Philippines ran on and on. Francis Ford Coppola – like Cameron after him on the similarly bad-press-plagued *Titanic* – was vindicated by his film's wild success.

But this last laugh didn't last long, as he would find out on his very next film, the incredibly costly *One from the Heart* (1981) – a case of the budget being reviewed and the film itself disappearing in a trice. Then came *The Cotton Club* (1984), a chaotic mess of a production in which he and producer Robert Evans were at constant loggerheads. This double whammy torpedoed Coppola's stature for years as a big-budget film-maker, illustrating what reputational damage multiple flops can wreak.

Some bad press is insurmountable. During the Montana shoot on Michael Cimino's *Heaven's Gate* (1980), an undercover journalist called Les Gapay went so far as to sneak on set as an extra, to confirm rumours of the absolute madness unfolding.[1] When the film came out, scraping together the grosses of any studio executive's worst nightmares, Cimino's film became a byword for Hollywood's most wasteful tendencies, and a convenient rebuke to the overblown importance of the auteur – a film to which studios could point forever more to justify playing it safe.

From then on, any film with a hefty price tag suddenly had a target on its back. Failures couldn't avoid being publicised, even smirkily given trophies. The Golden Raspberry Awards were inaugurated in 1981 – that rather juvenile institution purporting, as a kind of anti-Oscars, to celebrate the worst of everything Hollywood has to offer.

Duly nominated for Worst Picture in 1988, Elaine May's uncertain comedy *Ishtar* (1987), pairing Warren Beatty and Dustin Hoffman as talentless lounge singers, had been bedevilled by media attention crowing that it was a wildly overpriced vanity project. Ditto *Hudson Hawk* (1991), the lead-footed Bruce Willis caper that won big, but only at the Razzies.

Costner's *Dances with Wolves* (1990) had already been dubbed 'Kevin's Gate', and could easily have gone the same way, but proved everyone wrong, not only winning seven Oscars but making an extraordinary fortune for a three-hour-long, levity-free frontier western. But the nickname lingered, soon attaching itself to *Waterworld* instead – or 'Fishtar', if you prefer.

Studios now have a convenient burial plot for their most embarrassing product, which can be swiftly sold off to streaming services and thereby submerged with minimal public exposure. Such companies have no obligation to reveal stats on how many people are watching, say, Joe Wright's *The Woman in the Window* (2021), a shambolic $40m thriller funded by Fox, originally to be released by Disney, delayed by Covid, and then dumped, three years after it was made, on Netflix.

Streaming berths are these days a safe house for commercially dicey films, and have curbed the whole sport of guessing the flop. Netflix spent a king's ransom on such flicks as the sci-fi thrillers *Bright* (2017, $90m) and *Mute* (2018, $140m), George Clooney's *The Midnight Sky* (2020, $100m), Michael Bay's *6 Underground* (2019, $150m), the Scottish epic *Outlaw King* (2018, $120m), the megabucks heist caper *Red Notice* (2021, $200m), and such interchangeable spy romps as *The Gray Man* (2022, $200m) and *Heart of Stone* (2023, $140m).

Were any of these flops? Without viewing figures or opening weekends to give us a metric, that can be only a matter of speculation. Blushes can be spared that way; careers conserved. Besides, the whole concept of the flop as we used to know it has been further eroded by the box office impact of Covid-19, which for the best part of two years made *everything* into a flop, and pushed viewers in their droves towards the convenience of home cinema.

This is why the final film to get a chapter here could easily be the last banner fiasco of its kind, which merits pride of place as the grand finale to this survey of celluloid wreckage. How could it not? If it exists to prove anything, it's that the medium would actually be the lesser without its flops. We crave them, we need to know all about them, and sometimes we can't help but treasure them, even when we also can't believe what we're physically seeing. This is why I come, not to bury this ill-fated litter of miscellaneous catastrophes, but to dig them back up, one by one.

INTOLERANCE (1916)

Director: D. W. Griffith
Budget: ~$2.5m+?
Gross: ~$1m

WHITE ELEPHANTS – the god of Hollywood wanted *white elephants*, and white elephants he got – eight of 'em, plaster mammoths perched on mega-mushroom pedestals, lording it over the colossal court of Belshazzar, the pasteboard Babylon built beside the dusty tin-lizzie trail called Sunset Boulevard.

Kenneth Anger, *Hollywood Babylon*

It was one of the most ostentatiously vast film sets ever built – walls 300 feet high, enclosing a city within a city, with 3,000 costumed extras wandering about inside. These Babylonians-for-hire, all LA natives pocketing a tidy $2-a-day wage for their troubles, couldn't have helped ogling the hanging gardens, the giant thrones, the steps leading your eye in every direction. The office of the design department had to be put on stilts just so they could see what they were meant to be doing.

D. W. Griffith, then the most celebrated director in America, and already its most controversial, was not messing around. *The Birth of a Nation* (1915), one of the very earliest feature-length films, had been the *Titanic* of its day, achieving staggering profitability and cultural impact. It was the first movie ever to be screened for the White House and the Supreme Court.

It also fuelled the revival of the Ku Klux Klan. With its hate-mongering agenda barely veiled under a shimmer of antebellum nostalgia, it's tarred forever with that brush: today, it's the film taught to illustrate twentieth-century racism, rather than technical craft, as it used to be. This toxic artefact could be easier to forget if it hadn't been the original blockbuster, revolutionary in business terms, and a foundation stone for the entire industry.

Griffith was not unaffected by the *Birth* backlash, including attempts by the NAACP* to ban it, which succeeded for two years in Ohio, and newspaper columns (by the likes of Booker T. Washington) urging a public boycott. Far from being chastened, the Kentucky-born director's response was furious indignation, and he was able to take solace in the popular fervour backing up everything he was trying to say. One viewer was so incensed when Mae Marsh's Flora flees her attempted rapist in the film (played by white actor Walter Long in blackface) that he took out a handgun and started firing at the screen to try to help her.

Accused of intolerance by his political enemies, Griffith would have none of it – indeed, he considered them the intolerant ones. He went so far as to publish a cartoon pamphlet called 'The Rise and Fall of Free Speech in America', which used the word 'intolerance' repeatedly, depicting examples of censorship through history.[1]

From this thesis, the film sprang. A fallacy used to circulate that this grandiose follow-up was conceived as an atonement cum apology for *Birth*. The very opposite was the case. Griffith aimed to outdo his earlier film in spectacle, but was also doubling down on his statement, determined to parade the evil forces he was up against.

Intolerance wound up being four films in one, set across four historical time frames spanning 2,500 years of human civilisation, which were daringly cross-cut to illustrate his overarching theme. But this was not Griffith's initial plan. He first shot the most contemporary, starkly affecting story as a stand-alone feature – 'The Mother and the Law' – about a couple in the slums, played by Mae Marsh and Bobby Harron, who lose their baby to a corrupt orphanage.

* National Association for the Advancement of Colored People.

Lillian Gish, who'd played the lead role of Elsie Stoneman in *The Birth of a Nation*, went to a screening of 'The Mother and the Law' for studio employees in 1915. 'We all agreed with him that the film was too small in theme and execution to follow *Birth*,'[2] she remembered. Studio records prove that the other sections of *Intolerance* were initially to be filmed as separate productions by Griffith's Majestic Film Corporation, until he had the grand idea of uniting them into one overwhelming tapestry.

The project was 'a mighty improvisation',[3] according to Griffith's most exhaustive biographer, Richard Schickel. How were we to get from the Fall of Babylon in 538 BC, via a passion play on the last days of Christ, to the St Bartholemew's Day Massacre of the Huguenots by Catholic mob violence in sixteenth-century France, and thence to the gritty modernity of 'The Mother and the Law'?

The Italian epic *Cabiria* (1914), by Giovanni Pastrone, had made Griffith green with envy,[4] with its innovative roving camera and multiple story lines, and he became obsessed with outdoing it. The skeins of Roman history in that film, derived from Livy, featured such spectacles as Hannibal crossing the Alps with his elephants, and a palace set with two huge elephant sculptures on columns at the gate.

Griffith was undoubtedly quite taken with the pachyderm imagery. There was no evidence elephants had ever been a part of Babylonian iconography, but when he set about designing the most lavish section of his own blockbuster, he needed plaster elephants right away, and he needed eight, to kick Pastrone into touch.

No expense was spared in realising his vision for Babylon, which dwarfed everything around it. The second-unit director Joseph Henabery, who would also play a Huguenot admiral in the French section, bought hundreds of research volumes to assist in the designs, demanding two of each tome, so he could tear out pictures and paste them in a scrapbook, which weighed eight pounds by the time it was finished. Students of Assyrian culture – elephants aside – would be impressed by the accuracy of the end result.

In terms of the scale of what Griffith was building, this was next-level showing-off. Griffith wanted ramparts along the top of the set that were wide and strong enough for chariots to be raced along them. A giant balloon was attached to the scaffolding to promote what was still called 'The Mother and the Law', before *Intolerance* took over as the title.

While construction ran on and on, Griffith tinkered about idly with the remaining chapters – the Huguenot and Christ sections, which exercised his imagination far less than the other two. They wound up feeling truncated, and relatively perfunctory, compared with the conflict between Prince Belshazzar and Cyrus the Great in his Babylonian epic, and the plangent melodrama of the modern story.

In early autumn 1915, Santa Ana winds attacked the set, and Babylon had to be battened down: steel hawsers were used to attach its timbers to railroad ties buried in the earth. But significant damage had already been done, and from then on the whole thing felt like a death trap. The horses enlisted for the chariot race freaked out because the structure was so high and kept wobbling beneath them. Cameramen were made to lean dangerously out of their tower to capture those shots. While everyone held their breath, the structure swayed but it held. Griffith wasn't impressed. He ordered a faster second take.

As the camera operator Karl Brown remembered, 'He was leaning casually against a parapet, his cheap straw hat shoved back on his head, his mouth slightly open in a grin of purest delight. The man was actually *enjoying* the situation.'[5]

At some point, a kind of tyrannical madness, fitting for the war campaigns of Nebuchadnezzar, took over. Brown was left quaking in his boots when Griffith rigged one of the towers to crash down for effect, in a cloud of canvas and wood, all around the camera crew. The director needed live elephants too – of course he did – and he wanted them to be used not only as battering rams but mobile siege towers by the attacking Persians.

In these early days of film production, professional animal handlers were hard to come by. Griffith's assistants somehow succeeded in rounding up the beasts, but they were a jumble of male and female, proved averse to being given performance notes, and what mainly ensued was hormonal chaos. The battle shoot was bedlam: at the end of one shooting day, a total of 60 injuries received treatment at the production's hospital tent. The resulting sequence features two on-screen decapitations – thankfully faked.

Griffith also wanted human volunteers to leap off the walls into safety nets, and everyone thought he'd lost his mind yet again. Then he doubled the day rate to $5 for anyone who would jump, and he was suddenly inundated. 'Stop those crazy fools! I haven't enough nets, or enough money,'[6] he declared.

Over the more highly paid performers in his film, whom he failed to give screen credit – which would be a serious marketing error – Griffith continued to exert a control that was partway between hypnotic charm and devious manipulation. According to the cinematographer Billy Bitzer, he deliberately fostered a romance between the Babylonian leading lady Seena Owen (who played Attarea, the 'Princess Beloved') and a co-star called George Walsh, to stoke up the emotion of her performance. Then he whispered in her ear that Walsh was toying with her, and banned him from the set. While Owen pined away, she lost all the excess weight she had gained. (The couple would swiftly marry, have a daughter together, and then divorce in 1922.)

Many, many months later, in the winter of 1915, Griffith would finally declare that he was finished with the Walls of Babylon, and order them dismantled – but only to erect Belshazzar's court in the same spot, the giant set with the white-elephant pedestals, open to the sky. Building this imposed a further hiatus, which would delay completion of principal photography until the early summer of 1916.

Even at this stage, Griffith was optimistic about his picture's chances. Thanks to royalties from *Birth*, he was swimming in money; his income that year was a whopping $250,431. Unlike Charlie Chaplin, Mary Pickford or Douglas Fairbanks, who were careful about saving their personal fortunes, he was cavalier about spending his. He had the finest suits tailored, and swanned around in expensive cars. Plus, he had no compunction in bankrolling every last cent of overtime on *Intolerance* personally. Convinced that his own genius was the origin of these rewards, he reinvested his fortune, ecstatically, in himself.

Estimates for the film's budget have always swung all over the map. One unlikely figure floating around on the Internet puts it at a staggering $8.4m, which would have made it the most expensive film on record, even without inflationary adjustment, until 1954, when *20,000 Leagues Under the Sea* cost $9m. Griffith's more sympathetic biographers, including Richard Schickel, have worked hard to whittle that figure way down: $1.9m more often gets cited. Schickel contests even that sum as excessive, though: the result, he argues, of fraudulent publicity given to the *Scientific American*, which ran a feature on the film's production, listing one hard-to-believe expense of $360,000 for soldiers' uniforms.

Trumpeting and even overestimating your budget may have been a trick to pique public interest back then, though the very idea these days would give most producers a cardiac arrest. Whatever the actual scale of Griffith's investment on the shoot, it was about to be doubled, or even tripled, by the costs of distribution and marketing. He had only himself to blame. He wanted what would become known as a 'roadshow presentation'. *Intolerance* would travel around the country with an orchestra, and the only theatres allowed to show it had to be specially decorated. It was these sumptuous extravagances that sank all hope of it breaking even.

The rough cut of *Intolerance* ran for a bewildering eight hours, which Griffith originally wanted to show in two four-hour sittings. Exhibitors, who were gaining power to decide what they could or could not programme, baulked at the proposal. Fielding their complaints was Griffith's first external setback in the 20 months he'd taken putting the film together. On their advice, he cut it back to under three hours, tearing away swathes of subplots, especially in the French section.

Intertitles needed adding to supply the thematic coherence he worried – rightly, as it turns out – would be lost on audiences. That task was assigned to Anita Loos, who at that time was on Griffith's payroll as a staff screenwriter, a decade before she would pen *Gentlemen Prefer Blondes*. While pretending to have been moved beyond words when she watched his assembly, the actual words inside her head, as she remembers thinking, were 'I thought D.W. had lost his mind.'[7]

The premiere at New York's Liberty Theatre on 5 September 1916 went deceptively well. Griffith got a standing ovation from this first-night crowd. 'Stupendous, tremendous, revolutionary, intense, thrilling,' frothed *Film Daily*. In the early part of that autumn, it even looked possible that *Intolerance* would run and run as a box office rival to *Birth*. But, after a promising opening, it started to thin out alarmingly, topping out at a gross somewhere around the $1m mark. (*Birth* had made at least $20m worldwide, and by some estimates much more.)

No one quite knew what to say to Griffith as the fact of his epic disappointment sank in. The great mistake had been a determination to outdo *Birth of a Nation* so bombastically that he left his eager audience in the dust. The vulgar, demotic charge that had whipped them up into such a frenzy during *Birth* had no equivalent in this high-handedly artisanal lecture.

While Hollywood cognoscenti and many critics found the film awe-inspiring or at least technically remarkable, the wider public just couldn't get the hang of it: Griffith's obsession with cross-cutting kept them at a remove, as did his failure to supply emotional clarity by isolating faces in the crowd. What he was trying to say never travelled into the newspaper columns, or translated into word of mouth: indeed, it felt as though it *needed* translating.

It didn't help that all eyes were now on the war in Europe, which America was about to join. With his fulminating, self-involved pleas for harmony, and all the historical hopscotching, Griffith was guilty of badly misjudging the public mood.

Soon after the film's dwindling returns became apparent, Lillian Gish received a letter from Griffith that gets cited in all his biographies. He spoke of 'wandering through the darkened theatres, barking his shins on the empty seats'. 'I don't know where to go,' he told her, 'or where to turn, since my great failure.'[8]

Griffith could derive a modicum of solace from the film's warm reception at the Drury Lane Theatre for the film's London premiere in April 1917. And it was a huge success in Russia – although, as the copies shown were pirated and distributed without Griffith's permission, he never received a rouble in return. To recover, as an apologia and career-rescuing measure, he would throw himself into the wartime propaganda piece *Hearts of the World* (1918), starring Gish.

Artistically, he was far from done for – *Broken Blossoms* (1919), *Way Down East* (1920) and *Orphans of the Storm* (1921) would all follow, and do pretty well. But that reckless megalomania of his had peaked. 'Although none of us was aware of it,' wrote Gish, 'he had reached the apex of his career. He was still to make great pictures, but he'd be harassed by debts till the end of his life.'[9]

If Griffith ever needed cause to second guess himself, or rue the giant folly of trying to be a one-man film studio, he only had to drive past the intersection of Sunset and Hollywood Boulevards, where the Babylon set would remain standing, growing increasingly dishevelled, for the best part of four years. He didn't even have the money to finance its demolition. The Los Angeles Fire Department would declare this crumbling ruin a fire hazard, and finally have it torn down in 1919 – white elephants and all.

QUEEN KELLY (1929)

Director: Erich von Stroheim
Studio: United Artists
Budget: ~$800,000
Gross: not accurately recorded, but a near total loss

No other film-maker was more ardent in their admiration of Griffith than the Austrian émigré Erich von Stroheim. On his mentor's death in 1948, he delivered a radio eulogy explaining Griffith's pre-eminence in cinema as 'the first man who put beauty and poesy into a cheap and tawdry sort of amusement'. He also hailed him for inventing the close-up, thereby giving any poor man with a music-hall ticket access to the same emotional detail as an opera patron with box seats.

Stroheim owed Griffith: he got his first job in Hollywood under him, as an extra and horse handler on *The Birth of a Nation*, and hung around to play an uncredited role as Second Pharisee in *Intolerance* – while also serving as assistant director and general dogsbody to the D.W.G. production unit for four years.

First, though, he had to invent the 'von'. He was born mere Erich Oswald Stroheim in Vienna in 1885, the son of a middle-class Jewish hat-maker. By the time of his arrival on Ellis Island in 1909, having fled military service in Austria, he had mysteriously become Count Erich Oswald Hans Carl Maria von Stroheim und Nordenwall.*

The fiction of his aristocratic background would be sustained throughout Stroheim's career and rescue it repeatedly. When the USA

---

* Stroheim certainly wasn't the last auteur to add a fictitious 'von' to his name. Ask his successor Josef von Sternberg or, indeed, Lars von Trier.

entered the First World War in 1917, he became *persona non grata*, fired by an anxious Douglas Fairbanks, his name dropped from cast billings. Suddenly, though, a demand arrived for Prussian military villains to be played convincingly in propaganda films.

Stroheim happened to be an expert in German military uniforms, and set about becoming the decorated Hun everyone loved to hate – especially notorious for a scene in *The Heart of Humanity* (1918) when he chucked a baby from a two-storey-high window. After sound came in, not even the fact that he'd largely forgotten his native tongue was an impediment to playing the living archetype of Prussia's officer class in Jean Renoir's *La Grande Illusion* (1937).

Stroheim starred in half of the eight and a half films he directed, beginning with *Blind Husbands* in 1919, in which he typecast himself as 'Lieutenant Eric von Steuben', a caddish fellow who tries to ravish a doctor's wife in the Austrian Alps. This production set the tone for the extravagance and autocracy he would get away with for years in Hollywood.

Studio moguls, especially Universal's Carl Laemmle, were looking for a 'super-director' who could be promoted as the next Griffith, and Stroheim eagerly swallowed up all the resources they were willing to throw at him. His defiant overspending, bullying of his actors and obsession with orgy scenes featuring real sex workers courted infamy – and achieved it. He had a reputation for assaulting his actresses, including the likes of Fay Wray and Malvina Polo, if their performances weren't achieving the requisite levels of anxious hysteria.

The kinky melodrama *Foolish Wives* (1922) cost an eye-watering $1.1m, making it the most expensive film since *Intolerance*. On the monumental and aptly titled *Greed* (1924), Stroheim shot 85 hours of footage, before submitting a first cut that was 10 hours long. Both those films were re-edited against his will, and he butted heads repeatedly with Universal's boy-wonder executive Irving Thalberg, a stern watchdog who snapped and sacked him – sending shock waves through the industry – six weeks into the shoot of *Merry-Go-Round* (1923).

Most directors would be broken, or at least bowed, by these hard knocks; not Stroheim. He pounced back by scoring his biggest hit to date with *The Merry Widow* (1925) for MGM, and then cashed in that credit with *The Wedding March* (1928), another ridiculously lavish production, which created an exact replica of Vienna's St Stephen's Cathedral on Paramount's backlot.

The scenes in a whorehouse were so graphic, according to cinematographer Hal Mohr, that only about a fiftieth of what Stroheim shot was usable. 'If it wasn't screwing, it looked like it,'[1] Mohr recalled. This film got shut down after six months' shooting, having quadrupled its original budget because of Stroheim's fixation on printing all 40 takes of some shots. It eventually had to be released, desperately, as two entirely distinct features, with the last eight reels packaged by Paramount into a sequel called *The Honeymoon*.

The adage about an unstoppable force meeting an immovable object must now intervene in Stroheim's story. If he was the force, the luminous object was Gloria Swanson, until 1925 the most bankable silent film star of the day. She still had major respect in the industry – nominated for the 1928 and 1930 Best Actress Oscar – despite some poor financial decisions, especially turning down a $1m-per-year contract with Paramount to join United Artists.

On paper, *Queen Kelly* boded well enough: there was little to portend the derailing of both their careers. The plot was a typically Stroheimian bit of saucy nonsense about a convent girl, Kitty Kelly (Swanson), seduced by a philandering prince (played lifelessly, alas, by Walter Byron), who is betrothed to a sex-crazed queen, 'Regina V of Kronberg' (*Intolerance*'s very own vixen of Babylon, Seena Owen). Taking serious umbrage at this betrayal, Regina imprisons the prince and has Kelly whipped and exiled.

When Swanson met Stroheim to discuss making it, she found him 'gracious and charming but at the same time aloof and conceited'[2] – not an uncommon first impression. The financier/ producer who hooked them up was none other than Swanson's lover Joseph P. Kennedy, father of JFK, who was looking for the right project to reinstall her as a megastar and get the cash flowing once again.

All three dived into the shoot with blithe abandon. Meanwhile, Warner Bros had been experimenting with sound since 1926, and had woken up the whole industry with the impact of Al Jolson's part-talkie *The Jazz Singer* (1927). A scramble to produce full talkies began, with even B-pictures such as Warners' *The Lights of New York* (1928) making enormous profits, while the lavish likes of Fox's *In Old Arizona* (1928) and MGM's *Broadway Melody* (1929) were well into production when *Queen Kelly* started. Stroheim, Swanson and Kennedy were blocking their ears, and ploughing ahead with their old-timey silent bonkbuster as if no one would care about sound in a year or so.

The extent of their misjudgement was epic. But they were also about to become each other's worst enemies. Discord on set was brewing by late 1928; it didn't help that 20 out of the first 42 days of shooting had run past midnight, often later than 5 a.m. As *Film Weekly* reported on New Year's Eve, 'Extras are swooning daily on the set from overwork, and that work goes on all night and continues through the day without a break.'

Swanson and Kennedy were starting to worry about the amount of sex Stroheim was bent on including, which his script hadn't specified. After doing ten naked takes when strolling over to a balcony, Seena Owen wanted her modesty covered, and was given flesh-coloured tights to wear, then a white cat to caress and cover her breasts with. After two hours more of this, the cat, too, had had quite enough, and started to scratch her in protest. It had to be equipped with white mittens until the scene wrapped at 7 a.m.[3]

Because of Kennedy's connections with the Roman Catholic hierarchy, everyone was nervous to show him the rushes of, for instance, the scene where Kelly's knickers drop to her feet in front of the prince's cavalry. And this was even before production shifted, in early 1929, to the truly problematic latter half of the script, which had Kelly decamping to German East Africa, being forced by her dying aunt to marry a syphilitic suitor named Jan (Tully Marshall), and eventually becoming a brothel madam.

Swanson explained in her autobiography how Stroheim's spell over her gradually wore off. She was, at first, 'hypnotised by the man's relentless perfectionism', and no matter how few pages of script they managed to get through on a daily basis, 'his exactitude always paid off in the rushes'. The price of his control-freakery was that scenes most directors could have managed in an hour took all day, with him 'fondling and dawdling over the tiniest minutiae'.[4]

Cats did not have a great time on this set, generally. Another one, when it was meant to be throwing a hissy fit, fell into 'a state of lethargy from which it was impossible to arouse it', according to the press agent/critic Cedric Belfrage in *Film Weekly*. Eventually Stroheim gave up and just shot the creature sleeping.

Paul Ivano, the film's second cameraman and a one-time lover of Rudolph Valentino, remembered that Stroheim 'used to fire me four times a day', until Swanson bawled him out. He was rough with actors, often resorting to the crude approach of playing the scene himself, expecting them to copy him. And if things didn't go his way, he would descend to 'obscene ethnic epithets'.[5]

Swanson, meanwhile, watched the costs inexorably climb. It seems unclear whether she'd truly grasped the seedy implications of the brothel section: she claimed in interviews much later in life* that she'd been misled by the script, which specified this location as a dance hall. Her relationship with the director frayed further when she called a script meeting, insisting they drop an expensive set piece – Stroheim's favourite scene – in which Kelly was to cling to a tree in Africa as it sank 80 feet into a swamp.

At the urging of her friend and soon-to-be director Edmund Goulding, she wanted to convert some remaining sections of the film into sound sequences, which went down atrociously with Stroheim. And then, halfway through the African shoot, came the final straw.

This was a shot of Jan, the repulsive groom, dribbling tobacco juice over Swanson's hand, which Stroheim insisted on retaking over and over. Three hundred feet of film were exposed of this one moment, and he was happy with none of it. 'I had just eaten breakfast,' Swanson would write in her 1980 memoir, 'and my stomach turned. I became nauseated and furious at the same time.'[6]

In general, it added to her impression that the African scenes were 'rank and sordid and ugly, and full of material that would never pass the censors'.[7] 'The picture,' as she worried more than ever, 'was going to be in the wastepaper basket.'† With one call to Kennedy in Miami, she got Stroheim fired. 'Joseph,' she recalled the conversation going, 'you'd better get out here fast. Our director is a madman.'[8]

---

* The best of these has to be her appearance on *The Dick Cavett Show*, on 3 August 1970. Seventy-one-year-old Swanson came dressed as a glamorous flapper, with a platinum bob and Gatsby-esque headband. Her fellow guests were Margot Kidder and a reliably caustic Janis Joplin, in her last ever TV appearance. With Cavett ill-at-ease during so much sartorial chat, topics included the use of ice cubes on set in the silent days, to perk up nipples under silk gowns, and Swanson's invention of the panty girdle.

† Swanson, 'I Am NOT Going to Write My Memoirs!', *Sight and Sound*, winter 1969–70, p. 60. (She did anyway.)

There was nothing Stroheim could do but walk away, leaving his star and producer with a dilemma they would make no decisive stab at resolving. Something around $600,000 had been spent on the film already; another $400,000 might have finished it, but Swanson had no appetite to complete the African sequences. 'My brain twirled,' she wrote. 'I walked floors, I tossed in bed. How do we save it? Does one cut the first* third of the picture and still save the story? My imagination went wild.'[9] A merry-go-round of directors and script doctors (Irving Thalberg, Goulding, Richard Boleslavsky, Delmer Daves) were hired to save it over the next year or so, but they added only 12 minutes of usable material.

Just two weeks of additional shooting, in the opinion of one Stroheim biographer,[10] might have achieved a salvage job, with a few sound effects and some minimal lines of dialogue added. The option of 'synthetic sound' (dubbing it over silent footage) had just been used on William Wellman's *Chinatown Nights*, which Paramount released in the nick of time on 23 March 1929.

The doctors swarmed around *Queen Kelly*, but when Kennedy arrived in California to see the fruits of their surgery, he had a meltdown. 'He slumped into a deep chair,' Swanson recalled, 'put his head in his hands, and grunted and groaned like a hurt animal. His first words were, in a quiet voice: "I've never had a failure in my life."'[11]

Kennedy had to set Swanson straight, in no uncertain terms, on her obligations to the production: he would not be footing the bill, for which her terrible judgement in agreeing to his financial terms without good legal advice could be blamed. By the end of 1929, Wall Street was in horrendous turmoil, and their affair – conveniently for Kennedy – sputtered out, leaving Swanson entirely liable for the film's inevitable disaster.

---

* It seems more logical that she meant 'last'.

Delaying the issue, she jumped ship to *The Trespasser* (1929) – a bona-fide sound hit, directed by Goulding, for which she got the second of those Oscar nods. It was just about successful enough to enable her to think about *Queen Kelly* again, but she dithered, wasted time on two other films, and by then it was 1932, three years too late for *Kelly* to be in any way marketable.

A bolder, earlier attempt to convert *Queen Kelly* into a part-talkie could have clawed back some of the lost expenditure. Instead, Swanson had a beautiful ruin on her hands. It wound up getting no commercial showings in the USA at all, though it did play a Parisian art house called the Falguière, and possibly in a few other spots in Europe.

Having to carry the can for all the reshoots and vast delays ended up costing Swanson the entire budget, $800,000. Bankrupted, disillusioned, and tragically dethroned as a viable star, she stepped away from the limelight.

Stroheim's own story about the debacle was that Kennedy had pulled the plug, not because of his director's excesses, but because of talkies being 'the death knell of silent pictures'.[12] He did try one last time to work for the studios, hired under strict conditions by Fox to handle a pre-Hays-Code romance called *Walking Down Broadway* (1933; aka *Hello, Sister!*).

He kept it tightly on budget, and everything looked pretty dandy, until executives watched what he'd given them, and were horrified by the morbid sexual overtones. They wrenched it from him, hired two other directors to reshoot it, and released it in a bowdlerised 61-minute cut with no directing credit at all.

It was a steep dip from Stroheim's glory days, with the industry concluding there was nothing more to be done with him as a director. But at least he had his acting career as a fallback; the rise of the Nazis in Europe made that Teutonic menace of his indispensable again. He'd play a bullying SS officer in *So Ends Our Night* (1941), none other than Erwin Rommel in Billy Wilder's *Five Graves to Cairo* (1943), and a whole range of ghoulish, Mengele-esque experimental scientists in various low-budget horror flicks.

Restored versions of *Queen Kelly* have circulated over the years, including a painstaking effort by Kino International in 1985 to put together the most complete cut possible, based on Stroheim's scripted intentions. The film's intoxicating visual style, especially during the dynamite scenes of palace intrigue, makes the collapse of its production undeniably poignant. It's a landmark instance, not so much of too many cooks in the Hollywood kitchen, but exactly the wrong combination of egos at the wrong time. 'Do we have to go into poor, dear *Queen Kelly*?' Swanson once pleaded with a BBC interviewer. 'She'll never die . . .'

She does have a sequel, though, beautiful if bittersweet – and that's *Sunset Boulevard* (1950), that backhanded tribute to the silent age for which Billy Wilder had an inspired double notion. The first was to lure Swanson out of retirement, in a borderline self-portrait as the faded screen legend Norma Desmond. The second was hiring Stroheim as Max Mayerling, her devoted butler and inescapably sinister projectionist.

Feeding her delusions, playing her own films to her nightly in her private auditorium, Max is the proud custodian of Norma's legend. And the film we watch her watching, with Swanson lighting a candle in an ethereal convent chapel, is, of course, *Queen Kelly*.

FREAKS (1932)

Director: Tod Browning
Studio: MGM
Budget: ~$310,000
Loss recorded of $164,000

Any screening of *Freaks* today demands certain caveats, if not outright trigger warnings. Even on its release, this singular horror experiment, a tale of solidarity among circus misfits and their grisly revenge against the non-disabled, caused an uproar.

Opprobrium rained down on it from all sides. It would be two further years before the Hays Code came into proper force, precisely to stop the likes of *Freaks* ever making it past treatment stage. No Hollywood studio could have got it off the ground after 1934.

Over the years, *Freaks* has gained a uniquely vexed, uniquely complex place in the film canon. It's now a persistent cult favourite, which the critic Danny Peary included in his influential 1981 book *Cult Movies*, alongside the likes of *Eraserhead* (1977) and *The Rocky Horror Picture Show* (1975). Back in the day, though, the forces of censorship were too embryonic, and too panicked, to have any idea what to do with it.

Discomfort with the storyline and with the film's chosen ensemble tended to blur: no one could see past the 'freaks' Browning had cast to play versions of themselves, however sympathetically he wanted to draw them. The plot tracks how a community of circus people responds when a dwarf called Hans is tricked into marriage by Cleopatra, a heartless trapeze artist. This relationship alone was enough to weird people out, even before the retribution she faces from Hans's tight-knit posse of friends, who come in all shapes and sizes.

Browning's authorship of the film – or, certainly, his understanding of its setting – was profound. At sixteen, he ran away from his well-to-do Kentucky family to join the circus, and worked his way up the ranks: roustabout, sideshow barker, song-and-dance man on riverboats in Ohio and Mississippi. Next came a stint as a clown with the famous Ringling Brothers, and a live-burial routine as 'The Living Hypnotic Corpse'. Born Charles, he had adopted the professional name 'Tod' – the German word for death.

After touring in vaudeville as a magician's assistant and blackface comedian, he graduated to film, acting in slapstick comedies, and was hired by D. W. Griffith – up the old devil pops again – to play various bit-parts, including in *Intolerance*, where he appears uncredited as 'Crook', and, like Erich von Stroheim, helped out as an assistant director.

Browning came close to his own Tod in 1915, when he drunkenly drove through a railway crossing and collided with a train, sustaining terrible injuries and killing a fellow passenger, the actor Elmer Booth. The trauma of this event would inform his outlook forever. The films he then began to direct would focus on crime and punishment, guilt and obsession. And he'd keep returning to the carnival to play out these melodramas.

One breakthrough silent feature, one of MGM's biggest hits of the day, was *The Unholy Three* (1925), based on a circus-themed novel by Tod Robbins, who also wrote the short story 'Spurs', on which Browning based *Freaks*. Lon Chaney, the self-styled 'Man of a Thousand Faces', played a double role – a scheming ventriloquist who poses as a kindly grandma. Victor McLaglen, ex-boxer and future Oscar-winner,* was the strongman. And as the ruthless Tweedledee,

---

* For John Ford's *The Informer* (1935).

Browning cast Harry Earles, a young actor with dwarfism, who was one of a quartet of sibling entertainers called the Doll Family, immigrants to Hollywood from Stolpen in Germany.

It was Earles's film debut, and he made quite an impression as this brawling cherub. Come the sound remake in 1930, notable as Chaney's final film before his death from throat cancer, Earles had made it onto the poster – third-billed, and pictured in a black fedora under the strongman's arm. The story goes that it was Earles who drew Browning's attention to 'Spurs' as a possible vehicle for him and Chaney; three out of four of the Doll Family would wind up getting roles. Though Browning persuaded MGM to buy the rights for $8,000, he couldn't get a silent version off the ground in the mid-1920s, and Chaney's death seemed to put paid to it.

The reviving factor was Browning's huge success for Universal with the Bela Lugosi *Dracula* (1931), which triggered that studio's legendary first wave of monster movies. 'Other studios are looking for horror tales,' reported *Variety* in April 1931, 'but very squeamishly. Producers are not certain whether nightmare pictures have a box office pull, or whether *Dracula* is just a freak.' When James Whale's *Frankenstein*, released in November that year, did even better business, it was all systems go. Browning, who'd signed a $50,000-per-picture deal with MGM for his next three films, had managed to get his long-cherished pet project in front of cameras that very month.

Irving Thalberg – last seen grappling bitterly with Stroheim – was the man in charge of MGM's production slate at the time, busy overseeing the likes of *Grand Hotel*, which would be a glittering, Best-Picture-winning success story. He must have hoped *Freaks* would look after itself. When Browning submitted the script he wanted to use, Thalberg is said to have hung his head with serious buyer's remorse. 'Well, I asked for something horrible,' he muttered, 'and I guess I got it.'[1]

To dilute the film's one-off casting philosophy and reassure audiences, Thalberg wanted to cast marquee names as what the script calls the 'normals' – Myrna Loy* as the gold-digging villainess Cleopatra, and Jean Harlow as the good-girl foil.[2] But as the start date neared, these parts mysteriously migrated to the lesser-known Olga Baclanova and Leila Hyams, whose careers there was less concern about tainting.

Meanwhile, Browning conducted a widespread talent search for actors with a whole range of visible differences. According to Hyams, his desk was piled high with photos of hopefuls from across the States, many hundreds of whom were rejected, including an 'elephant-skinned' girl, an army of 'pygmies', and a boy with supposedly canine legs. She remembered Daisy Earles, Harry's three-foot-tall younger sister, perusing this stack one day and reacting with exclamations of disbelief.

To cosset the sensibilities of the non-disabled at MGM, shooting had to proceed with a separate outdoor mess for almost all of the so-called 'freaks'. Before this apartheid was put in place, F. Scott Fitzgerald happened to be on MGM's payroll as a screenwriter (though only for one week longer). He was sitting in the commissary when a pair of conjoined twins featured in the film, Daisy and Violet Hilton, came in, discussing what they were going to eat. Fitzgerald, according to one witness, 'turned pea-green, and putting his hand to his mouth, rushed for the great outdoors'.[3] He would put a more benign spin on the incident in his short story about Hollywood's social whirl, 'Crazy Sunday'.†

* Loy, who was under contract to MGM, remarks in her autobiography that she was horrified by the script, and begged Thalberg to let her out of the part.
† '. . . the sad, lovely Siamese twins, the mean dwarfs, the proud giant from the circus picture . . .' (F. Scott Fitzgerald, 'Crazy Sunday', published in *American Mercury*, October 1932).

In other respects, shooting on *Freaks* went like clockwork, with its performers housed for convenience in Culver City's Castle Apartments, next door to MGM. The bearded lady, Olga Roderick, was 'very grand and ritzy', according to Hyams. 'You almost expected her to peer at you through a lorgnette.'[4] Everyone called her 'The Duchess'. Browning didn't want her to do anything to her beard, but she showed up with it dyed black – 'and *marcelled!*'* recounted Hyams. 'Tod nearly died.'

There was a fair amount of backstage bitching. Whether he's to be trusted on this or not, Browning flippantly told a reporter in Los Angeles that the freaks' professional jealousy was amazing. 'Not one of them had a good word for the other,' he declared, while also claiming one of the cast had vented their rage by biting him.

The actors in question have never enjoyed any right of reply on such remarks. In fact, little information has come down to us on how they found themselves treated professionally on the *Freaks* set, or by Browning personally. Many appeared on film here for their one and only time. Many had been subject to a long history of exploitation, such as the Hiltons, who had been taught song and dance from the age of three, to be set to work by their legal guardians.

Angelo Rossitto (playing the dwarf Angeleno) was the prolific one. He went on to appear in more than 70 films, all the way up to *Mad Max Beyond Thunderdome* (1985), but ducked questions about Browning later in life. Olga Roderick, known to be the least content of all the cast, would denounce the film as an insult to circus performers everywhere, and regretted her role in it.[†5]

---

* A hairstyle technique using hot curling tongs, popularised in the 1920s.
† The actor Jerry Maren, who was the last Munchkin from *The Wizard of Oz* to survive, supports her remarks: 'When I was a kid, I wasn't crazy about it, because it put us in a bad light . . .'

Putting on his P. T. Barnum hat, Browning liked to paint his ensemble as prima donnas of the sideshow world, seizing their moment for a shot at the big time, donning shades to act like film stars. Who could blame them? Prince Randian, 'The Living Torso', who memorably rolls a cigarette using only his mouth, would amuse himself between takes by lurking in dark corners, then terrifying unsuspecting passers-by with sudden, bloodcurdling screams.[6]

Browning was a complicated man. Without his comfort in the company of these circus folk, the film would never have achieved the open curiosity and unpatronising sympathy it manages. He did become great friends with some of the actors, especially the 'Half-Boy', Johnny Eck, born without the lower half of his torso, whose ongoing film career Browning would help foster.

The director's worst behaviour, in any case, was directed elsewhere. According to a camera assistant called David S. Horsley, '[He] was a bastard as far as his crews were concerned. Hardworking but pitiless.' The film's editor, Basil Wrangell, called him 'very sarcastic, very unappreciative of any effort, and very demanding . . . In my book, [he was] a sadist, and I imagine that's why he picked those kind of subjects. It titillated his amusement.'[7]

Commonplace dangers imperilled the shoot: everyone kept getting electric shocks from the lighting rigs. A script clerk called Willard Sheldon nearly died when trapped next to a pyrotechnic device called a 'lacapodium', which was used to create lightning for the film's climactic storm scene, when the freaks enact their terrible revenge on Baclanova's character.

It was this part of the script – the only time when the freaks are truly presented as frightening – that Browning had fought about the most with MGM, ultimately losing this battle. 'They wanted macabre,' according to his biographer David Skal; 'he wanted sad.' The mutilation of Cleopatra, whom the freaks punish by transforming her from

'The Peacock of the Air' into a mute, squawking 'human duck', and the castration of her strongman lover Hercules (Henry Victor) were, astonishingly it seems, edicts directly from Thalberg.

When the fruits of this meddling were shown, the panic and finger-pointing provided the first inklings that *Freaks* was in serious trouble. Several MGM executives wanted the film shut down altogether, and Louis B. Mayer was horrified. It was Thalberg who persuaded them all to hold on.

Then the public got their first view of *Freaks*, in early January 1932, at a sneak preview in San Diego. An uncredited art director called Merrill Pye wouldn't forget the way the evening went.

'Halfway through the preview, a lot of people got up and ran out,' he recalled. 'They didn't walk out. They *ran* out.'[8] One woman who attended even tried to sue MGM, claiming the film had induced a miscarriage.

Abruptly, all the studio machinery went into damage-limitation mode. Browning no longer had any say over his film, which a despondent Thalberg took away, eventually cutting it from 90 minutes to just a squeak over an hour. The most ghoulish shots, with the muddy freaks swarming over their victims at the end, were excised, as was the pay-off scene with an emasculated Hercules singing falsetto, and some comic notes, including a bit with the 'Turtle Girl' being amorously pursued by a seal.

Originally, there was a lengthy epilogue in a second-storey museum of curiosities in London, called 'Tetrallini's Freaks and Music Hall', which was completely discarded, save for a final shot of Cleopatra quacking. A closing scene designed to exculpate Hans, the film's sympathetic centre, from being the architect of her horrific fate was shot, tested, foreshortened – and still didn't work.

MGM's release strategy remained brazen, if thoroughly confusing: too much money had been spent on *Freaks* to dump it altogether. The hope was that it would still succeed, even in this hobbled form, in cashing in on the horror craze. 'Can a full-grown woman truly love a MIDGET?' asked one poster salaciously. This stooping to exploitation, though, sat alongside the hypocritical efforts of the publicity department to trumpet the film's gritty compassion: 'A LANDMARK IN SCREEN DARING!' ran one ad.

It carried on in that vein, with hyperbolic punctuation typical of the day, and a touch of Shylock's anguished monologue from *The Merchant of Venice*: 'WHAT ABOUT ABNORMAL PEOPLE? THEY HAVE THEIR LIVES, TOO! What about the Siamese twins – have they no right to love? The pinheads, the half man/half woman, the dwarfs! They have the same passions, joys, sorrows, laughter as normal human beings. Is such a subject untouchable?'[9]

The trade paper *Motion Picture Daily* saw exactly the game MGM was playing: 'The picture is unkind and brutal,' it concluded. Most critics laid into it with venom, often seizing on it as an example of the disgraceful slump in Hollywood morals. 'In *Freaks* the movies make their great step towards national censorship,' wrote John C. Moffitt in the *Kansas City Star*. 'If they get it, they will have no one to blame but themselves.'

Opening officially at the Fox Criterion in Los Angeles, the film died a slow and characteristic death over two weeks, despite Louella Parsons* (of all people!) giving it one of its few favourable reviews. In Atlanta, a judge banned it for breaching the city's decency laws.

Women's groups, rallying to the censorship cause, pushed for boycotts. When it opened in Washington DC, the committee head for the National Association of Women's film division, one Mrs Ambrose Nevin Diehl, wrote sternly to Will Hays, talking of 'that offensive

---

* 'Queen of Hollywood gossip' thanks to her widely syndicated columns, at least until the rise of Hedda Hopper gave her a fierce rival for that accolade.

film *Freaks* which seems to be causing us all so much concern and embarrassment' and accusing MGM of 'stoop[ing] to the disgrace of making money out of hurt, disfigured and suffering humanity.'[10] In truth, she sounds equally appalled by the film's risqué double entendres as repulsed by how many varieties of disability Browning had seen fit to parade.

The tenor of the marketing may have been off base, but the shuddering attacks on the film itself were, ironically, redolent of the very disgust shown on screen by Cleopatra, when she recoils – appallingly – from the convivial welcome of the assembled freaks, during the rightly famous wedding banquet scene. As they pass around a loving cup, chanting, 'One of us! One of us!', Cleopatra steps back aghast, then makes a cackling mockery of their ceremonies. For this shameless display of inner ugliness, she'll be fittingly tarred, and literally feathered, come the Poe-esque denouement.

Browning never got over the perception of his film as a tasteless misfire, alongside its galling commercial failure. Despite a long reputation for turning a profit – he had several dozen features to his name before *Freaks* – he would make only another four films.

One of these was the nifty *The Devil-Doll* (1936), but he received no screen credit on that, and was summarily shown the door at MGM when *Miracles for Sale* (1939) flopped. Retiring to his Malibu Beach retreat, he became a recluse, forgotten by Hollywood – so much so that when his wife Alice died from pneumonia in 1944, *Variety* mistakenly published an obituary of Browning himself. In fact, he lived for almost another twenty years, an alcoholic shut-in, before dying, just like Chaney had done, of laryngeal cancer in 1962.

That very year, *Freaks* started coming back from the dead. It was screened appreciatively at the Venice Film Festival, and began to gain a whole new afterlife as a countercultural landmark. In 1963, a 30-year ban by the British censors was lifted, allowing it to be screened with an X certificate. As of writing, this deceptively non-graphic horror movie is a mere 12 certificate in the UK, a measure of faith in the sensibilities of younger teenagers, who are trusted to be more enlightened now than to respond to visible differences with the knee-jerk repulsion of yesteryear.

In a 2020 feature for *IndieWire*, the disabled critic Kristen Lopez praised the naturalism of Browning's lens, also pointing out that *Freaks*, to this day, is the only American feature to have a predominantly disabled cast.

The Toronto-based critic Bill Chambers, who shared some further thoughts, considers the film 'a key disability text – it's ours'.

'You'd definitely fight a losing battle,' he told me, 'convincing a studio to put real disabled people at the centre of a mainstream film today, which is what true ableism looks like.

'*Freaks* certainly has the lure of exploitation, like a sideshow, but all of those characters are on screen so long that you become desensitised to their difference. It's striking, actually, when able-bodied characters enter the frame and the camera has to adjust for them.

'What makes the movie not ableist is that the so-called freaks aren't entirely virtuous and they're not entirely evil; they're not saints and they're not sinners.'[11]

Where iconic horror films of the time, including *Frankenstein* and *Dr Jekyll and Mr Hyde* (1931), tended to pathologise external appearance as a guarantee of deviance within, *Freaks* effectively did the opposite – clearly one reason that it confounded so many viewers in 1932. It's been argued[12] that Browning was putting over an anti-eugenics message, partly by making the true monsters of his tale the exploiters who prize their 'normality' so very highly, but also because he familiarises us so well with the daily lot of the freaks, using a daringly sitcom-like tone to bring us into their midst before the shift to horror.

36

Most of the running time is devoted unassumingly to watching these people simply living their lives – including their sex lives – in ways 1932's viewers plainly struggled to handle. It's worth remembering that the exodus at that accursed preview started during the sweet, seriocomic scenes halfway in – long before the malevolent finale.

While the marketing clearly whiffed in trying to have it both ways, there's no denying that the film *is* forever double-edged. Partly because of the tone foisted on him by MGM, Browning confronts us with elements of heebie-jeebie voyeurism, but what's blended in – his sense of a community that loves and protects each other to the bitter end – creates a fusion that's radically strange, not to mention remarkably brave. The victory of the freaks' rough justice, once so unthinkable, holds up in retrospect as the least they deserve.

SYLVIA SCARLETT (1935)

Director: George Cukor
Studio: RKO
Budget: $641,000
Loss recorded of $330,000

Katharine Hepburn, that trilling chatterbox, that defiant human question mark, shears off her hair in *Sylvia Scarlett*'s first scene to become a boy named Sylvester. This is an illusion she sustains to make her way jauntily in a man's world for most of the next hour, like Shakespeare's Viola in *Twelfth Night*, or Barbra Streisand in *Yentl* (1983). The romantic confusion sown by this gender switch, in both male and female members of the ensemble, is quite fascinating, as is the pesky mannishness of Hepburn's heroine even when she reverts to frocks near the end.

'Fascinated', though, is not how anyone would describe audiences of the day. They took one look at this whimsical trifle and revolted against it – and by extension the twenty-seven-year-old Hepburn – almost as stridently as they'd reacted to *Freaks*. Pure public displeasure enforced a form of *de facto* censorship – effectively causing both Hepburn and her director, George Cukor, the biggest setback of their careers.

'Box Office Poison', Hepburn would brutally be dubbed three years after this debacle, in a notorious *Hollywood Reporter* advert, taken out in May 1938 by Harry Brandt, the President of the Independent Theater Owners' Association. 'WAKE UP! Hollywood Producers' ran the headline, before Brandt set about naming and shaming a litany of stars 'whose box office draw is nil'. It was pretty much all women: the likes of Mae West, Greta Garbo, Marlene Dietrich and Joan Crawford.

On behalf of cinema owners everywhere, Brandt begged for such stars to be cut loose: whatever their talents, he grumbled that their contracts were an insupportable burden on the industry. Hepburn was singled out for her 'negligible' public appeal, something that the comparative failure of her two most recent films, *Stage Door* (1937) and *Bringing Up Baby* (1938), had further borne out.

Much of this hostility to Hepburn can be traced right back to *Sylvia Scarlett*. Incensed by her tomboy antics, some might have wondered why the censors hadn't warned them. By now, the Hays Office had set to work enforcing its Production Code: the office had ordered brief nude scenes to be cut from *Tarzan and His Mate* (1934), and began stifling the career of Hollywood's sauciest icon, Mae West, by trimming out all her trademark double entendres.

Even if it was later condemned by the Legion of Decency, the Hays Office had no beef with *Sylvia Scarlett* at the script stage. And, indeed, it seems thoroughly innocuous today for a megaflop: it holds up uncontentiously as simply an eccentric, episodic romantic comedy about cross-dressing. It starts with Hepburn's Sylvia fleeing France on the cross-Channel ferry with her mischievous embezzler of a father (Edmund Gwenn), in the male disguise that becomes her second skin.

This is notable as Hepburn's first pairing with Cary Grant, in the role of a roguish cockney adventurer, Jimmy Monkley, whom father and 'son' befriend on the crossing. As this trio start living out of each other's pockets, teaming up as small-time con artists and then travelling circus buddies, Sylvia/Sylvester can't help but get the hots for this oblivious beefcake, especially when he takes his shirt off. He's earthy, rugged, and played by a thirty-year-old Cary Grant, and she is, after all, only human. Jimmy's reaction to her eventual gender reveal, in one of the deftest developments, is little more than a well-I-never scratch of the head.

Thanks to Cukor's direction, the touch remains charmingly light, especially in the scenes where a womanising bohemian artist called Fane (played by Brian Aherne at his most Errol Flynn-like) can't put his finger on why he finds this lad so appealing. He even refers to the 'queer feeling' he gets in Sylvester's obviously smitten company. Both men offer to share their bed with the boy – the gregarious Fane to be accommodating, and Jimmy to use him as a human hot-water bottle, which makes Hepburn positively fizz with impure thoughts and run away.

When she parts from Fane, beaming and lovestruck, she does this happy leap from his bedroom window into the garden. The moment is scarcely more than a grace note to end their scene, but there's supreme elegance to the way it's timed, in one fluid motion. 'I like the window!' Sylvester first explains. I'd go so far as to call this Chaplinesque flourish one of the most captivating things Hepburn ever did. Sylvester must also fend off the advances of a runaway maid-servant called Maudie (the delightful Dennie Moore) who thinks he's the real deal, daubs a moustache on his upper lip, and steals a kiss, from which Hepburn recoils in blushing shock.

It was an open secret in Hollywood that Cukor was gay, but 'queer feelings' in his films tended to be sublimated through their career-long identification with women – not least in *Little Women* (1933) and, indeed, *The Women* (1939), but also his many star vehicles for great actresses, from Garbo in *Camille* (1936) to Ingrid Bergman in *Gaslight* (1944) and Judy Garland in *A Star is Born* (1954). *Sylvia Scarlett*, with its plot entirely built around gender-bending trans-gressions, and that way-ahead-of-its-time 'queer' moment, is the closest thing to an 'out' Cukor picture you might find.

The script, by Gladys Unger, John Collier and Mortimer Offner, had been filleted down from a whopper of a 1918 novel by the Scottish author Compton Mackenzie, which Cukor often suspected Hepburn hadn't bothered to finish reading. It hardly mattered, given their ongoing rapport and mutual confidence. The director had plucked her from the stage to star opposite a stricken John Barrymore for her film debut, the earnest domestic drama *A Bill of Divorcement* (1932), and was instantly impressed, as were RKO, who signed her to a long-term contract.

Hepburn's second film, Dorothy Arzner's *Christopher Strong* (1933), cast her as an impetuous aviatrix pursuing a married aristocrat. Her no-fucks-given glamour peaked in that film when she arrives at a fancy-dress party in a glittering, ravishingly alien moth costume.

Already the toast of Hollywood, she won her first Best Actress Oscar* for *Morning Glory* (also 1933) but had a much bigger hit the same year with Cukor's *Little Women*, the first talkie version of Alcott's book. The full force of her coltishness and bright verve makes her many people's definitive Jo March. ('I defy anyone to be as good a Jo as I was,'[1] Hepburn said with classic vim in her later years.) Other projects had panned out less well, but she was so terrific in George Stevens' *Alice Adams* (1935),† from Booth Tarkington's novel about a deluded social climber, that she nearly won a second Oscar post-haste, coming second to Bette Davis for *Dangerous*.

Sylvia Scarlett wound up being one of those star-derailing projects – a *Gigli* of its day, if you like. There were few intimations on set of how badly the film was going to go down: it was largely shot around Trancas Beach in Malibu, with a cast and crew in hog heaven. As Cukor put it, 'Every day was Christmas.'[2]

---

* The other three would come decades later, for *Guess Who's Coming to Dinner* (1967), *The Lion in Winter* (1968) and *On Golden Pond* (1981).
† See also p. 52.

Swapping endless presents, they all sunbathed and picnicked on the cliffs, far away from any RKO meddling, or the eyes of 'supervising' producer Pandro S. Berman. One day, they spotted a small plane circling overhead, which landed in the adjacent field. This turned out to be Howard Hughes, a friend of Grant, who had let it be known that he wanted to meet Hepburn[3] – and would soon do so on the golf course, as you'll perhaps recall from Cate Blanchett's first scene in Martin Scorsese's *The Aviator* (2004).

Hepburn was loving the social life, but did have private reservations about what they were getting on camera. 'This picture makes no sense at all,' she confided to her diary, 'and I wonder whether George Cukor is aware of the fact, because I certainly don't know what the hell I'm doing.'[4]

Later in life, the pair would tend to gang up on the movie, dismissing it – Hepburn especially – as an unfunny shambles they'd realised was going wrong. 'For Kate and myself, our attitude has frozen into being comic about it,'[5] Cukor told Gavin Lambert. But they were still shocked by the first, 'ghastly' preview, which happened in San Pedro, Los Angeles, in early December 1935. As the film unspooled, no one was laughing, and any comic flow was upstaged by a steady trickle of exits. 'A nightmare,' as Cukor would reflect. 'People rushing out up the aisles!'[6]

RKO's president, B. B. Kahane, got up from his seat and paced nervously at the back. 'Those that stayed kept laughing in all the wrong places,' Cukor recalled.[7] A typical report card from one audience member: 'My only reaction was one of repugnance at witnessing such a lewd portrayal.'[8] Hepburn, for her part, would tell the story that she'd repaired for a breather to the ladies' room, and found a woman who had just fainted lying prostrate on a sofa. 'Did our picture finish you off?' the actress ventured, with the woman replying by raising her eyes to the rafters.[9]

Directly after this horror-show screening, Cukor and Hepburn took a tense ride back to Beverly Hills to meet Berman at Cukor's house – so tense that Hepburn bashed her head as she climbed in. 'Thank God – I've knocked myself out!' she quipped.

Their producer did not, on any level, see the funny side of what would pan out as RKO's worst box office failure of that year. Trying to be light-hearted, they begged him simply to scrap the film, offering to make another one for nothing. 'Don't bother, please!'[10] Hepburn records him saying in her memoir, while Cukor had an even darker memory of Berman's fuming words: 'I hope I never see either of you again.'[11]

In time, all would be patched up. Berman would produce plenty more Hepburn films (including the likes of *Stage Door*) and, many years later, Cukor's *Bhowani Junction* (1956) and *Justine* (1969). Having considered *Sylvia* a lost cause for so long after the 'terrible outcry' attending its release, Cukor would eventually warm to his own film when sympathetic interviewers quizzed him about it. 'The first part was terribly amusing,' he'd concede, calling it 'a picture in which the central idea simply got out of hand.'[12]

Still, no matter how flippant they tried to be about *Sylvia*'s failure at the time, the fact that it was considered RKO's worst ever A-picture stung, and had consequences. 'It wasn't pleasant,' Cukor told Lambert. 'It didn't really injure me – I think it injured Kate much more. But I certainly didn't like it.'[13]

If he was underplaying it there, he went on to confess in the same interview, 'The picture did something to me. It slowed me up. I wasn't going to be so goddamned daring after that. I thought, "Well, kiddo, don't you break all sorts of new paths, you just watch it."' His next film was MGM's *Romeo and Juliet* (1936), with (infamously) forty-three-year-old Leslie Howard and thirty-five-year-old Norma Shearer as the leads – a dutiful, sexless adaptation, little loved by Cukor later on; it has 'safe retrenchment' written all over it.

As for Hepburn, the frighteningly modern figure she cut for the viewing public marked her card as a performer who simply couldn't be trusted. Off screen, she would continue the crusades of her mother, the suffrage leader Katharine Martha Houghton Hepburn, in campaigning for abortion and birth-control rights. Her next three films for RKO, all period pieces positioning her as women of destiny, bombed: *Mary of Scotland* (1936), *A Woman Rebels* (1936) and *Quality Street* (1937). This string of failures compounded the *Sylvia* effect and sent her career into 'a real nosedive'[14] that could easily have been terminal, for all her efforts to shake it off.*

None of it was fair. She's utterly wonderful in Cukor's equally wonderful *Holiday* (1938) – her finest collaboration with Grant, too – and it still barely broke even. Not until they all tried again with *The Philadelphia Story* (1940), tailored to Hepburn specifically on Broadway as a return ticket to stardom, did the comeback click. (It was partly masterminded by Hughes, during their 18-month love affair.) And even then, Cukor's film had to begin (shockingly, to our tastes now) with Grant pushing Hepburn to the ground through her own front door. Strategically, it was key to Hepburn's rehabilitation that she first had to be taken down a peg or two, before being tamed as half of an evergreen double act, with cranky, dependable Spencer Tracy, that would see them paired nine times.

All the while, Grant had sailed through a string of flops practically unscathed – three of them right alongside Hepburn – and somehow ascended to the peak of his pulling power. Sure, he'd had a wobbly time at Paramount in the early 1930s, but no one took out adverts labelling *him* box office poison. Indeed, he would credit *Sylvia Scarlett*

---

* 'No other star has emerged with greater rapidity or with more ecstatic acclaim. No other star, either, has become so unpopular so quickly for so long a time.' Andrew Britton, *Katharine Hepburn: Star as Feminist*, p. 13.

as a watershed moment in his career. He wasn't required to carry it as a romantic lead, so was able to cut loose, playing a character much closer to his raffish cockney roots than any of the dinner-suit charmers he'd previously embodied.

It's dismayingly logical that the star who cross-dressed got the flak for *Sylvia Scarlett* – there had to be a scapegoat, and it had to be Hepburn. What did she have in common, after all, with those fellow vials of poison, Dietrich, Garbo, Crawford, Mae West? They're all gay icons for a reason, and their best characters are rarely on screen to make friends.

We know now, as audiences perhaps only vaguely clocked at the time, that bisexuality among Hollywood's A-list was something close to a norm, and that an impressive majority of the dramatis personae in this chapter – Hepburn, Grant, Crawford, Hughes, Tracy – were at the very least bi, if not predominantly (Edmund Gwenn, Garbo) or wholly (Arzner, Cukor) gay.

Not box office favourite Bette Davis, however. Or Will Hays, whose Code expressly forbade any overt references to homosexuality in the scripts his office read – a straitjacket (straightjacket?) that the slippery *Sylvia Scarlett* must have narrowly wriggled out of. Decades later, if we needed more evidence for the general feeling of embarrassment around the film, *All About Eve*'s writer-director, Joseph L. Mankiewicz, would recall thinking it was 'very fey, and very wrong'.[15]

It became a cautionary tale for female stars across the century, as Barbra Streisand explained in her 2023 memoir, *My Name Is Barbra*. 'Obviously I knew *Yentl* was not exactly commercial,' she wrote. 'And there was the obvious hurdle that I would spend most of the movie dressed as a man. The last actress who had tried that was Katharine Hepburn in *Sylvia Scarlett* back in 1935, and it didn't turn out too well.'

This notoriety may have depended specifically on Hepburn's gender. When Grant released *I Was a Male War Bride* in 1949, it was a bumper hit – as was *Some Like It Hot* (1959), of course. Were filmgoers more relaxed about watching top-flight stars dabbling in drag* by then, or was it simply that men doing it was considered funnier? In Grant's case, it's closer to pantomime – a stunt, with him making a fool of himself. It *is* funnier, while also being more facile.

Hepburn was nobody's fool. Her *self-assurance* in drag, surely, was the underlying cause of the outrage – there was a cockiness, a strut, to it. Her character isn't humiliatingly forced into it, but flings herself eagerly into a male persona, stays in that skin long past the point where it's strictly needed, and thrives.

Sylvia Scarlett remains neglected: it ought to have accrued more of a twenty-first-century cult by now than it really has. Cukor might not have intended this on any conscious level, but Sylvia's transition to becoming Sylvester was presented from the start as a species of life choice, not just a fleeting punchline. If they weren't going to laugh at this prototypical display of gender fluidity, the impressionable public in 1935 didn't know what options remained – except booing.

---

* Only for about ten minutes, in Grant's case, and at the very end.

THE MAGNIFICENT
AMBERSONS (1942)

Director: Orson Welles
Studio: RKO
Budget: $1.1m
Loss recorded of $625,000

We've dealt so far with pictures that missed their mark, misjudged public appetites, or were derailed, after panicked screechings of brakes, by their own confusing novelty. With *The Magnificent Ambersons*, one of film history's most devastating might-have-beens, we now have to confront an instance of wilful sabotage from on high.

Infamously recut and substantially reshot without Orson Welles, *Ambersons'* runaway maestro, getting any say from afar, this grandiose elegy to a lost America was unceremoniously desecrated by a bankrupt studio that had run out of faith in what the film was trying to say.

The bombing of Pearl Harbor, which triggered this crisis of confidence between shoot and edit, was only the second worst thing that ever happened to *The Magnificent Ambersons*. The worst – galling to this day – was the routine destruction of Welles's original cut, the negatives of which were incinerated by executive order the following December, to free up space in RKO's vault. This wasn't even personal: it was standard industry practice to burn unused nitrate negatives after six months, to salvage the silver in the emulsion.*

---

* As pointed out in Robert Carringer's *The Magnificent Ambersons: A Reconstruction* (p. 2), the leftover material from Hitchcock's *Suspicion* (1941),

49

There is a world in which all this damage might have been undone – if we could only find the work print of that 132-minute original edit, which Welles is known to have been sent in Brazil, as he flung himself into his next (unfinished) project, *It's All True*. Weirder things have happened in the byways of film history, and even in the realm of Orson Welles studies, long a haven for obsessives and dreamers after his own heart.

After all, an unfinished work print of Welles's 1938 short farce *Too Much Johnson*, previously thought lost, showed up in an Italian warehouse in 2013. Meanwhile, several cans of the aborted *It's All True*, labelled 'BRAZIL' and amounting to 20 hours of negative, were found in Paramount's vault by a researcher named Fred Chandler in the early 1980s.

Plus, twice, Universal's bowdlerisation of Welles's *Touch of Evil* (1958) has been redressed – first when the studio unearthed a 108-minute print in 1976, and then in 1998, when Walter Murch oversaw a close-to-definitive 111-minute reconstruction using Welles's own editing notes.

With *Ambersons*, though, there remains this yawning gulf between the only version we still have – the RKO-dictated 88-minute one – and the holy grail of that 132-minute version, shown only once to an audience, at a Pasadena preview in March 1942.

For all the storyboards and shot lists that have survived, bridging that gap remains a feat of the imagination, and it's the only way now to appreciate everything Welles wanted his film to be. We have to extend him exactly the faith that RKO would not, when they cut him off at the knees.

---

another RKO production, was destroyed at the same time, so it hardly seems likely that selective vindictiveness was at work.

From one angle, the whole sorry saga is an Icarus story, with Welles as the boy wonder scorched – destroyed, he would later say – by his own incandescence. He was only twenty-six, had just made one of the greatest debuts of all time, and was subject to the twin pressures of rapturous acclaim and mounting industry resentment. Though *Citizen Kane* got nine Oscar nominations, we shouldn't forget that it was booed in every category at the Biltmore Hotel on 26 February 1942, and won only for Best Original Screenplay, an award that neither Welles nor Herman J. Mankiewicz was present to collect.

Of course, Welles had made powerful enemies with his ostensible calling card, above all William Randolph Hearst, the media mogul Kane was obviously based on, who counted many of Hollywood's elite among his cronies. But the upstart director, from an artsy theatre and radio background, was also being punished for achieving too much too young. He wasn't 'movie people', disdained commerce, and already had a target on his back.

RKO hadn't made a dime on *Kane*, and its then president, George Schaefer, who had first offered Welles his astonishingly liberal contract (including final cut), was fighting a losing battle against his board about bankrolling Welles at all. Two pipe dreams Welles had talked up grandiloquently had failed to come to fruition – his adaptation of Joseph Conrad's *Heart of Darkness*, and a romantic espionage thriller called *The Way to Santiago*, which neither RKO nor the Mexican government was particularly keen on. He was meant to direct the Eric Ambler spy thriller *Journey into Fear* (1943), as well as co-writing, producing and co-starring in it, but passed the reins onto Norman Foster.

After all this chopping and changing, Welles chose to follow up *Kane* with *The Magnificent Ambersons*, a much-admired, now-little-read

1918 novel for which Booth Tarkington had won the first of his two Pulitzer prizes.*

This stately saga of a Midwestern family's decline amid the turbulence of industrialisation had grand themes, potential for florid period detail, and plenty of juicy roles for Welles stalwarts (Joseph Cotten, Agnes Moorehead, Ray Collins, Erskine Sanford). There was a logic, too, in Welles luring the silent star Dolores Costello out of semi-retirement to play the widowed heiress Isabel, even if this throwback actress seems too matronly for the younger phases of her role.

Conversely, Anne Baxter, just eighteen at the time, would give a luminously mature performance as Lucy, the daughter of Isabel's suitor Eugene (Cotten). And meanwhile, the cowboy actor Tim Holt, hardly a typical Wellesian player, had a tricky assignment in rendering Isabel's son, the last-of-the-line Amberson scion George, into more than just a spoilt brat – the 'princely terror' of the clan, with his fraught, Oedipal attachment to his mother.

Welles's biographer Simon Callow comes down hard on Holt: 'stocky, plebeian in manner, sulky and impetuous',[1] where the George of Tarkington ought to have had a haughty, aquiline bearing. Depending on your point of view, it's either a coarse instance of miscasting or a rather bold reconception of the role. Welles had toyed with playing that part himself, but decided instead to handle the lightly mocking, omniscient narration, which manages to set a genteelly self-aware tone, then modulate towards melancholy – a trick Wes Anderson continues to imitate often, and sometimes well, especially in *The Royal Tenenbaums* (2001).

Ambersons might not have been perfect, or even ideally cast, but it could still have taken shape as an exquisite monument to faded ideals; a sad, haunted, dying fall of a movie, with a last scene at a

---

* The other was for *Alice Adams* (see p. 42).

dismal boarding house that was Welles's own invention, quite different from Tarkington's happy-ish denouement. Welles was proud of
this ending – by all accounts justly so. It should have been the finest
scene of Moorehead's and Cotten's careers: their characters, Eugene
and the fragile, long-smitten Aunt Fanny, can barely hear themselves
over the clatter of her cheap lodgings.

As Welles described the scene to Peter Bogdanovich, 'There's nothing left between them at all. Everything is over – her feelings and her
world and his world; everything is buried under the parking lots and
the cars. That's what it was all about – the deterioration of personality, the way people diminish with age . . . But without question it
was much the best scene in the movie.'[2] Alas, like so much else in the
film, it was ripped away the moment the film first previewed, not in
Pasadena, but Pomona, two days before.

Welles had good reasons to be out of the country, but would regret
them bitterly in his later years. He'd already been in Rio for six weeks,
shooting footage in and around the Carnival for *It's All True*, a portmanteau project suggested to him by Nelson Rockefeller after Pearl
Harbor. This was to be Orson's contribution to the US war effort,
hatched as a way to maintain good relations with Latin America.

RKO was slightly held over a barrel to fund this ultimately
abandoned enterprise, because Rockefeller, then US Coordinator
of Inter-American Affairs, was a major stockholder on the board.
Scrabbling to get a rough cut of *Ambersons* together before his departure on 2 February, Welles left his baby in the custody of supervising
editor Robert Wise – the man who would later direct *West Side Story*
(1961), *The Haunting* (1963) and *The Sound of Music* (1965).

Oscar-nominated at twenty-six for cutting *Kane*, Wise had an
impossible go-between role in the fate of *Ambersons*, leading him to
be accused forever more by Welles and his acolytes of rank treachery
at the studio's behest. Wise, who lived to ninety-one, would become

tired of raking over the whole affair, and defended his actions largely by reference to Welles's long absence in Brazil. '[Orson] was happy to go down there and get out of the draft,' Wise countered in his last-ever interview. 'He was draft age, remember [. . .] And, according to the stories that came back, he was having some parties and a pretty good time.'[3]

These pages are rife with ruinous test screenings. But this one perhaps takes the biscuit, thanks to a variety of mutually aggravating factors. The Los Angeles suburb of Pomona, at the time, was a proving ground for Hollywood product among middle-class audiences, but the ones who attended on 17 March 1942 were largely restless teenagers, needing an escape from wartime worries and world news. The film they'd come to see, at the top of the bill, was *The Fleet's In*, a musical comedy about sailors on leave, starring William Holden and pin-up-girl-of-the-moment Dorothy Lamour. RKO's decision to roll *Ambersons* after this frivolous romp is the rough equivalent, in 2003, of scheduling *Mystic River* after *Legally Blonde 2*.

The boredom of this rowdy crowd scarred the film forever. This is in spite of a nervous intervention from Welles himself, who possibly had a hunch that 132 minutes of a sad, haunted dying fall were not going to keep the joint buzzing, and instructed Wise to chop around 22 minutes from the middle.

When the report cards came in, they sent Schaefer and Wise into a tailspin. Wise would call it the worst test screening he'd ever attended. Their high hopes that the film might be taken seriously were savaged by the slew of walk-outs, the 72 out of 125 negative assessments, and the sarcastic laughter that plagued so many dramatic scenes, especially those involving Aunt Fanny's descent into hysteria.

'Never, in all my experience in the industry,' Schaefer wrote to Welles, 'have I taken so much punishment or suffered as I did at the Pomona preview [. . .] The picture was too slow, heavy, and, topped off with somber music, never did register.'[4] Welles's 22-minute excision can hardly have preserved emotional continuity, and this atypically panicky move counted against him: if it wasn't working with an audience even at that shortened length, what hope did it have at all? 'The picture does seem to bear down on people,' Wise cabled in desperation to Welles.

Two days later, in Pasadena, Wise made the honourable move of reinstating the section Welles had jettisoned, and the response was a lot more positive. But it was already too late. Welles knew the film was slipping away from him, and the long cables he was sending to his production manager, Jack Moss, detailing every nip and tuck he wanted, were effectively attempts to shut the stable door after the horse had bolted.

After *Kane*, he'd revised his contract with RKO, and lost the right of final cut in the process, a concession that came back to bite him brutally. Meanwhile, Schaefer gave Wise full authority in April 1942 to get the film down to releasable length, whatever it took. 'I just knew that we had a sick picture and it needed a doctor,' Wise would explain. 'It would have been so much easier if [Welles] could have been there.'[5]

There are stories of the older Welles's reluctance ever to watch the film in its extant form, and tales of him silently crying when he caught snatches of it over the years. When watching it once with his friend Henry Jaglom on cable, he was appreciative up to a point, then grabbed the remote 20 minutes before the end and switched it off. 'From here on it becomes *their* movie,' he explained. 'It becomes bullshit.'[6] Gone, indeed, was the entire drift of his final act, and patched in were a string of clunky remedial scenes, shot as pick-ups without him.

The boarding house was substituted by a reshot ending, closer to the upbeat one Tarkington wrote. Filmed by assistant director

Freddie Fleck with Cotten and Moorehead in a hospital corridor, it delivered this embattled film its final slap in the face. On every viewing of *Ambersons*, the scene looks worse: a banal, smiling-through tears exchange about everything being fine and a brighter future beckoning. We barely recognise the two characters involved, and you can well imagine Welles shuddering with horror when he first saw it.

Nothing went well for *Ambersons* from this point forth. The delays releasing it had only worsened the film's blatant incompatibility with what audiences were after. 'Guys were going off to training camp,' Wise would put it, 'as people and the whole country were gearing up to go to war. Women were getting jobs in aircraft factories.'[7] It was hard to get anyone to care, as he put it, 'about the problems of Georgie Minafer, the Amberson family and Indianapolis at the turn of the century.' With American industry mobilising right then for an enormous test of its mettle, Tarkington's laments about the price of progress – all the factory smog blighting the old charm of the Midwest – made Welles's film look like a fusty antique.

And then, a regime change at RKO that summer saw Schaefer ousted, to be replaced by the much less sympathetic Charles Koerner, who fired Welles, scrapped *It's All True*, and threw the Mercury Theatre staff off RKO's lot. He had no confidence even in an 88-minute *Ambersons* with a naff happy ending, and released it with minimal fanfare, in just two Los Angeles venues, on the bottom half of a bill with the Lupe Vélez comedy sequel *Mexican Spitfire Sees a Ghost*.

The *Ambersons* we have is a long way from nothing. A seductive aura has grown around it. As two-thirds of a great film, poignantly stymied, it speaks to us of cinema's best-laid plans and their aptitude to crumble. If Welles had made it at a more experienced age, when he knew his way around the pit-traps of the business, could it have stayed intact?

Tempting though these speculations are, *Ambersons'* singularity is that it arrived out of time – you wouldn't say ahead of its time – with its lambent classicism. It took a remorseful overview of American lives at the least propitious moment in modern memory. Through a fateful kind of alchemy, the tragedy it wanted to relate wound up baked, instead, into the film's clay – as a site of yearning, unfulfilled ambitions, and broken dreams.

LAND OF THE PHARAOHS (1955)

Director: Howard Hawks
Studio: Warner Bros
Budget: $3.15m
US gross: $2.7m

In April 1954, a scorching day of slave labour was afoot, in a stone quarry near the unfinished Egyptian pyramid of Zawyet El Aryan, outside Giza. Many thousands of extras were needed to achieve one of the grandest location shots in Howard Hawks's *Land of the Pharaohs*, which had just started production in an extreme state of unreadiness.

An uncharacteristically nervous Hawks hoped to put his best foot forward by getting at least one huge money shot in the can. To court favour, he sent the rushes post-haste to Jack Warner at Burbank, to show where the $1.75m budget was going.

The sequence was all heave-ho – the shouldering of stone blocks to start work on the funeral complex of Pharaoh Khufu (Jack Hawkins), the film's dictatorial main character, whose life's work becomes focused on building humanity's blingest death monument. Many of the extras were Egyptian army recruits, lent to the production by the beneficence of President Neguib, as if to prove that 4,000 years of human history hadn't wholly rejigged the country's power structures. But the toil and boredom of these nearly naked men, after three lengthy rehearsals, was taking its toll. It was murder to choreograph them in unison.

The second unit director, Noël Howard, who would write a book-length memoir in French about the shoot, *Hollywood sur Nil,* came up with an idea. He managed the crowd by getting them to chant a few sing-song phonetic phrases as they heaved and ho-ed. Few of these were words they understood: 'Lift that barge!'; 'Get a little drunk!'; 'Smoke Chesterfield!' But then a scurrilous mood must have taken over. To Hawks's amazement as he looked on, the sound of thousands of Egyptians chanting 'Fuck Warner Brothers!' came rising from the quarry's depths.[1]

As Hawks took a car back to his hotel, his driver remembered him smiling and muttering this to himself the whole way. But the signs of him being in over his head, a rare event in his prolific career, were obvious to all. Newly married in February 1953 to his third wife, the TV actress Dee Hartford, Hawks was entering his late fifties (Dee was twenty-four) and had a lot of expensive alimony to sort out. He struck a deal with Jack Warner that would net him $100,000 plus 50 per cent of the profits – then an unheard-of package for a mere director – for a film of their choosing, with a Hitchcock-style possessive credit thrown in, along with $1,000 in weekly expenses, a car, and a secretary.

The trouble was picking a subject. 20th Century Fox had just had a whopping hit with *The Robe* (1953),* the first production in ultra-widescreen CinemaScope, which broke industry records and had every studio racing to cash in. So it was that the vague idea for *Land of the Pharaohs* was born – not Judeo-Christian, this one, but still a sandy epic about obsession on a grand scale.

Hawks was in plaid swimming trunks, lounging around the pool of the Hotel du Cap-Eden-Roc in Antibes, when he got the green light from Warner. Howard remembers the director asking in what

---

* Directed by Henry Koster, starring Richard Burton as the Roman tribune, Marcellus Gallio, who was responsible for Christ's crucifixion. It cost around $4m and grossed $36m, making it the No. 2 hit of 1953 behind Disney's *Peter Pan*.

direction Egypt lay across the Mediterranean. 'Noël,' he drawled, pointing towards it. 'I am going to build a pyramid.'[2]

The next months were a mad rush of getting the picture planned, designed, cast, and written, all mostly at the same time. But written last. Hawks hired the renowned Hungarian-French Alexandre Trauner (*Les enfants du paradis*) as his art director and the aspiring director Howard as his right-hand man. Noël Howard's greatest talent was in subterfuge: he would get the best tables at all the restaurants by calling ahead and adding a slight cough to his surname.

The script was a constant sticking point. Always much more comfortable with the wiseacre banter of cynical newspapermen or jaded gunslingers, Hawks knew next to nothing about the ancient world. He needed some serious weight on the page, but neither Anthony Veiller (*Beat the Devil*) nor Ben Hecht (*Scarface*) liked the look of the project. Nor did the potential godsend Robert Graves (*I, Claudius*). Hawks turned instead to a triumvirate of scribes, only two of whom made significant contributions to the finished film: the divorced expat screenwriter Harry Kurnitz, seasoned veteran of Errol Flynn swashbucklers, and a twenty-nine-year-old New Yorker called Harold Jack Bloom, about to be Oscar-nominated for his first job, on Anthony Mann's *The Naked Spur* (1953).

The third writer, unfortunately, was William Faulkner, a Hawks bosom buddy who'd helped adapt two of his best films, *To Have and Have Not* (1944) and *The Big Sleep* (1946). The recent Nobel laureate needed cash as badly as Hawks, and pounced on what he assumed would be hack work for the $15,000 fee plus living expenses. On arrival, Faulkner was dumped in Hawks's Paris hotel suite entirely drunk and bleeding from a head wound, having over-imbibed on his journey to Europe and been assaulted by thugs in a late-night bar. 'Hawks – Plaza' were the only words he managed to say to the local gendarmes before collapsing in a stupor.

It rapidly became clear to Kurnitz and Bloom that Faulkner's heart was certainly not in the actual writing. 'He didn't see movies and didn't like them,' Bloom would recall. 'He thought they were for children.'[3] His idea to have the pharaoh talk like a Southern plantation owner – pure Faulkner – competed with Kurnitz's notion that he ought to be modelled on King Lear. 'I don't know how a pharaoh talks,' Hawks would explain to Peter Bogdanovich in 1962. 'And Faulkner didn't know. None of us knew.'[4]

Amid these tugs of war, they were falling well behind the other departments. Trauner's sets were good to go, after consultation with the world's leading Egyptologist, Jean-Philippe Lauer, about the contentious question of how the world's tallest structures were actually built, as well as the ingenious methods used to seal off their burial chambers, which would provide the film with pretty much its entire third act.

Howard, who had been put in charge of research and historical accuracy, had bad news for Hawks when construction began on thirty chariots for the pharaoh's entourage. According to hieroglyphics of the twenty-sixth century BC, Egyptians didn't have the wheel yet, so they didn't have chariots. Nor, to the huge dismay of the film's animal wrangler, did they have horses. Or camels. Hawks took Howard aside and begged him, 'I'll make a deal with you – I give up the horses, but for God's sake, Noël, let me have camels!'[5]

While Hawks burrowed down into these details, the plotting and dialogue were in a state of chaos, not helped when the director swanned off for a skiing holiday with Dee and their miniature poodle. Faulkner, meanwhile, was on a side quest of his own, to obtain as many bottles of a 1949 Chassagne-Montrachet as he could from a favourite French restaurant. After five weeks of binge drinking and barely a single line of usable dialogue to show for it, Hawks finally let Faulkner go, marking the inglorious end of the writer's Hollywood career.

With such expense going into the set-building, there was never much in the budget left over for big-name stars. Jack Hawkins was respected at the time, but not exactly a Wayne or a Bogart, and his British military bearing gave him a hard time getting fully into character, especially given the dialogue at hand. 'Some of the lines we were expected to speak were unspeakable,'[6] he later complained, having largely signed on in the hope of having some Faulkner poetry to recite. He would call the film 'perfectly ridiculous'.

For the lead female role – the wicked Princess Nellifer, a Cypriot ambassador who offers herself to Khufu and becomes his avaricious second wife – Hawks wrote to Warner that they needed 'the most beautiful, sexy girl we can find'.[7]

On the strength of a screen test much trumpeted in Hollywood, they pursued the seventeen-year-old Ursula Andress,* but Paramount had already snapped her up. Hawks's wife Dee was briefly mooted – by him – but she was pregnant, saving some embarrassment all round. Gina Lollobrigida's name got thrown into the hat, too. The supermodel Ivy Nicholson was flown into Cairo for a test, but when she had to act biting Hawkins on the hand, she gnashed through it right to the bone, enraging him, and was dismissed as 'a little cuckoo'.[8]

With camp inevitability, they wound up with Joan Collins. Hawks had met the sultry twenty-year-old brunette in Paris a year earlier, and cast her somewhat reluctantly, because her sexuality wasn't the cool, aloof type he usually favoured. She'd played a series of bad girls in various British quickies, and continued that theme – indeed, not just on-screen but off-screen too.

---

* Andress's reluctance to learn English meant she profited nicely from Paramount's and Columbia's stipends without making a single film for either. Even in *Dr. No* (1962), she was dubbed.

Straightaway, she started a fling with Sydney Chaplin, son of Charlie, who was playing the Captain of the Guard whom Nellifer seduces. When the shoot moved to interior scenes in Rome, the pair would stay up all night cavorting on the Via Veneto, much to Hawks's displeasure.

All the pasta and red wine took their toll, and both became over-weight for their parts. 'You do not have the appearance of starving,' which Khufu says to Nellifer in their first scene, sounds suspiciously like a nervous rewrite. Collins had to suck in her stomach to fit into the bejewelled costumes made to measure for her when she was eight pounds lighter. On one take, a fake red ruby, stuck in her bare navel to placate the censors, popped right out onto the floor. 'Get some airplane glue!' Hawks barked to the crew. 'Get anything to keep the damn thing in place.'[9]

The lovebirds found it difficult to take their ultra-solemn dialogue at all seriously. Chaplin kept corpsing when he had to declare his love for Nellifer, and soon cracked Collins up too, spreading an irreverent mood to the entire crew. Hawks was furious at this insult to his author-ity on set, and called off shooting for the rest of the day, warning both actors they were putting their future careers in jeopardy.

Todd McCarthy's classic Hawks biography has a detailed account of all the other issues that made this shoot such a nightmare. There were countless problems of heat, language barriers, censored inter-national communications, equipment failure, the arrival of Ramadan, and even a headline-causing incident in which Egypt accused Warner Bros of smuggling because Trauner had bought a mummified bird, and his assistant was caught with it at customs.

'At one point, a fight broke out among some extras, resulting in the death of one man; at another, some army extras mutinied and charged the film crew, resulting in Hawks and [director of photo-graphy] Russ Harlan having to fend them off by throwing rocks.

Later, the threat of hostilities with Israel caused the disappearance of virtually all the extras overnight.'[10]

Through all this, you might have expected rising anxiety from the executives, but the PR job Hawks kept doing with Jack Warner had been working almost too well. On the strength of his epic crowd footage, the studio was sure it had a massive hit on its hands. Charles Feldman, Hawks's powerful agent, speculated it could make $20–30m, and wired him to say, 'Jack Warner is really overboard about the rushes . . . Confidentially, he feels [it] is the greatest stuff he has seen in his life.'[11]

Mirage as it was, the idea of hitting the jackpot put a gleam in Hawks's eye – his highest grosser before that, the wartime rabble-rouser *Sergeant York* (1941), had netted a mere $6m. One day, Noël Howard snuck in to find him in the set of the pharaoh's treasure chamber, looking to and fro at the huge piles of fake gold and jewellery, until he gave a start when Chaplin, too, abruptly entered. 'Sydney, look at all this,' he recovered to say to the actor. 'Isn't it . . . beautiful?'[12]

It was only in the final weeks of the shoot, when production manager Gerry Blattner calculated the final cost, that Warner went ballistic. 'In my wildest imagination never would believe could go this figure,'[13] he wired apoplectically to Hawks. He didn't like the new footage he was seeing from Rome, either, complaining that the camera was too far from the actors, a problem inherent in trying to use the CinemaScope format indoors.

Hawks was disillusioned with the wide-screen process and would never use it again, not even for the open-range safari scenes in *Hatari!* (1962). Because of the awkwardness of splicing close-ups and master shots together, it made the cutting process hell. The original editor, Vladimir Sagovsky, was fired. His replacement, Rudi Fehr, took one look at the assembly and pointed out that the story didn't begin until page 54. 'I tried restructuring but it didn't work,' Fehr would recall. 'Howard knew it. They never solved their problems.'[14]

Even though test screenings of the film were apparently excellent, and even the early reviews quite kind, it slowly dawned on everyone that *Land of the Pharaohs* was going to be nothing like the blockbuster they'd dreamed of. 'We really had a scabby bunch of characters in that picture,' Hawks later reasoned. 'That was my fault. It could have been very easily fixed.'[15] It lacked the stars or biblical prestige of rival attractions, so Warners panicked with a low-brow ad campaign trading on lurid, *Duel in the Sun*-style sensationalism instead: 'Her Treachery Stained Every Stone of the Pyramid!' ran one tagline.

It would never reach higher than No. 4 at the US box office, and took a measly $4.2m worldwide, leaving Warners $1.5m out of pocket after prints and advertising. Going down as Hawks's costliest failure, it would send him into a brooding hiatus for three years before his comeback with *Rio Bravo* (1959).

Watched today in the right Sunday-matinee spirit, *Land of the Pharaohs* is a daft delight, and actually one of Hawks's most entertaining films of that period, both for reasons he intended and some that he didn't. It's quite apparent that Hawks's habitual cleverness and control, which resulted in several flinty masterpieces, deserted him on this occasion, but there's something about the film's combination of puffed-up spectacle and soapy melodrama that makes it an engagingly trashy artefact. At 107 minutes, it's a good hour shorter than the roadshow spectaculars Cecil B. DeMille was putting out at the time, which undeniably helps.

Especially hard to shake is the finale, when Nellifer realises her murderous schemes have led to her sitting pretty, atop all the untold wealth in the pharaoh's kingdom . . . until it dawns on her that she's trapped inside the self-sealing burial chamber, just another trinket in his tomb.

With all the detail it lavishes on this one exorbitant building project, the film's a folly about a folly, a monument to megalomania that gets carried away in its own right – as if Ozymandias had commissioned a commemorative poem and found himself stuck with Shelley's.

'When I first saw it as a kid, *Land of the Pharaohs* became my favourite film,'* has said no less a light than Martin Scorsese, who was thirteen when it opened – perhaps the perfect age to appreciate its tawdry sense of the exotic, and Joan Collins as a conniving temptress in lashings of shiny fake tan. She looks a lot like Elizabeth Taylor in *Cleopatra* (1963) – a role for which Collins would even screen-test when Walter Wanger was casting it.

If you want to look for the film's influence in Scorsese's later output, the place to go is *Casino* (1995), his own treatment of amassing a fortune, losing your soul, and marrying an exuberant, unfaithful gold-digger who wants to take you to the cleaners. It's practically an unofficial remake. De Niro's Ace Rothstein is an abusive tyrant cut from Khufu's cloth, while Sharon Stone, shaking those dice and rolling around in armfuls of sumptuous Bulgari, never had a more Collins-esque role.

The sphinx and pyramid of Vegas's Luxor Hotel even feature in *Casino*'s cynical closing montage: 'Where did the money come from to rebuild the pyramids? Junk bonds,' rues Ace. Hawks may have looked back on *Land of the Pharaohs* with a similar sense of waste, but as a gaudy pile of wreckage it still glitters and tempts.

---

* *Film Comment*, September–October 1978, when Scorsese inaugurated the magazine's long-running 'Guilty Pleasures' column. Other than *Pharaohs*, few of his other choices feel at all worthy of guilt, with the possible exception of *Exorcist II: The Heretic* (1977).

DOCTOR DOLITTLE (1967)
(and the collapse of the roadshow)

Director: Richard Fleischer
Studio: 20th Century Fox
Budget: $18m (before marketing)
Loss recorded of $11,141,000
Further test cases: *Camelot* (1967), *Star!* (1968),
Hello, Dolly! (1969), *Paint Your Wagon* (1969),
Goodbye, Mr Chips (1969), *Darling Lili* (1970)

When is a crushing flop also a Best Picture nominee? It happens – but usually when there's a certain bouquet of critical respect sprucing up the film's chances. Both Spielberg's *West Side Story* (2021) and *The Fabelmans* (2022) found dismayingly little commercial favour, but were warmly received in the circles that mattered, as weighty prestige pictures by a beloved film artist, and so bagged seven Oscar nominations apiece.

We've had one such anomaly already: amazingly, *The Magnificent Ambersons* snuck into the running for the Academy's top prize, as one of ten Best Picture nominees in February 1943. Tempting as it might be to interpret this as some consolation prize for everything Welles suffered in its post-production, it's not as if he was nominated for Best Director; indeed, studios hoovered up even more of the Best Picture glory back then. To see RKO given this hat-tip is, we might speculate, unlikely to have made Welles's day.

Come the 1960s, there was no studio that mounted an awards campaign with the blithe extravagance of 20th Century Fox. Budgets skyrocketed in this era, as Hollywood threw everything it could at top-dollar attractions to win viewers away from their TV sets.* Only the ultra-widescreen spectacle of so-called 'roadshow' presentations, harking back to the pushy hucksterism of Griffith's day, could make the biggest releases worth leaving the couch for.

In this era, roadshows meant reserved-ticket engagements, at a premium price tag in a handful of giant screens, to hype up a block-buster before it unspooled for the masses. Such rollouts could then run and run for a year or more, like MGM's *Ben-Hur* (1959) did, raking in profits. Festooning your film with the spurious bunting of Oscar recognition was all part of the game.

Then, in 1963, came *Cleopatra*. The staggering cost of this four-hour epic had already nudged Fox to the very brink of bankruptcy. It took an almighty promotional drive to convince audiences this over-blown pageant was worth the bother. Elizabeth Taylor and Richard Burton had been coaxed into starring with juicy back-end deals atop already hefty salaries, which made clawing out of the red, from a studio accountancy standpoint, next to impossible.[†]

If you're wondering why *Cleopatra*, a famously hellish shoot and by far the most expensive film of its day, didn't demand a chapter unto herself here, there's a simple reason: that film did eventually break even, while earning very little money for anyone bar Elizabeth Taylor. It managed to squeak to No. 1 in the box office charts for 1963, with a domestic gross of $57.7m on its eye-watering $44m[‡] budget.

---

* Nine out of ten American households owned a set by 1960.

† Fox executives were sent to Rome to try to fire Taylor as late as June 1962. In 1964, the company would launch a $50m suit against Taylor and Burton for 'depreciating the commercial value' of *Cleopatra* through 'conduct and deportment' – a clear reference to their tumultuous, alcohol-fuelled on-set affair.

‡ Includes marketing costs; adjusted for inflation in 2024, this is something in the range of $440m.

No one involved had much of a kind word for it, with Taylor calling it 'a botch-up', the soon-to-be-ousted Fox president Spyros Skouras admitting it had cost $20m too much, and the director, Joseph L. Mankiewicz, commenting that it 'was conceived in a state of emergency and wound up in a blind panic'.[1] And yet, thanks to Fox's undeterred push and an exceptionally weak year for quality film-making, this chintzy behemoth, which you could repackage as an entire season of MTV's *Entombment Cribs*, gorged itself on nine Oscar nominations, including Best Picture, and ultimately won four tech awards.

Financially, Fox was headed on a rollercoaster ride. The company's fortunes had been in the gutter – they'd sold off their backlot in 1961 to pay for *Cleopatra*'s rising costs – but would soar two years later, when they capitalised on an explosive renaissance in full-scale musicals. They obliterated every box office record with Robert Wise's *The Sound of Music* (1965), which nearly outgrossed the combined takings of two other huge hits from rival studios – Warner Brothers' *My Fair Lady* and Disney's *Mary Poppins* (both 1964).

Collectively netting 18 Oscars, this trio of evergreen classics would prove a false dawn for a much-loved but notoriously disaster-prone genre. For this excitable moment, an atavistic nostalgia for song and dance certainly looked like the mass entertainment that everyone (bar a few grumbling critics) craved. All the studio chiefs were persuaded that musicals were a guaranteed goldmine. Whether they featured soot-cheeked chimney sweeps, animated penguins or even non-singing Nazis, it didn't matter, especially if Julie Andrews* starred.

---

* Andrews, famously, had been rejected for *My Fair Lady* in favour of Audrey Hepburn, despite originating the role of Eliza on stage. This was Jack Warner's call. She got her own back by sarcastically thanking him in her Oscar acceptance speech for *Mary Poppins*.

The view from the top of this log-flume ride was admittedly dazzling, but no one had yet figured out how precipitous the plunge might be. In the race to find the next *Sound of Music*, Warner Brothers had their own contender in the wings: *Camelot*, based on the 1960 Lerner-and-Loewe stage show, which had been developed, then held at a yellow light, while the same team concentrated on *My Fair Lady*. *Camelot* wasn't a dead cert, mind. Warners hadn't managed to sign Andrews or Burton, who'd starred on stage, but settled for Richard Harris and Vanessa Redgrave, who were conspicuously less good at singing.

It was in this competitive flurry that *Doctor Dolittle*, for Fox, was born, proving both a nightmare from the start and a brutal nail in the coffin of the entire roadshow business model. The runaway hell of its production, and grim lessons for this flagging genre, were first chronicled in John Gregory Dunne's *The Studio*, about the inner workings of Fox during the exact time of the film's release, and then in Mark Harris's *Scenes from a Revolution*, a blow-by-blow account of the 1967 Oscar race. Both books are essential, but if you find yourself needing even *more* tales of on-set animal insubordination than either had room to include, *Dolittle* is the mangy gift that truly keeps on giving.

Certain elements were dictated when Darryl F. Zanuck, who'd replaced Skouras as the studio's head, got his chequebook out: hummable songs, star names of proven cachet, a literary source, family appeal. And it had to be done the roadshow way, or not at all. Bullish about selling cinema as escapism and using roadshows to do it,[2] Zanuck wanted everything he green-lit to have a built-in intermission, pumping these dirigibles up with hot air to spell 'hot ticket', and thereby guarantee pre-sales.

Finding fresh material was the rub. The idea of adapting a quaint series of children's books by Hugh Lofting, about a pudgy Victorian vet who talks to the animals, was brought to Zanuck by fledgling producer Arthur P. Jacobs, a cigar-chomping ex-publicist who would suffer a near-fatal heart attack mid-shoot. 'Apjac', as he was known, tried the same pitch on Jack Warner, who made one of the best calls of his life in turning it down. Jacobs had only a vague impression of what the film would be, but he did have a heap of ideas for mer-chandising tie-ins, so much so that *Dolittle* would become the most relentlessly cross-promoted film of its day, with animal toys set to spill out of over 200 million cereal boxes.

Given the title character's gender, Jacobs and Fox must have known they'd struggle to interest Julie Andrews,* but this didn't stop Jacobs taking her to lunch before a script existed.[3] She passed – after all, she wasn't short of offers to stay on board the doomed musical band-wagon at that time. She chose one, Universal's *Thoroughly Modern Millie* (1967), which did pretty well, followed by two in a row, *Star!* and *Darling Lili*, which would, in their own turn, be end-of-an-era catastrophes.

The *Dolittle* team succeeded instead in enticing Rex Harrison, puffed up since his Best Actor Oscar for *My Fair Lady*, with the flattering idea of a star vehicle – the key being to team him again with that film's librettist, Alan Jay Lerner. Harrison's speak-along-with-the-music 'singing' style – Frederick Loewe once remarked that he had a vocal range of one-and-a-half notes – even made a certain amount of sense for the role, but his refusal to have any other actors sing at him, especially any who *could* sing, obscured the film's musical potential in an ominous cloud of controlling ego. Richard Fleischer (*Compulsion*, *Fantastic Voyage*) was hired to direct as someone who would basically do as he was told.

---

* She did pre-record the voice of Polynesia the parrot, though, for a 1998 stage version of *Dolittle* starring Phillip Schofield.

Meanwhile Lerner, who was going through a very public divorce, took a long time delivering no script whatsoever. Jacobs's decision to fire him, while inevitable, triggered a Harrison tantrum for the ages. Only when Christopher Plummer was briefly considered as a more pliable leading man did 'Tyrannosaurus Rex' calm down and accept Lerner's replacement.

This was the much less experienced Leslie Bricusse, known for his collaborations with actor-singer – and, suddenly, *Dolittle* co-star – Anthony Newley. While acquiescing to this double intrusion of upstart talent, Harrison flatly refused to star alongside Sammy Davis Jr, insisting that the role of Bumpo Kahbooboo, an African prince in Lofting, go to a 'proper' actor – specifically, the much-in-demand Sidney Poitier, whose rising salary, after months of rewrites, meant they paid him off handsomely, before realising they couldn't afford to have him appear.

Bumpo was reconfigured, perhaps mercifully, as a much smaller role for Geoffrey Holder, but they'd got there by first jettisoning Davis (to his devastation*), then Poitier (to something closer to relief): not great optics. Amid all this prevarication, to quote Fleischer's memoir, 'The budget was starting to look like a bloated stomach ad for Alka-Seltzer, but we hardly noticed it.'[4]

Half the film was to take place in the idyllic English village of Puddleby-on-the-Marsh, for which the Wiltshire town of Castle Combe was used for the shoot in June 1966, and a menagerie of over 1,500 animals bussed in. Exhaustive preparations were needed – six months were spent teaching Chee-Chee the chimpanzee how to fry bacon and eggs.[5] 'Puddleby' was all too apt, though: it rained on all but five of the shooting days, and the ground turned to bog. Rendering it picturesque caused no end of trouble.

---

* Indeed, he threatened to sue Harrison and denounce him to the NAACP.

When the crew dammed a trout stream for aesthetic reasons, locals were up in arms: literally, in the case of a twenty-two-year-old Ranulph Fiennes, before his second act as a writer/explorer, who was arrested for trying to blow up the dam with a gas bomb. His stated aim was to stop 'mass entertainment from riding roughshod over the feelings of the people'.[6] Having used army explosives for this sabotage, Fiennes was dismissed from the 22nd Regiment of the SAS, and served out the rest of his military career in the Royal Scots Greys.

There were few vertebrates on set with which Harrison did not lock horns. The problem with picking live sheep, not singing cast members, as his preferred co-stars was their tendency to force retakes by weeing on him. A mutinous goat at one point broke loose and ate Fleischer's script, and a giraffe, who hardly appears in the finished film, held up shooting for days when it reportedly stepped on its own penis.

Tales of animal woe on this set emerged only after the fact, or the American Humane Association would surely have taken an interest.* Several ducks were placed in a pond to look nice, but it was moulting season: they didn't have their water-repellent feathers, and sank. A restless squirrel had to be sedated to co-operate during a brief scene – but when trainers used a fountain pen to drip-feed it with gin, all they managed to get were a few moments of this featured

---

* Michael Cimino's *Heaven's Gate* (1980) – a megaflop we shall meet again, of course – would be a watershed moment for scrutiny of Hollywood's animal handling. The stories from that set, quite honestly, are no fun whatsoever. Barred from monitoring the shoot, the AHA issued press releases to organise a boycott, when allegations emerged that steers were being bled from the neck as a source of stage blood, real cockfights initiated, and cows disembowelled to provide intestines. Four horses were killed during the climactic battle scene, including one that was blown up by dynamite – footage that Cimino kept in the final cut. After the outcry surrounding all this, the AHA was contractually authorised to keep tabs on all use of animals in filmed media from that point forth, and the 'no animals were harmed' disclaimer became an important feature of end credits.

player swaying on a railing before it lost consciousness.[7] Meanwhile, a bored fawn needed her stomach pumped for eating a quart of paint during a scene break.

Harrison fumed, but he was arguably the worst behaved cast member of them all. No wonder Polynesia the parrot kept squawking 'cut', to the star's immense confusion, while he tried to get through multiple takes of 'The Reluctant Vegetarian'. He insisted on singing live, without pre-recorded backing tracks, which made post-production extra-taxing for everyone else.

His dubious idea of on-set camaraderie is summed up by his treatment of Newley, his Hackney-born co-star, whom he took to insulting openly as a 'cockney Jew' and 'sewer rat'. Throughout the shoot, Harrison's unstable wife, the actress Rachel Roberts, shocked everyone with her nightly alcoholic rampages, at one point feigning a suicide attempt when production shifted to several disease-plagued weeks of tropical hell in Saint Lucia.*

The film-makers weren't to know that the island's population had just been through a food-poisoning epidemic caused by freshwater snails, but this may have helped explain why the giant sea snail they built on the beach got pelted with stones by furious local children. Back on the Fox lot in Los Angeles, the set of Dolittle's home had to be built on a slope, upholstered with plastic and hosed down with ammonia to let the daily accrual of animal waste wash away.[8]

Jacobs remained gung-ho about soundtrack sales, pursuing the likes of Andy Williams, Bobby Darin and even Sammy Davis, who swallowed his pride, to record cover versions of the entire thing. The original LP wound up selling 500,000 units, making it the 66th best-selling record of 1967 – a far cry from the No. 1 smash of *The Sound*

---

* The island still maintains a restaurant called 'Doolittle's' (*sic*) with faded production stills dotted about.

of Music. The film was merchandised to death without audiences ever feeling they'd wanted it in the first place.

All of Jacobs's efforts to boost brand recognition – including a *Time* cover with Harrison riding that accident-prone giraffe, over 14 months before the film even opened – just added up to an aggressive glut, a sense of being forcibly sold a pup. Tie-in merch, including a talking version of the two-headed llama 'Pushmi-Pullyu', would gather dust in toyshops everywhere as the release date came and went. No matter how many of its animal stars stepped out for the premieres in black tie, *Dolittle* was doomed.

Despite being an undisputed turkey, which tripled its planned production cost of $6m, the extraordinary twist is that it *still* managed a total of nine Oscar nominations, including – yes – Best Picture. This wasn't a banner day for the probity or good taste of the Academy membership, many of whom Fox employed.

In desperation, the studio wined and dined *Dolittle's* way onto all the ballots it could, booking 16 consecutive nights of screenings on its Hollywood lot and offering free champagne dinners to voters who showed up – the kind of buttering-up now outlawed under official Academy rules. These banquet screenings were certainly a better deal than paying audience members got, but the desired outcome – salvaging a commercial success from a nose-pinching critical disaster – was by this point impossible.

Dolittle was and was not a musical, and here – even beyond its derelictions of storytelling and gruelling absence of real charm – was the fatal miscalculation. Of the two Oscars it actually won, the one for Visual Effects was mainly a testament to the cost of constructing that giant sea snail,* and so on. The award was effectively for Most

---

* The Great Pink Sea Snail, to name it correctly, weighed 8 tonnes and cost $65,000, all by itself.

Money Lavished on Elements of the Fantastical. When *2001: A Space Odyssey* won the same trophy a year later, it was the rough equivalent of handing consecutive literary prizes to Dan Brown and Aeschylus.

Best Original Song went to 'Talk to the Animals', an irritatingly pedestrian Bricusse ditty that was actively disliked by all involved, including Fox music chief Lionel Newman, who had to conduct it, and Harrison. 'A humorous song is meant to be funny,' Rex complained. 'This isn't funny.' He had a point – the song tries to rhyme 'rhinoceros' with 'ofcourserous', among other crimes. But Harrison's reluctance to treat it *as* a song, like all of his songs, certainly didn't help audiences in their quest for a decent tune.

Busy and colourful, at best, but impersonal, overstuffed and overproduced, *Doctor Dolittle* had already met its nemesis in the shape of *The Jungle Book*, which opened two weeks after it during Christmas 1967, sported the best songbook Disney had ever put together, and featured animated creatures enjoying themselves, not real ones looking sedated or woebegone. (Two jolly exceptions are the seal in a straw hat, Sophie, to which Harrison speak-sings an especially absurd ballad, and the gruff Great Dane belonging to an apoplectic judge, with which Rex conversationally barks on the witness stand.)

Even *Camelot*, which crawled to a mediocre No. 12 at that year's box office, succeeded in tripling *Dolittle*'s grosses. The film's profound failure had numerous repercussions: bruised by its unpopularity, Harrison withdrew from his relatively new-found film stardom, and would shoot only two features in the next ten years.

More dramatically, it sent shockwaves through Fox, whose executives assumed putting musicals on their front foot was a strategy to see out the decade. It was too late to backtrack by now: they were already deep into production on *Star!* (Andrews's biopic of cockney idol Gertrude Lawrence) and had built the sets to start on *Hello,*

Dolly! (Barbra Streisand in giant Victorian hats, a year after *Funny Girl* (1968) made her famous).

The rot set in. Neither of these huge female stars with legendary pipes could single-handedly make hits out of the throwback boondoggles being erected around them. Robert Wise, who directed the former, even found himself at the receiving end this time of a studio recut, when Zanuck tried to recoup some of *Star!*'s $14m budget by lopping a third out of it, including several big numbers, and re-releasing a year later. No dice.

Vogues were changing at bewildering speed in the era of Vietnam and campus unrest. Rather than forcibly upbeat spectacle, a cinema of restlessness and alienation was knocking at the door. The clock was ticking for musicals in particular, roadshows in general, and the tenure of both Zanucks at Fox: Darryl would soon fire his son and head of production Richard, only to be ejected himself in a vote of no confidence. When Franklin J. Schaffner's three-hour-long *Patton* (thankfully not a musical) came out in early 1970, it wasn't Fox's last rodeo. But it was their very last roadshow.

SORCERER (1977)

Director: William Friedkin
Studio: Universal/Paramount
Budget: $21–22m
Worldwide gross: $9m

'*Star Wars* came out like a juggernaut, and took everything.'

William Friedkin

A stubborn myth holds that William Friedkin's *Sorcerer* – a white-knuckle thrill ride about risk and predestination – opened a week after *Star Wars*, and therefore didn't stand a chance. The truth is not quite that: the gap was a whole month, and so, *Star Wars* being *Star Wars*, *Sorcerer* stood even *less* of a chance. The era of the all-conquering blockbuster, in the wake of *Jaws* (1975), had begun, and that feeding frenzy had many, many sequels.

You could have fooled George Lucas. He was certain *Star Wars* would be the casualty, not the victor, of these rabid new economics. Few around him had kept confidence in his film since the early enthusiasm they'd professed when green-lighting it. While his ILM effects boffins ran themselves ragged, Lucas showed his inner circle a work print in February 1977, mocked up with placeholder footage from Second World War dogfights. It did not go well. The only person who jumped up at the end, predicting that this would be the biggest film in history, was Steven Spielberg. Everyone else thought he'd gone insane.*

---

* Wagering that Spielberg's *Close Encounters* would be the bigger success, Lucas suggested they trade 2.5 per cent of the profits on each other's films. The deal still holds, netting Spielberg tens of millions over the years.

Star Wars opened sheepishly, then, on the Wednesday before Memorial Day, 25 May 1977. A mere 32 cinemas across the USA agreed to play it at first,* for all the pressure of Fox, who expected their Sidney Sheldon adaptation *The Other Side of Midnight*† to be the bigger summer attraction.

Even on that first day, though, the lines forming in Hollywood outside Mann's Chinese Theater, which Lucas witnessed first-hand, betrayed a public appetite no one could have dreamed of. Before long, Harrison Ford couldn't walk into a record store without having his shirt torn off. Action figures flew off shelves. Fox's stock price doubled.‡ The UK didn't even get the film until December, triggering the biggest foyer crushes since Beatlemania.

These were bad times for any other film to come down the pike, especially one that was such a pessimistic inverse of *Star Wars* in mood as well as subject – essentially a hell-on-earth experience, when everyone was busy dreaming of a galaxy far, far away. The same one-screen cinemas that had pooh-poohed *Star Wars* a month earlier were begging to get in on the action come 24 June, and crossing out every other release with thick black markers. In other words, *Sorcerer*'s goose was cooked well before it got out of the oven.

Shown Lucas's script in the mid-1970s, William Friedkin had turned down a chance to produce *Star Wars*, which he couldn't imagine taking a dime. He also wasn't impressed with *Jaws*. But he had a macho confidence in *Sorcerer*, right up to opening day. The

* It wouldn't reach its maximum screen count until a wide reissue the following summer, on an unheard-of 1,750 screens, raking in $10.2m over a single weekend.
† A Second World War-era romantic melodrama, featuring a young Susan Sarandon. It did fine.
‡ Before 1977, the company's highest annual profits were $37m. That year, $79m.

trailer had actually debuted before Lucas's film in a few sites, promising something grim, gritty and portentously downbeat. It wasn't wrong on any count, but still, underscored by Tangerine Dream's purgatorial synth motifs, it was a heavy trailer for a heavy film. Three minutes long, it had a listen-to-the-man voiceover typical of the day, which starts by trumpeting the Oscars Friedkin won for *The French Connection* (1971) and doomily declaring that *The Exorcist* (1973) 'made history'.

Back then, leaning in on an auteur's track record was the only known way to sell a film like *Sorcerer*, which had the medium star power of *Jaws*' Roy Scheider* in the lead, three foreign actors alongside him, and not a lot of merch potential, to say the least. Cinephiles would have known that it was based on a 1950 French novel, *Le salaire de la peur* (*The Wages of Fear*), which had been filmed already, in breathtakingly tense fashion, by Henri-Georges Clouzot in 1953.

Some punters might have found themselves grumbling, as critics would too, about the indulgence of mounting an expensive US remake at all,† even if Friedkin would never use that word for it. But for the hordes of kids who'd been queuing all day, out of their minds with excitement to see *Star Wars* for the fourth or fifth time, the trailer, indeed the very idea, of *Sorcerer*, was simply getting in the way. 'When our trailer faded to black,' as the film's editor, Bud S. Smith, remembers it, 'the curtains closed and opened again, and they kept opening. And opening.'[1]

---

* After giving Scheider his sidekick part in *The French Connection*, Friedkin accepted William Peter Blatty's argument that he was wrong for the role of Father Damien in *The Exorcist*. They fell out. Reunited on *Sorcerer*, their relationship would remain testy and mistrustful, by both accounts.
† Clouzot himself, close to death in Paris, neither blessed nor opposed it.

'I thought anything I did at that point would work,' Friedkin admitted to Nicolas Winding Refn in a 2015 interview.* This is what would make *Sorcerer* such an especially stark setback, a moment of reversal, within the storied narrative of 1970s Hollywood. The studios had lately allowed a rampant auteurism loose, with their backing of Francis Ford Coppola, Robert Altman, Martin Scorsese, Peter Bogdanovich, Hal Ashby and so forth. All of these careers would face gruelling vicissitudes in the 1980s, with only Spielberg and Lucas charging ahead (indeed, teaming up) as popular entertainers whose films were unashamedly franchise fit, with their firmly identifiable heroes and villains.

Where were these to be found in *Sorcerer*? The script Friedkin commissioned from Walon Green† begins with four vignettes, in different parts of the world, to establish our four main characters. Nilo (Francisco 'Paco' Rabal, in his Hollywood debut) is a hired killer, who shoots a mark in Veracruz, Mexico, and coolly walks off. Kassem (French-Moroccan actor Amidou, riveting throughout) is a Palestinian militant setting off bombs in Jerusalem, who's the only one to escape death or capture from his unit.

Victor (Bruno Cremer, France's future Maigret) is a Parisian banker accused of fraud, whose business partner commits suicide. And Jackie (Scheider) is a getaway driver for New Jersey's Irish mob, who collides with a truck, killing everyone else on board. In Friedkin's

---

* *Sorcerers: A Conversation with William Friedkin and Nicolas Winding Refn* (directed by Cass Paley, 2015). This chat is quite a study in personalities. Later, a segment went viral, when Refn refers to his own rightly slated neo-noir thriller *Only God Forgives* (2013) as a 'masterpiece', and Friedkin calls off-camera sardonically for medical help.

† The erudite, multilingual screenwriter best known for his Oscar-nominated script for Sam Peckinpah's *The Wild Bunch* (1969), and later for the likes of *Robocop 2* (1990) and *Eraser* (1996).

own summation, they had 'no redeeming characteristics',[2] which was exactly the unheroic jumping-off point he wanted.

To a degree, these four men could be said to have chosen their lots, but Friedkin and Green challenge this notion to the core. After all, it's by sheer fluke they've survived this far already. Destiny unites them, somewhere in Colombia under assumed names, where we find them scratching out a godforsaken existence. The rest is all slings and arrows.

Forty-one minutes into the picture, a nearby oil well explodes. The only way to extinguish the fire is with nitroglycerine, which the oil company has incompetently stashed 218 miles away, across impossibly hazardous terrain. As in Clouzot's version, the film's harsh equation is chalked up. Two trucks; four men with nothing to lose; a shit-tonne of unstable explosives; and a bumper payout to let them start new lives – on the reckless assumption they don't all combust. 'The premise seemed to me a metaphor for the countries of the world: find a way to work together or explode,'[3] Friedkin would write in his memoir.

The title, it's generally admitted, was a mistake – 'an intentional but ill-advised reference to *The Exorcist*,'[4] per Friedkin. He'd been listening to Miles Davis's 1967 album *Sorcerer*, and simply became attached to the word. It made him think of an evil wizard – taking a leap, in this film's conception, to argue that 'the evil wizard was Fate'.[5] Audiences were primed by *Sorcerer* for something expressly supernatural, though – and then duly confounded.

Casting was a huge migraine. Friedkin had the four roles tailored to particular stars, but would land only one of his first choices: Amidou. For the Scheider part, he'd wanted Steve McQueen, then the highest-paid actor in the world, who was thrilled by Green's script. It so very nearly worked out.

Friedkin went scouting first in the most exotic parts of Ecuador, falling in love with the country's semi-active volcano, Cotopaxi.

McQueen baulked at travelling somewhere so remote for such a long stint. He had recently married Ali MacGraw and didn't want to leave her behind. The star's two other suggestions – either write MacGraw a part, or make her an associate producer – met with Friedkin's blunt refusal. 'How arrogant I was,' he later wrote. 'I didn't know then what I've come to realise: a close-up of Steve McQueen was worth more than the most beautiful landscape in the world.'[6]

After McQueen stepped away,* Marcello Mastroianni also withdrew as Nilo. Gene Hackman, Paul Newman, Kris Kristofferson and Robert Mitchum all declined, with a delightful explanation in Mitchum's case. 'Why would I want to go to Ecuador for two or three months to fall out of a truck?' he asked Friedkin. 'I can do that outside my house.' Scheider was suggested by Universal as someone they could endorse in the lead – but Lino Ventura, earmarked for Cremer's role, refused to take second billing unless it was to McQueen, and dropped out, too. 'The portents were clear, but I dug in deeper,' Friedkin remembered. 'I thought I was bulletproof.'[7]

Then he lost Ecuador. Universal's chief, Lew Wasserman, put his foot down. He might have been willing to insure a Steve McQueen vehicle out there, but the new package was much more precarious. Only by splitting the risk with another partner would Universal stump up the budget of $15–20m. The head of Paramount, Charles Bluhdorn, proposed shooting the bulk of the film not in Ecuador, but the Dominican Republic, which at the time was a major outpost of Paramount's parent company, Gulf and Western. Tax-free labour and Paramount shouldering half the cost rescued *Sorcerer* from the scrapheap.

For Friedkin's despairing vision of life at the edge of the world, the dirt-poor locations they found would, in fact, be horribly fitting. 'A prison without walls,' was how he described the village of La Altagracia,

---

* Though his stunt double, Bud Ekins, remained a vital member of the crew.

'with a sense of timeless poverty and persecution.'[8] The irony of corporate interests dictating the locations for this decidedly anti-corporate parable was certainly not lost on its belligerent director. He used a Gulf and Western photo, featuring Bluhdorn, on an office wall in one scene, to represent the corrupt board of the oil company. According to Green, when Bluhdorn spotted himself in the scene, 'He had a shit haemorrhage.'[9]

Before all that, there was the prologue to contend with. In Jerusalem, with the help of Israel's security forces, the crew set off a mock explosion in a bank, which was so powerful it broke a window in the mayor's office across the street. At the same time, an *actual* terrorist bombing happened two blocks away, and Friedkin's camera crew raced there to steal shots of the aftermath. In New York, they burned through ten days and seven cars trying to nail the mid-air stunt flip that kills everyone but Jackie.

Danger and delay marked nearly every phase of the shoot. Around the film's three-quarter mark, the four men must blow up a giant caoba tree, forty feet long and ten feet wide, that has blocked the trucks' path in the jungle. This was to be achieved on camera with explosives slotted into the trunk. The moment they were all set up, the whirr of a chopper arrived overhead – it was Bluhdorn, flying in for a check-up. 'This Fweedkin is ah genius!'[10] he announced to his entourage when the effects shot was explained.

They all waited, on tenterhooks. But this blast was too feeble, flicking a few twigs into the air, and Bluhdorn choppered off without a word. Ironically, given the plot, additional explosives had to be dialled up, which came from one of Friedkin's old buddies, a dubious character in Queens nicknamed 'Marvin the Torch', who made his living from blowing up failing businesses for insurance money. He arrived with two suitcases labelled 'beauty supplies', obliterated the tree, and got out.[11]

On and on, exhaustingly, the shoot rolled. Almost half the crew had to be hospitalised or sent home with amoebic dysentery, gangrene or malaria.[12] Friedkin dropped 50 pounds and fired five production managers. (It was on this film that his stormy temper earned him the nickname 'Hurricane Billy'.) He also lost his trusty line producer, Dave Salven, because of a divorce ultimatum from the man's wife if he didn't quit.

Friedkin's camera operator Ricky Bravo, who had shot the Cuban revolution at Castro's side, lasted the course. But the cinematographer Dick Bush (*Tommy*, *Culloden*) lost confidence after realising he'd underexposed all the jungle footage they'd shot so far. He was replaced by John M. Stephens, more commonly employed as a second-unit guy (e.g. on *Titanic*), who switched lenses and film stock to handle the rest.

The most spectacular sequence – unforgettable once you've seen it – involves the trucks crossing an old wooden suspension bridge, atop a torrential river during a tropical storm. Captured in camera and on location, without recourse to the visual-effects elements that would standardly be used these days even in a stunt jamboree like *Mad Max: Fury Road* (2015), it's the most impressive set piece of Friedkin's whole career. You feel every visceral lurch, twitch with every jolt. No surprise that shooting it was a horror show for the ages.

Friedkin came at it without any script or storyboard, just a clear idea in his mind. Production designer John Box, a David Lean veteran, built the bridge at a cost of $1m, with a concealed hydraulic system, metal supports and invisible cables attaching the trucks, so they'd sway without capsizing. It had to be 200 feet long – the width of the best river they'd found – and took three months to build.

Rainfall ceased as construction proceeded. Gradually, the depth of the chosen river diminished from 12 feet until it was literally just a dry bed – so much for the raging deluge in Friedkin's head. They'd built a $1m bridge over nothing. 'This was becoming a cursed project,' the director grimly realised.

Executives urged him to come up with a simpler sequence, but Friedkin 'had become like Fitzcarraldo,' as he put it, 'the man who built an opera house in the Brazilian jungle.* My obsession was out of control [. . .] No one in his right mind would have continued on this course, but no one was in his right mind.'[13] At the very same time, all the way over in the Philippines, Francis Ford Coppola was also deep into his maddening jungle shoot on the way-behind-schedule *Apocalypse Now* – or 'Apocalypse Later', as wags of the press would dub it. These were very much the days of feted auteurs pushing up-river à la Colonel Kurtz.

Friedkin sent scouts to the Papaloapan river outside Tuxtepec, in Mexico, which was in roaring good health – for the time being. Cashing in all the credit he'd earned in the industry, he demanded permission to dismantle the bridge, fly it over, and re-anchor it there instead. While waiting, they at least managed to fit in the brief prologue scene for Rabal's Nilo, in a hotel overlooking the Veracruz town square. But otherwise production was shut down for a month, with every member of the cast and crew on retainer.[†]

On Friedkin's arrival at the ancient Aztec village where they would base themselves for the bridge shoot, he was met by a bizarre sight. A mass exodus seemed to be taking place, with men,

---

* As played with full-tilt megalomania by Klaus Kinski in Werner Herzog's *Fitzcarraldo* (1982), an epic flop that attempted to re-enact this very adventure, and gets chalked up as another of cinema's most lunatic – yet majestic – endeavours. Les Blank's enthralling documentary *Burden of Dreams* (1982) chronicled that arduous shoot, just as Eleanor Coppola's *Hearts of Darkness: A Filmmaker's Apocalypse* (1991) would do for *Apocalypse Now*.
† Recreation may have got a little out of control: several crew members were forced to go home when a federal agent fingered them for drug possession.

women and children tramping away from their homes with all their belongings. He asked one of his scouts why. 'They were a deeply religious people,' he was told, 'and the man who made *The Exorcist* was coming to their village.'[14]

Even the Papaloapan river got the heebie-jeebies. The current dwindled – again! – to a trickle, needing other sections upstream to be diverted to it with pumps. A half-dozen giant sprinklers brought the rain, wind machines the monsoon. And the cameras finally rolled. Despite being attached, the trucks toppled off the bridge seven or eight times, with stuntmen in flotation devices (mostly) taking the fall.* But, after months and months, they finally got it. It was the last sequence but one to be finished, cost $3m, and would stand tall as the centrepiece of the hellish existential odyssey Friedkin had always planned.

When it screened to them pre-release, American critics didn't get *Sorcerer* at all, and, unfortunately, this mattered. Indeed, it's hard to say whether the brutal reviews or *Star Wars* did it more harm. The critiques had a tone of nemesis to them – 'personal attacks, probably deserved, based on my callous, self-involved behaviour', as Friedkin reckoned in his later years. 'What went wrong?" began Charles Champlin in the *Los Angeles Times* – a man who knew Friedkin well, and had praised his previous movies to the skies. Fetching the paper in his slippers on the morning of release, Friedkin opened to those words and his heart sank. Jack Kroll of *Newsweek* would prove just about the film's lone initial champion.

---

* Friedkin interviewed by Adam Pockross, Yahoo Entertainment website, 25 April, 2014: 'I was in it once when it dumped, so were the actors [. . .] We just repaired that section of the bridge and kept going. You fell in the water. And it was raining. And you counted yourself lucky that the truck didn't fall on you or anyone else.'

Blindsided, Friedkin realised with shock that his predictions about the film's box office takings – 90 per cent of *The Exorcist*, he'd guessed for Sid Sheinberg – had been misjudged by a factor of ten. Whatever had gone wrong during the ten-month *making* of *Sorcerer* – many things, as we've seen – had carried through into the press response. There was a myopic refusal to step up to the precipice of the end result, challenging as it was.

The film remains a savage, delirious ordeal, packed with images that give it the feverish quality of a nightmare: a baying mob of villagers falling still as they carry aloft their charred dead from the oil field; Rabal sitting cross-legged on the bridge, mid-maelstrom, like some mad cultist prostrate before his truck; Amidou whittling and weighing, atop the felled trunk, to MacGyver his ingenious solution. All astonishing moments.

Friedkin always believed this was the best film he was capable of making. His self-confessed hubris, which pushed this production through its dire straits, may have mellowed a great deal over the years, but the punishment doled out for it continued to sting. 'It was payback time, and I was the piñata.'[15]

No salvation awaits at the end of *Sorcerer* – an assertion equally true at the end of its making. The indignity of its release was shattering, a hammerblow to Friedkin's reputation, worsened by the fact he'd alienated the top management of not just one but two studios in the process. It replaced *Star Wars* at Mann's Chinese in Los Angeles for just one week, before it was kicked out and *Star Wars* eagerly reinstalled. Universal had more good news: they terminated Friedkin's production deal in a flash.

In the months that followed this professional evisceration, a weak, nauseated Friedkin would realise he was still feeling the lingering effects of contracting malaria on the shoot. He flew to Paris with his wife Jeanne Moreau, to recover, pause and take stock, before the remainder – very much the lesser portion – of his career would resume.

It wouldn't have comforted him to learn that a shortened *Sorcerer*, about to be dumped before European audiences, had been recut without his consent, with the entire prologue missing and a few shots peppered in as flashbacks. In his chosen version, it's some kind of deadly masterwork – peak Friedkin for me, and I'm not alone. If only it hadn't been guided to release in such a perfect storm of bad karma. For a thriller grappling with the cruel joke of destiny, it was dealt one heck of a black eye by the hand of Fate.

DUNE (1984)

Director: David Lynch
Studio: Universal
Budget: $47m
US gross: $30.9m

We destroy in the editing room the movie.[1]

Dino De Laurentiis

There's no way of entering the 1980s without passing through *Heaven's Gate*.* Duck as you go, mind. This most fabled of Hollywood's fiascos has been flogged to death, reappraised back to life, and its critical reputation continues to yo-yo between puzzlingly extreme poles. But fresh angles on it are fundamentally spent. The bottom line: it ended the autonomy of a studio, United Artists, which had been founded in 1919 by Mary Pickford, Charlie Chaplin, Douglas Fairbanks and D. W. Griffith, and was soon bought in 1981 as a corporate asset for Kirk Kerkorian's MGM.† A great deal of creative freedom followed it down the drain.

UA's vice-president of production‡ in that last phase, Steven Bach, published an account of the whole fiasco in 1985, *Final Cut: Dreams and Disaster in the Making of Heaven's Gate*, around which

---

* Michael Cimino's career-ruining, numbingly beautiful, fitfully interesting 1980 epic about an obscure land dispute in 1890s Wyoming. Budget: $44m. Box office: $4.5m.

† After decades of dormancy, it has lately been rebranded as United Artists Releasing, responsible for co-producing the *Creed* franchise (2015–), *Booksmart* (2019), *No Time to Die* (2021), and a couple of dozen other titles.

‡ Also head of global distribution.

two dominant opinions have formed. From one perspective, it's the definitive executive's-eye-view of a megaflop. Or, if you happen to take Michael Cimino's line, it's 'a work of fiction' by 'a degenerate who never even came on the set'.[2]

Either way, the film became a prize scapegoat for battening down the hatches at that time, used as a cautionary tale by executives reasserting control over the Hollywood order. All those high-flying 1970s auteurs found their mobility hog-tied; suddenly, the Altmans of this world were on watch.

Equally, the genre police were on high alert. Scan the studio pictures that came out from, say, 1981 to 1984, and you'll find precious few westerns,* four-hour-long battle epics, or vehicles for Kris Kristofferson – such was the *Heaven's Gate* effect, the miasma spread long afterwards.

Instead, by studio edict, this was the era of reaching warp speed, getting swords and/or sorcerers on as many posters as possible, and concentrating on all things that looked and sounded out of this world. Science fiction? Kind of – but preferably not too much of the science, please. Make a *space* western and they'd give you all the rope you desired.

It's through this Jedi-rivalling logic that a film of *Dune* finally came about – in a back-to-front fashion, seeing how much of Frank Herbert's sandy mythos and mind-control wizardry George Lucas had cunningly drawn upon in conceiving *Star Wars*.[†] What requires quite a bit more digging to explain is how David Lynch wound up

---

* Down but not out, the genre made minor comebacks with *Silverado* (1985), *Pale Rider* (1985) and then *Young Guns* (1988).

† So much so that when Herbert and some fellow SF writers spotted the borrowings, they jokingly formed the 'We're Too Big to Sue George Lucas Society'.

94

directing the *Dune* of no one's dreams, nearly capsizing multiple careers, including his own.

———

Frank Herbert published *Dune* in 1965, when it became a stoner favourite – a slow-growing bestseller among the Age of Aquarius hippie set, with its themes of ecological doom, mind-altering substance abuse, and the Byzantine intrigue between its rival planetary dynasties.

A knockout imaginative feat that would win both the Hugo and inaugural Nebula awards, it was rejected by 23 publishers before Chilton, best known for its range of automotive manuals, took it on. In time, it would have crossed the desks of numerous studio executives who had no immediate idea what to do with *Dune* – there was simply *so much* of Herbert's book. The amount of whispery internal monologue gained it a stubborn reputation as unfilmable.

Our old friend Arthur Jacobs (narrow survivor of *Doctor Dolittle*) was the first to have a go. He optioned the rights in 1971, and got a screenplay off the ground, but was busy prioritising the first sequel to *Planet of the Apes* (1968). Among the directors he courted were David Lean – who knew his way around a sand dune, of course – and an even squarer possibility, Charles Jarrott.* But nothing solidified before Jacobs died of a heart attack in 1973.

The most infamous unmade *Dune* nearly busted out of the desert in the mid-1970s. Alejandro Jodorowsky, an underground god for his surrealist Mexican head-trips *El Topo* (1970) and *The Holy Mountain*

* Fresh from all the Tudor in-fighting in *Anne of the Thousand Days* (1969) and *Mary, Queen of Scots* (1971), this journeyman Brit was rather cruelly dismissed by Pauline Kael as a 'traffic manager'.

(1973), somehow persuaded a consortium of French producers that his vision for it could be achieved, despite a script Herbert saw ('It was the size of a phone book'[3]) that would have lasted at least 11 hours on screen and cost $15m.

For Jodorowsky, Salvador Dalí alone demanded $100,000 per hour* to play the Emperor of the Known Universe, Shaddam IV, alongside Orson Welles as 'floating fatman' Baron Vladimir Harkonnen,[†] Mick Jagger in what would later become Sting's role, Feyd-Rautha, and a generally insane international cast: Gloria Swanson, Alain Delon, Hervé Villechaize, Udo Kier, Geraldine Chaplin, David Carradine. Jodorowsky's own twelve-year-old son Brontis would play the messianic hero, Paul Atreides. Impressively, around $10m was raised, with $2m spent in pre-production on creature designs by Moebius, sets by H. R. Giger, and special effects by *Dark Star*'s Dan O'Bannon. Music, naturally, would be Pink Floyd's domain.

The documentary *Jodorowsky's Dune* retells this quixotic saga, which ate up years of many talented lives before that budgetary shortfall snuffed it out. A huge silver lining is that, without it, we'd never have had *Alien* (1979), which a bankrupt O'Bannon wrote on the rebound, haunted by Giger/Moebius concept art that had seeped into his nightmares.

Thanks specifically to that film's gestation, it was Ridley Scott who had the next crack at *Dune*, which Dino De Laurentiis[‡] bought off

---

* Jodorowsky agreed, but configured the part so that he'd use a body double from most angles, and would shoot Dalí for one hour only.

† Welles was again approached for this role when Lynch was casting, but then found out that he would spend most of his scenes dangling from wires. 'I weigh 600lbs,' he quipped. 'Do you want to be known as the people who killed Orson Welles?'

‡ The astonishingly prolific Italian producer, whose career spanned multiple Fellini and Rossellini films, *Barbarella* (1968), *Serpico* (1973), *Death Wish* (1974),

the consortium in 1976, paying Herbert to write a more sensibly compressed script* and planning to shoot straight after *Alien*. This attempt failed, mainly because Scott, suddenly red hot, had a distaste for shooting in Mexico.[4] He bounced to *Blade Runner* (1982), putting the book back in De Laurentiis's hands.

It was the latter's daughter Raffaella, a *Dune* fanatic and the more hands-on producer of the film as it evolved, who alighted on the newly alluring Lynch option. Their first phone call wasn't the most auspicious: 'June?' he quizzed her, unfamiliar with Herbert's novel. After the one–two of *Eraserhead* (1977) and *The Elephant Man* (1980), which scored eight Oscar nominations, Lynch had all kinds of options before him.

He'd been offered *Return of the Jedi* by Lucas, despite having 'next to zero interest'. Out of respect, he agreed to fly in for a meeting – Lynch was shown 'these things called Wookiees'† in the LA production office – and then Lucas took him for a ride in his Ferrari to go eat a salad. '[My] headache was getting stronger,' Lynch recalled, as if the migraine he'd felt since landing was begging him to flee. Lynch saw no way to put his personal stamp on a film Lucas had 'three-quarters designed already', as he told the Associated Press in 1984.

Dune, once he'd put the book down, was different. With four planets to visualise, a whole range of creatures no one had yet depicted, and all the potential it dangled for exploring interiority and dreamscapes, it was a tempting invitation to step up to blockbuster budget league, while trying for a pop surrealism that might flatter

---

and the 1976 remake of *King Kong*; later, he would produce all the Hannibal Lecter movies except the one that got away, *The Silence of the Lambs* (1991).

* Reworked, at Scott's behest, by Rudy Wurlitzer.

† I wondered if he meant to say Ewoks, before a friend clarified that Lucas's original concept was for the climactic battle to take place on Chewbacca's home planet of Kashyyyk.

his own point of view. It should have been his playpen. As he said in 1992, 'I saw tons and tons of possibilities for things I loved, and this was the structure to do them in. There was so much room to create a world . . .'[5]

At what point, we have to wonder, did Lynch's confidence falter? On those rare occasions when he entertains the subject of *Dune*,* he talks of lying to himself every day, as 20,000 extras milled around in Mexico City's Churubusco Studios, often waiting for the right amount of sand to be wafted over them. Had he kept final cut, he might be able to look back on the whole experience with more sangfroid, but it's hard to know how much happier he'd be with the end result. 'There's something wrong with that movie,' he frowningly admitted to *Cinefantastique* in 1986.[6]

If that phrase 'creative differences' ever sank a film, it did this one – not as a euphemism for particularly bad personal spats, but in the truer sense of a stark, unresolved friction between what a director and his producers had in mind.† Even in Ed Naha's *The Making of Dune*,[7] a contemporary tie-in with a clear brief to stay on message for the film's release, much can be read between the lines: a barely concealed sense of frantic paddling to fend off disaster, and the skimpiest of illusions that it's likely to succeed.

The book starts with a sketch of Lynch directing Kyle MacLachlan, as Paul crawls backwards through red dust away from a putative sandworm, while goggled-up crew members cough and wheeze all around. A hundred and fifty tonnes of sand, we're told, were imported

---

* When asked by Yal Sadakin about Denis Villeneuve's version, for *Cahiers du Cinéma* (April 2023), he stated categorically, 'I will never watch it.'
† I can't improve on the assessment of Nick Davis, in a Letterboxd capsule review, that 'Lynch and the De Laurentii [are] never on the same page, rarely even in the same wing of the library.'

from the Samalayuca dunes and spread over the set, where trying not to get it in your lungs was the primary goal. Everett McGill, the deep-voiced actor who played the Fremen leader Stilgar, kept his timbre intact by stuffing wet paper inside a cut-off Dr Pepper bottle to filter his breathing, impressing everyone else with his ingenuity as they rasped and gagged.

The production designer Tony Masters, building the oily, industrial sets for the Baron's infernal lair on Giedi Prime, mentions Dino De Laurentiis visiting one day and worrying it was all too dark. The producer was increasingly fixated on the VHS market, and worried the film would look too murky in that format. 'As I was lightening things up and putting more colour around, David showed up. He wanted things darker.'[8]

With its 53 speaking parts, 70 sets and 900 crew members, *Dune* was a gigantic enterprise that De Laurentiis, chronically averse to paying taxes, was determined to make on the cheap. Churubusco was chosen as a place to get maximum bang for buck on screen. But everything that could possibly have gone wrong in Mexico did, down to the customs office randomly impounding crucial apparel, hundreds of thousands of dollars' worth of effects machinery, and even dailies. 'Everybody had to go down with bribes to get anything in,' remembers Francesca Annis, who played Lady Jessica.[9] Sting had several cassette tapes of his freshly recorded songs go missing.

With all its 'smog and altitude and food', Mexico was not Sting's idea of a good time. 'I was down there five weeks. It seemed like five years,'[10] he complained to Naha. One fellow actor who had not been forewarned of the singer's arrival, and had no idea why he was famous, was Patrick Stewart, whose attempt to break the ice soon stranded him in an excruciating cul-de-sac. 'You play in a police band?'[11]

Meanwhile, electricity and phone lines kept going down, leaving the whole operation in the dark for days. 'David was like the White

Rabbit, always rushing down the corridor escaping,' remembers his costume designer, Bob Ringwood. 'There was this sense that he didn't want to be questioned.'[12]

Large sections of the Arrakis shoot took place in a rubbish dump, once the corpses of dogs and tonnes of broken glass had been cleared out of the dirt. (They nicknamed it 'the Dead Dog Dump'.) Temperatures soared to over 120°F – even 145°, inside the dunes – with hundreds of tyres set on fire to emit thick black clouds for the battle scenes.

Smoke inhalation, heat exhaustion and dehydration were all in a day's work for those playing the Fremen and their allies, especially thanks to their accursed rubber 'stillsuits'. They found with chagrin that these full-body garments did not bestow the magical properties of air conditioning and fluid recycling with which Herbert had invested them. Many extras were homeless Mexicans, found on the street and paid in shoes. (The unventilated costumes became incubators for lice.) An entire army division showed up in a parking lot for a sequence that wasn't scheduled until the following week.[13]

Dune was a supposedly high-tech filming assignment everyone was forced to bring off in exasperatingly low-tech production facilities. 'We might as well have gone into a coal mine and done it,'[14] declared Lynch's usually chipper cinematographer Freddie Francis, of lighting the fixed, monolithic sets he was given.

Resourcefulness did, sometimes, win the day. Shimmering tendons inside the sandworms were created using thousands of condoms cut in half, then pasted together and moistened. 'What a manly movie!'[15] Lynch quipped when the order was placed.

He might have saved that comment for the overhead shots of worms bursting out. There was frequent anxiety that these looked too phallic, and that Universal might have 'the first X-rated science fiction film' on its hands, to quote Raffaella De Laurentiis. After viewing the footage, 'Every man in the room went home with a large inferiority complex.'[16]

Some cast members look back on the whole adventure as a wild, drunken time. But dangers were real. Second-unit director Jimmy Devis stumbled off a cliff near fatally during a stunt, breaking numerous bones. When a 5K light bulb exploded, Jürgen Prochnow – tied down by the Baron – had to dive off his stretcher to avoid being savaged by shards of molten glass. When the traumatised actor got back on it two weeks later, it was for his last scheduled shot. This time, he suffered first- and second-degree burns when the green gas billowing from a device attached to his cheek overheated.

'Lynch doesn't know whether to laugh, cry or perhaps seek another line of work,' Naha writes in his book during the wrangling of a Mexican extra's dialogue. 'Combat photography would be easy by comparison,' muttered Lynch, who would later dub the experience of filming it 'maybe 75 per cent nightmare'.[17]

―――――

'There's something wrong with that movie.' Lynch is not mistaken, even if – by the accounts of most on set – he tried hard to hide it.* There's a great deal wrong with *Dune*, festering below and waiting to strike, as we're blindsided by everything that's richly memorable on the surface.

Kenneth McMillan's pustulent Baron is genuinely revolting. I will never not love the inspired Siân Phillips, with her seething exhortations as the Reverend Mother Gaius Helen Mohiam: 'Kill this child, she's an abomination!' Then there are Freddie Jones's deranged eyebrows as Mentat security chief Thufir Hawat, and the creepily

---

* 'I don't think it's a silk purse. I know it's a sow's ear.' Lynch, 2022 interview with The AV Club.

intense Linda Hunt, who deserved a better showing as the Shadout Mapes,* 'the *house*keeper'.

Carlo Rambaldi went to great lengths designing the Third Stage Guild Navigator,† a super-evolved human floating in its spice tank like a giant slug, which 22 crew members operated from behind. It sums up the film's vision – much higher concept than anything featuring that slavering mound of rubber Jabba the Hutt, at least until Rambaldi's creation is let loose to fold space in some grossly dated optical effects shots.

If more amounted to more, *Dune* might be the greatest film ever made. But there *is* more. Paul's visions, of dark pools and a foetus in a birth canal, are like sumptuous experimental shorts (handled by the second-unit cameraman Frederick Elmes, who went on to shoot Lynch's next two features). There's an immensity to the echoey sound environments, conjured by Lynch's favourite, Alan Splet.

Sure, the electric guitars in Toto's score lead to some proggy horrors, but the more becalmed moments, with input from Brian Eno, are quite beautiful. It would be hard to lavish too much praise on the tactile aspects of Tony Masters' production design: his sets (the jade-floored throne room is a marvel) and props; and Bob Ringwood's costumes for nearly 4,000 citizens in *Dune*'s universe.

We can't quite get around Sting's winged codpiece, though. Nor can we leave out the wholesale collapse of the film's storytelling *and* music *and* visual fabric in the final third, when the majority of worm-based effects come in. Behold a massive, misguided vehicle visibly running out of money, energy, and steam.

---

* Shot but cut was her splendid demonstration of the crysknife to Lady Jessica; it's out there as a deleted scene.
† An early model of this was taken through customs in a trunk, absolutely bewildering the officials who opened it.

No one could disguise their panic in post-production, even when shots had notionally been completed. (Lynch admits he knew, now.) The original effects team was Apogee Productions, formed by industry legend John Dykstra after he won an Oscar for *Star Wars*. After three months' work in Mexico and a great deal of splurging – including untold hundreds of thousands spent on a miniature ornithopter with electronic control panels – Dykstra and his team walked off. According to his replacement, Barry Nolan, Apogee was 'constantly jacking the prices' and Raffaella De Laurentiis put her foot down. 'It came down to money,' Dykstra agrees.[18]

A make-do-and-mend ethos took over, and the film's effects were corroded by a thousand compromises. In October 1983, the stage housing the biggest blue screen* ever made for a film caught fire, destroying all the equipment and props within. Nolan's team hastily built a much more basic replacement outside, importing gallons of blue paint to do so. Meanwhile, one dune away, production on Raffaella's concurrent *Conan the Destroyer* (1984) was under way just as *Dune* was racing to get finished. Amid the general chaos, it's hardly any wonder that Lynch's film wound up with a bad, threadbare climax you can't imagine anyone involved revisiting with much pride. 'We'll fix it in post!'[19] Sean Young remembers Lynch saying cheerily, almost every day.

The thing that cost Lynch most dearly was not having final cut. The seventh and final draft of his script envisaged a three-hour running time, but Dino De Laurentiis was under pressure from Universal – and cinema owners – to get it down closer to two, settling on 137 minutes as the ostensible sweet spot. Many of the cast and crew who'd seen Lynch's four-hour rough cut in Mexico were mortified by

* More commonly green screens in the digital era.

what was lost.* 'We were all so shocked at how bad the film was,'[20] Ringwood recalls.

Much of the third act was jettisoned for brevity, requiring new chunks of voiceover from Virginia Madsen's Princess Irulan to stitch it together. They settled on the awful 'make it rain' ending, which put paid to the sequels Lynch had planned. Another actress, Molly Wryn, had shot her part as the Fremen widow Harah, and emerged heartbroken from the premiere at how little of her was left. Wryn could never get work afterwards; even MacLachlan initially struggled.

Dune indicates forevermore Lynch's lack of interest in handling wide-scale spectacle, but the sadness of it comes from looking on while all his hopes for a more intimate conversation with Herbert dribble away. All the best scenes are one-to-ones: the box of pain, Paul and Jessica together, Leto and Thufir grasping Paul's destiny.

The fact that so many vivid characters die midway is an issue bedevilling Denis Villeneuve just as much in his recent two-part adaptation. Released in 2021 and 2024, this followed Herbert's original structure, since the book was first published as two separate serials in *Analog* magazine. Has anyone *entirely* solved *Dune* in adapting it? I'm less sure than either Lynch's apologists or Villeneuve's bullish champions, for all the latter's commercial vindication.

On that level, it failed Lynch dismally. Herbert's fans, who knew the story, generally reacted with disappointment at the 1984 version's stunted form. Uninitiated critics were savage about its murk and

---

* Various attempts have been made at reinstating deleted footage to produce 'extended cuts' of *Dune* (cf. *Alexander*, p. 238), but none at the behest of Lynch, who usually sounds depressed by the whole idea. Universal cobbled together a haphazard 186-minute version for TV, which Lynch disavowed, taking his name off the credits. The most acclaimed composite cut is a 178-minute fan edit made by 'SpiceDiver' in 2012, eliminating the rain at the very end, and judiciously fleshing out the story with all the available elements.

incoherence – once they finally got to see it. It was withheld from press screenings until the eleventh hour, exacerbating already bad buzz. 'Universal became confused, anxious and finally dismissive,'[21] remembers one of their marketing executives, Paul M. Sammon.

The reason for the botching of the promotional message was simple: they'd wanted to sell it as the next *Star Wars*, which it plainly was not. Action figures, jigsaws and everything else were lined up, but the film itself, high-handed and opaque, refused almost hilariously to play in the same sandpit. It certainly wasn't for six-year-olds. The two-page glossary Universal had issued in cinema foyers, explaining all Herbert's language and character names, plainly smacked of desperation.

'Most of those things are decorating the corpse,'[22] shrugs Frank Price, the studio's incoming president at the time. For Columbia, he'd just overseen *Krull** (1983), another whopping science-fantasy flop, so he didn't exactly welcome this troubled foster child: 'It wasn't something I would have made,'[23] he confesses now. As the release date neared, none of Universal's older top brass were falling over themselves to take charge: indeed, nobody could agree on who had even green-lit it.

Dune opened at No. 2 on the second weekend of *Beverly Hills Cop*, the star-making Eddie Murphy smash that cost $13m and made $234m in the US alone. No one had any trouble understanding the plot of *that*.

Lynch is lucky to have been given a life raft straightaway. We're even luckier. Dino De Laurentiis, in something more akin to a gesture of love than a cold-hearted gamble, agreed to finance Lynch's next film, to the tune of a mere $6m, and to give him the all-important privilege of final cut this time. It saved MacLachlan's bacon, too. This

---

* See *The Adventures of Baron Munchausen*, note 4.

was *Blue Velvet* (1986), a crucial reset – and marvel – which pointed Lynch forward to *Twin Peaks*, a Palme d'Or, and two decades of extraordinary film work. Perhaps he needed *Dune* out of his system to get there.

THE ADVENTURES OF
BARON MUNCHAUSEN (1988)

Director: Terry Gilliam
Studio: Columbia Pictures
Budget: $46.3m
US gross: $8.1m

Singling out just one Terry Gilliam project for this book was the hard part. Even his most highly regarded film, *Brazil* (1985), lost the shirt off its back theatrically, after Gilliam fought an infamous knock-down battle with Universal Pictures even to get his version released.[1] Among his dozen other movies, a mere three – *Time Bandits* (1981), *The Fisher King* (1991) and *12 Monkeys* (1995) – truly ignited at the box office.[2] His career has been a boisterous pinball game with many lives, third and fourth chances, and only these rare jackpots keeping the lights on.

The floppiest of all his flops, though, was *The Adventures of Baron Munchausen*.

You could make the argument that the best and worst of Terry Gilliam are stuffed into the rickety frame of this archetypal 1980s auteur folly. By design, the film's a mad flight of fancy, like the hot air balloon it sends soaring over eighteenth-century battlements. We watch it climbing high, reaching for sublime absurdity, but deflating just as fast. It huffs and flaps as it sinks back raggedly to Earth, crashing without burning.

It's remarkable how often film-makers in this decade were drawn to fantasy – even more so, how willing executives were to keep bank-rolling so many unprofitably nerdy quests involving wise-cracking thieves, fairy folk and pumpkin-headed sidekicks. The dimly remem-bered likes of *Dragonslayer*[3] (1981), *Krull*[4] (1983) and *Ladyhawke*[5] (1985) never found much of an audience; nor did the costly *Legend*[6] (1985), Ridley Scott's headachey follow-up to *Blade Runner*, ridicu-lously pitting Tom Cruise's gawping ingénu against Tim Curry's truly scary Lord of Darkness.*

Labyrinth[7] (1986) may have had David Bowie yodelling 'Sarahahah!' under the spikiest hair-metal mullet of the day, but was too fudged, too inane, to find a winning commercial formula. It's hard to pinpoint why *The NeverEnding Story*[8] (1984) and Lucasfilm's *Willow*[9] (1988) clawed back a profit, unless it was their cute-and-cuddly bedside manner. In this, they're the opposite of Walter Murch's spellbindingly chilly *Return to Oz*[10] (1985), with its stop-motion Nome King, terrifying Wheelers, and Princess Mombi (played by *Willow*'s sorceress, Jean Marsh) with her interchangeable heads in cabinets. Murch's lone directing credit, this bravura fantasy understood the primal shivers of the genre better than all those others combined – and was cold-shouldered brutally by the public.

Munchausen – an epic of tall tales, which spring from the myth-making of a fictitious eighteenth-century German aristocrat[†] – was Gilliam's extravagant bid for a commercial breakthrough after all the squabbles that had embroiled him, then gained him a deep pocket of critical respect, when *Brazil* came out. He was perfectly poised, in other words, for his very own *Dune*.

Both films have come down to us as cautionary tales. Here were

---

* Decades after I first saw it as a kid, aspects of *Legend* still give me the creeps – especially what happens in and around the dungeon's magic mirror, with Mia Sara's black dress doing a waltz before she's wearing it, and then Curry's cloven-hooved demon stepping right through to molest her.

† Lightly based on real-life 'baron of lies' Hieronymus Karl Friedrich Freiherr von Münchhausen.

artists of outlandish sensibility, suddenly allocated way more money than they'd ever been given before, and burdened with a staggering array of logistical challenges, only some of which they brought on themselves. In Gilliam's case, the toil was enormous, the methods dangerously chaotic, and the results . . . well, we'll get to those. But it was the fateful match between the ex-Python and his producer, Thomas Schühly, that made this whole film a tinderbox waiting to go up, very expensively, in smoke.

It ought to have been so straightforward. Going back to the original stories of Rudolf Erich Raspe, with their illustrations in later editions by Gustave Doré and others, Gilliam and co-writer Charles McKeown found a structure to house the manifold exploits of this beaky-nosed Baron – his derring-do combating the Turkish army, visiting the moon in said hot-air balloon, and being swallowed by monstrous sea creatures. It would have a dash of *Gulliver's Travels*, a pinch of *The Wizard of Oz* and – thanks to eight-year-old Sally Salt, the Baron's near-constant companion – a soupçon of *Alice in Wonderland* for good measure.

The initial plan was to build everything in a British facility, most likely Pinewood Studios, for a projected cost of $25m – a figure Schühly disputes was ever the official budget. 'It was always $36m,'[11] maintains this German producer, an obsessive bodybuilder, who was brought in by Gilliam's *Brazil* partner, Arnon Milchan, before that pair fell out.

Schühly had worked back in the day with German cinema's bad boy Rainer Werner Fassbinder, but latterly picked up bragging rights as executive producer on *The Name of the Rose** (1986), a tricky shoot

---

* Directed by Jean-Jacques Annaud, starring Sean Connery as Umberto Eco's Franciscan sleuth, William of Baskerville. It deservedly did well, grossing $77.2m around the world from a $17.5m budget.

he claimed to have ruled with an iron fist, leading this modesty-free chap to declare himself 'the Rambo of film production'.[12] His main achievement was dragging *Munchausen*, with ruinous consequences, to Italy, having simply fired all the obstructive accountants who totted up the tab at $40m or more.

The carrot Schühly dangled before Gilliam was the baroque lure of Italian scenery, along with esteemed Italian heads of department: production designer Dante Ferretti and costumier Gabriella Pescucci both followed along from *The Name of the Rose*.* They secured the great, but notoriously slow, services of cinematographer Giuseppe 'Peppino' Rotundo, a lauded veteran of Fellini and Visconti.

What soon became apparent, though, was that Schühly, who was all about preserving an illusion of forward momentum, had been vastly downplaying the time and money *Munchausen* would take to be shot in Cinecittà. Indeed, he kept claiming that shooting in Rome would be 40 per cent cheaper than in England, a promise that would come to seem laughably vain, if not plain deluded.

At the scheduled start of the shoot, to quote the increasingly exasperated McKeown, 'Nothing was ready. Nothing was right!'[13] Ferretti had 100 carpenters working overtime to build 67 sets, but they were already two weeks late even to pick up a camera. With cast and crew milling around at a cost of $700,000 per week, these were some expensive delays. A sweltering autumn in Rome meant beginning with relentless night shoots – never anyone's nirvana – and while the whole machine limped into action, a serious depression settled over the enterprise.

Schühly, who'd envisaged *Munchausen* as 'a kind of *Indiana Jones* in fantasyland',[14] wanted the future Indy Snr, Sean Connery, to star

---

* They'd even repurpose Ferretti's astonishing library set, filling it with water features, to serve as the ballroom of Oliver Reed's Vulcan.

as the Baron, and quarrelled with Gilliam over his contrary casting philosophy. To suit the dusty dignity of the character, Gilliam wanted 'a great actor who had been forgotten', and landed on sixty-two-year-old John Neville, a respected British stage veteran of the 1950s, who had emigrated to Canada in 1972.

Instead, Connery was offered the King of the Moon – a part he didn't fancy when that segment of the film got downscaled. They petitioned Marlon Brando to consider stepping in, but having been sufficiently wined and dined, he demurred. Eventually, it fell to Robin Williams, who turned in his aggressively maniacal cameo as a favour, uncredited and unpaid.

Where everyone was in agreement, from her first screen tests, was that they could hardly have found a more ideal Sally than eight-year-old Sarah Polley, an established child star in Canada, who had film-stealing presence as the smudge-faced urchin who must chivvy the Baron along. Ominously for the experience she was about to endure, the rumour got out that one of Gilliam's own daughters might have had the role, if it weren't that he didn't want to expose her to the arduous difficulties of the shoot ahead.

'Apart from boarding school,' claims their co-star Eric Idle, 'it's probably one of the most unpleasant experiences I've ever been through in my life.'[15] Long, long hours spent in freezing water tanks had a lot to do with this. While everyone went crazy from lack of sleep, Schühly, for all his vaunted skills, was arguably too inexperienced to whip *Munchausen* into shape. A crippling lack of day-to-day preparation kept stalling progress while money poured down the drain. The English and Italian crew contingents were violently at loggerheads, too, with racist epithets flying about when they couldn't see eye to eye.

Tales of corruption and inefficiency from this set make it amazing the film ever crossed the finish line. Make-up artists would do one pass on a single character, then simply doss around, shunning more work for the day. Before the scene in the sultan's tent, hours were spent ageing up Neville into the Baron's eighty-year-old self, because no one got the memo he was meant to be at his youngest. The usually even-tempered Neville, continually frustrated that the part wasn't throwing up richer acting opportunities, understandably saw red.

It was good news in Rome for anyone's cousin who needed a job. They got one – usually fixing whatever someone else had just been paid to do wrongly. Instead of rental cars, bangers belonging to someone's relative would provide transport, then claim the right to have their dodgy brakes fixed at the unit's expense. Supporting player Bill Paterson compares the cost of Cinecittà to being tricked by an Italian restaurant with the basic price for pasta at the door, then astonished to find that cover charges, bread and water have somehow quadrupled the overall bill.[16]

Schühly, for his part, was rumoured to have three identical black Porsches parked at different gates around the studio, so no one ever knew when he was in or not.[17] He was supposed to have had a sneaky habit of never being available when the worst problems arose, such as the gale at one location, off the coast of Almería in Spain, which ripped the masts off the ships in the harbour. 'He had vanished off the face of the Earth,'[18] remembers Gilliam of that day, unlike Schühly himself, who insists he was always on set. There are stories – perhaps apocryphal, but quite persistent – of the power-crazed producer brandishing guns after hours, and using empty sound stages for target practice.

Don French, taken on as first assistant director, had just performed the same role in Morocco on Elaine May's *Ishtar*, which was Columbia's reigning flop right before this one. 'He'll be right at home,' was everyone's first thought. But he resigned early on, because of alleged demands from Schühly, in French's own words, 'to do false budgets and underschedule the film',[19] by way of pulling the wool over Columbia's eyes. Schühly's commitment to Italy meant all the local contractors had him over a barrel, but he found any excuse to delay payments elsewhere. As Gilliam put it, 'Everyone from England was "an asshole". Everyone who expected to get paid was an asshole.'[20]

The casting director, Irene Lamb, had no end of trouble with Schühly and contracts, especially when Paterson and fellow supporting player Alison Steadman were put on standby. Schühly wouldn't sign off on their furlough pay, and then, when he finally did, he'd Tipp-exed out their start dates to try to cap what he owed them.[21] This time, the only person not complaining about his hours was Sting, who knocked off his cameo as a condemned soldier in one day.

As the budget soared, Gilliam nearly got sacked when production went on emergency hiatus. The company that had underwritten *Munchausen* to protect Columbia's pockets, Film Finances, sent in an emissary called David Korda amid a flurry of threats: not only were they thinking of replacing Gilliam, but they intended to sue him for fraud and misrepresentation, and to seize his personal assets. Gilliam stormed out of his first meeting with Korda in a blistering rage, almost picked up a rock to throw back into the room, and instead punched through the windscreen of a parked car to let off steam. Only after the adrenalin had worn off did the director realise this was actually his own car.

Already, David Puttnam, then head of Columbia Pictures, had been given the chop, which spelled inevitable calamity to all who could read the signs. Battle hadn't even fully commenced at that point, but the war was lost. Puttnam, in fact, had hemmed and hawed over green-lighting *Munchausen* – it was his second-in-command, David

Picking, who'd ushered it to the start gate. But the incoming regime at the studio did not like one bit of what they were seeing.*

Dawn Steel, the new head of production, was told relentlessly by Gilliam 'that this was not a David Puttnam movie. It was a Terry Gilliam movie.'[22] The reassurances he got back planted him in quicksand. When Steel pledged to give it a well-supported release if Gilliam could cut the running time below two hours, he duly obeyed: an out-of-character decision he bitterly regretted when Columbia still dumped it in the trash. Despite plenty of sympathetic reviews, *The Adventures of Baron Munchausen* opened on an astonishingly derisory 48 prints across the USA, not even tripling that score by the end of its run. It opened the same week that *Police Academy 6: City Under Siege* had 1,627 screens to play with.

————

Sarah Polley, then eight, cared nothing for all these director–producer spats or studio politics as she laboured through her role. 'I just wanted to go home,' she confessed in a 2008 documentary.[23] More recently, in her remarkable memoir *Run Towards the Danger*,† Polley has excavated the trauma of feeling terrified on set on a daily basis – sprinting again and again through explosions that seemed pretty real, for all the minimising insistence of Gilliam, then and now, that she was never

---

* It's an infamous tactic for new studio chiefs to sabotage whatever their predecessors got into production, much like legislation by axed governments. The very same policy, when David Puttnam was hired by Columbia in 1986, hobbled the release of *Ishtar*, a film Puttnam claimed never to have even seen, and which Elaine May and Warren Beatty were convinced he wanted to fail.

† *Run Towards the Danger: Confrontations with a Body of Memory* (2022). The *Munchausen* essay is entitled 'Mad Genius'. I could hardly recommend the collection more highly, especially the audiobook read by Polley herself.

in genuine peril, since 'we couldn't afford to lose you'.[24] She describes flinching at loud bangs ever since.

The darkest moment arose when Polley was on a rowing boat with several other castmates. A small squib spooked the Baron's horse, Bucephalus, which jumped overboard. There was a larger explosive primed in the tank, so powerful it had been set at the bottom. The horse's hooves dislodged this and, as it surfaced, it detonated.

'I remember not hearing anything,' Polley recalls, 'Eric [Idle's] terrified face, the crew looking panicked at the edge of the tank. I remember a hard, crushing sensation in my chest and being carried towards an ambulance as the crew looked on, alarmed. I remember that the doctors were kind, that my parents were told there was nothing wrong with me and that I went back to work the next day. The scenes with explosions continued, each one terrifying me more than the last.'[25]

Beyond her own distress, Polley also remembers that of Uma Thurman, 17 at the time, and cast as the goddess Venus in one of her earliest acting roles. She remembers Thurman crying behind a set piece one morning, while the men around her joked about the drunken lechery of her on-screen husband Oliver Reed, who wouldn't leave her alone the night before. 'I was very aware that there was a vast distance between how scared and angry her eyes were and the jocular recounting of whatever had happened,' Polley writes. Another day she saw Reed stomp, 'very hard', on Thurman's foot, bringing her again to tears. No one intervened. 'If it was a joke,' thought Polley, 'adult jokes seemed scary, and I wanted no part of them.'[26]

Useful and detailed as it often is, I can't say that Andrew Yule's 1991 book *Losing the Light*, an insidery account of the *Munchausen* disaster, strikes a sympathetic (or even decent) tone as far as the 'statuesque', 'luscious' Thurman is concerned. 'The matter of her deflowering' gets an icky paragraph – a subject of 'nothing less than national pride' to the Italian crew. 'The undulating Uma [was] the one common cause,'[27] Yule claims, venturing a lewd limerick by line producer David Tomblin, about her being 'lithe as a puma' and 'close to the age of consent'.

There's more, unfortunately. Thurman rebuffs Reed after a boozy lunch ('Stop behaving like a cunt!' he sportingly yelled at her), and we get a truly gross description of what happened during the shooting of her topless scene, as Venus emerging from the shell. Gilliam restricted access to the set, but 'every available vantage point and peephole' was used to get a glimpse. 'Jee-sus, these *tits*!' Yule even quotes 'one worthy' as exclaiming.[28]

This is all deeply grim, whether the tone of such anecdotes tarnishes your view of the film itself or not. Briefly, Yule's book does describe the explosion Polley remembers as a near-death experience: 'Two hours elapsed before young Sarah was able to stop crying.' He confirms that all 17 seconds shot of that accident were used in the final print.[29]

Personally, I might struggle more with the dilemma of *Munchausen* fandom if I truly saw in it what some adore. No doubt it's possible to nod along with Gilliam's mantra on Yule's back cover: 'I will sacrifice myself or anyone else for the movie. *It* will last. *We'll* all be dust.' One can try to enjoy all the parallels he loves throwing up between this wild visionary of a character, with his many misadventures and narrow escapes, and Gilliam himself, in the process of making it.

For me, the myth of *Munchausen* has really grown to dwarf the film itself – a daffy pleasure for sure, with its helter-skelter pacing, but also a stunted epic I find pretty hard to love. There's a musty, plasticine aroma to it, which has only got mustier as the lore around it has got more bleak. Isolated shots – the smoke blasting from Reed's ears, a pull-back through the sultan's army – delight more than entire scenes, though Eric Idle's zippy running sprees do stand out for their giddily cartoonish quality. Gilliam's take is that, somehow, the film floats magically free of all the trouble they had making it, but I beg to differ: something heavy and exhausted about it sets in, and these moments of true lift-off are rare. It's nowhere near the worst film I've picked for this book, but nowhere near the best, either.

Polley, despite rating it highly, has a naturally complex relationship with the film, and also with the not-exactly-repentant Gilliam. The irresponsibility he displayed towards her, as she sees it, goes hand in hand with an old archetype – 'the idea of the *enfant terrible*, the out-of-control mad white male genius'. That model of a quixotic auteur is much less easily indulged these days, less recklessly fetishised by the industry, because the ethos of film-making has thankfully changed. Few would agree that the Gilliams of now (or the Griffiths of whenever) are quite so welcome to sacrifice anyone they like, or terrorise eight-year-olds, at the altar of Art.

Ultimately, the film confects more joy than it properly earns. When it ends with the Turks vanquished and everyone beaming outside the citadel gates, it's the most Disneyish 'happy' ending of Gilliam's career – all stiffly waving extras and forced euphoria. Whether it was worth the pain behind some of those smiles is not only for Terry Gilliam to decide.

NOTHING BUT TROUBLE (1991)

Director: Dan Aykroyd
Studio: Warner Bros
Budget: $45m
Worldwide gross: $9.2m

Git. Road to Ruin. Trickhouse. Valkenvania. These were all working titles for Dan Aykroyd's sorry brainchild, a truly berserk horror-comedy that didn't so much come out in mid-February 1991 as splat on impact. While opening wide (unlike *Munchausen*) on 1,671 screens, it entered the US charts at No. 8 and never improved. So sulphurous were the American reviews, Warner Bros gave it an apologetic UK theatrical release the following August, when it scraped the bottom end of the top ten for one week only.

For years, the only home-viewing format for us Brits was a pan-and-scan, 4:3 DVD, doing little to help the film's putrid reputation. Seen that way, it purely bewildered me on a probably drunken first pass. (I scanned it and panned it, you might say.)

When they trumpet 'the budget is all up there on the screen!' – unusually true, for this batshit oddity – it's hardly fair to chop off the left and right of the image, compress it to a murky, low-res transfer, and still expect this kind of campy horror show, intended as equal parts *Beetlejuice* and *The Texas Chain Saw Massacre*, to hold up. When the brief in making it was, at all times, 'overstuffed nightmare', it certainly won't do to rip half the stuffing out.

Aykroyd was hobbled in the edit badly enough already, and he's never been allowed to direct again. No one's arguing that he's Michelangelo, or that Warner Bros hacked away segments of the

Sistine Chapel here. But try to imagine the most ambitious trash-cinema equivalent. You round a corner in it, and meet something else to goggle at.

There are two giant, gurgling mutant babies (one, called Bobo, played in 'might-as-well' spirit by Aykroyd himself) that wetly molest Demi Moore. John Candy does half his work in drag, with delightfully saucy come-hither looks, as a mute horror bride named Eldona. Aykroyd has the juiciest part as her granddad, a doolally hundred-and-six-year-old Justice of the Peace, with a fake nose that's intentionally penis-shaped. This sadistic hoarder convicts passing motorists for minor traffic infractions and churns them up into, we infer, hot dogs. Which he then eats. All the driving licences of his victims (among them Jimmy Hoffa) are pinned up in his attic.

How the bejeesus did we get *here* from the Manhattan glitz of the opening credits, with Ray Charles crooning through 'The Good Life'? You'd need to ask Chevy Chase, dickish and coasting as a yuppie finance whiz who agrees to drive Moore's ditzy lawyer to a meeting in Atlantic City, purely because she's hot. One ill-advised detour off the New Jersey turnpike, one failure to notice a stop sign in the decrepit old mining town of Valkenvania, and these city slickers are at the mercy of Aykroyd's Judge Alvin Valkenheiser, who simply won't let them leave without treating them to one of his hot-dog dinners, along with a measure of his spleen. In fact, he won't let them leave at all.

There's more – way more. A pyramid of actual batshit in one upstairs room, with critters clinging to the rafters? Sure. The Valkenheiser manse is a booby-trapped American Gothic funhouse, like snakes and ladders gone Universal Horror.* In the humongous scrapyard

---

* In these ways, it has much in common with Wes Craven's similarly creepy-wacky cult classic *The People Under the Stairs* (also 1991), though you wish we actually got to spend more time exploring the house in *NBT*.

outside, we find an execution device called Mister Bonestripper, a chomping hydraulic maw into which anyone incurring the judge's disfavour is fed by rollercoaster.

The film's whole edifice is gleefully rancid, and you can see why people really, really hated it. Plenty of elements go awry. But it's also pretty wild, like an overblown *Saturday Night Live* sketch that someone indulged with a monster budget and fatefully took their eyes off. Which is more or less precisely what occurred.

———

The story goes that Aykroyd, along with his brother Peter and their producer buddy Robert K. Weiss (*The Blues Brothers*, *Dragnet*) had a movie date together in the autumn of 1987. Weiss had recently fractured a rib, and it hurt to laugh, so he begged them not to pick a comedy. Unfortunately for him, they opted for Clive Barker's *Hellraiser*, a chiller so outlandish it had half the audience in hysterics. The idea of a gross-out horror romp, getting crowds to laugh and scream simultaneously, was hatched on their way out.

Aykroyd had form in this arena. His original draft of *Ghostbusters* (1984) was far more out-there than the one Harold Ramis and Ivan Reitman eventually beat into shape. Aykroyd's 'Ghost Smashers' wouldn't have been horror, per se, but cosmic science fiction, with a bevy of spectres to vanquish across planets and dimensions in the near future. Reitman thought it plain unfilmable at that scale, unless it came heavily back down to Earth (i.e. Manhattan).

After *Hellraiser*, up popped into Aykroyd's head a weird episode from years before, when he'd been pulled over for speeding in upstate New York, and was hauled before what he referred to as a 'kangaroo court', with an eighty-eight-year-old female judge presiding. Having dished out his $50 fine, this garrulous old-timer insisted he stay for tea, and essentially held him hostage for four hours.

Thus was hatched the Valkenheiser character, a self-described 'fishing-licence dispenser and stamp-pad jockey' whose lavish verbal diarrhoea is the most wickedly enjoyable element of Aykroyd's screenplay. He's plainly having a ball in this part, too, and all the crew, who had Aykroyd's back and treated him like a hero through-out, could see it.

Alvin assures the arraigned visitors they'll be processed in no time – '*quick as sump grease through a ten-year-old goose!*' he spits out. No one else's dialogue is anywhere near as good – except one line, when the hip-hop group Digital Underground are, *incredibly* randomly, the last to pull up, and cop a load of their whereabouts. 'Man, would you look at this place?' asks one guy in shades (I believe it's Schmoovy-Schmoov), clocking the derelict facade. 'It's, like . . . *extremely* Draculated.' Yep, that's also Tupac Shakur in their midst, credited as '2 Pac' in his movie debut, and grinning ear to ear in a Yankees jersey.

As for the giant babies – these are the judge's deformed grand-sons, by the way, who aren't allowed inside – these somehow stepped fully grown out of Aykroyd's dreams. Meanwhile, the story behind Valkenvania as a junk-strewn ghost town* was prompted by Centralia, Pennsylvania, which has dwindled from a peak population of 2,671 to a current population of just five,† thanks to the mine fires burning under it since 1962, blasting up lethal fumes and sinkholes, which have sent all but the most tenacious residents packing.

---

* They dressed the town on the western backlots originally built for *High Noon* (1952).
† Based on 2024's census. Centralia's mine fire also inspired the plot of *Silent Hill* – the 2006 film, not the original Konami games.

Anyway. All of this absolute lunacy was set down on paper, then put out to various directors who ran a mile. John Hughes wasn't interested in anyone else's scripts. John Landis, who'd made several hits with Aykroyd,* felt like a logical choice with his horror background, but read it and loathed it. (His wife, Deborah Nadoolman,† still wound up designing the rather excellent costumes.)

Aykroyd had no particular desire to take the reins, but when Warner Bros offered a home for the film, he realised he could save on the directing fee if he took it on personally. Somehow, they'd stump up a budget of $40m – not *Terminator 2* money,‡ but a hefty figure for the time. John Candy in his dual supporting role§ was gravy, and they scored a coup signing Demi Moore, after she'd shot *Ghost* (1990), but before it proved such a smash.¶

The studio's main condition was getting Chevy Chase in the lead, not Aykroyd himself, which was the original plan. Chase, according to his own memoir, 'knew it was going to be the worst film [he] would ever make'[1] before the script was even finished. Without his loyalty to Aykroyd, his friend and co-star since the early 1970s, he claims he'd never have done it.

Being paid three times as much can't have hurt, either. Locked in to write, direct and play the major role of the judge, Aykroyd was a glutton for punishment on this one – and, indeed, reaped all the penalties

---

* *The Blues Brothers* (1980), *Trading Places* (1983), *Twilight Zone: The Movie* (1983) and *Spies Like Us* (1985).
† Particularly feted for devising Indy's wardrobe in *Raiders of the Lost Ark* (1981).
‡ $102m, smashing the then record.
§ He also plays Eldona's brother Dennis, the deeply reasonable chief of police who brings them before the judge. Being Candy, he manages to become the film's sympathetic centre when he's not even *at* the centre.
¶ The No. 1 hit of 1990, in fact, beating even *Home Alone* and *Pretty Woman* with $506m worldwide.

when it failed. He did find one other actor (John Daveikis) willing to strap on a grotesque blubber suit and play a giant baby, but only the one. As Bobo, Aykroyd would therefore direct significant portions of the movie while wearing one of the silliest get-ups of all time.

In retrospect, WB's confidence may look slightly insane. It wasn't just a calculation based on everyone's track records in comedy, but a sign of the studio's risk-taking largesse at the time. Having supported Tim Burton through the successes of *Pee Wee's Big Adventure* (1985) and *Beetlejuice* (1988), they'd just struck gold attaching him to *Batman* (1989), which took over $400m worldwide from its $48m budget. These were the right days – perhaps the *only* right ones – to be pitching a weird, dark, maniac-mansion star vehicle that clearly owed a lot to *Beetlejuice* in tone, even sporting a set-piece dinner in someone's wacky home (alas, no Harry Belafonte singalong, though). After all, *The Addams Family* came out in the same year, and was huge.

The other reason *Nothing But Trouble* managed to happen, go $5m over budget, and become the stink-bomb pariah it did? All the studio's panicked heads were pointing in another direction. While their Burbank backlot was being stuffed to bursting point with junk for William Sandell's sets* – dozens of crushed old bangers, stacked school buses, Ford Model Ts, washing machines, fridges, sewing machines, a Stonehenge made of Lincolns, and thousands of toasters, all piled up outside the Valkenheiser mansion – there was another right mess reaching critical mass in New York.

The *other* half of this bicoastal migraine for WB's accounting department boasted similar levels of star power – and even a strangely cognate plot, about a slick businessman and his squeeze, who run

---

* The wizard of his craft who'd just done *Robocop* (1987) and *Total Recall* (1990) for Paul Verhoeven.

into danger with fatal consequences in their own executive car, then fall foul of the criminal justice system.* This was Brian De Palma's *The Bonfire of the Vanities*† (1990) – a lunge for prestige and/or Oscar attention that backfired in every imaginable way.

The one terrific outcome of that botch-up, with its fatal miscasting, is the book that sprang from it, *The Devil's Candy*,‡ widely thought the best account of a flop ever published. *Wall Street Journal* film critic Julie Salamon was granted total on-set access by De Palma, when everyone hoped his adaptation of the rollicking Tom Wolfe novel was off to the races. Even as misjudgements piled up before and during the shoot, and when it became clear none of the main cast was comfortable or suitable in their roles, De Palma kept his word.

There's not one thing I could say about the *Vanities* debacle that Salamon didn't do a beautiful job chronicling. The mistakes were legion: Bruce Willis alone got $5m as the sodden limey hack Peter Fallow, and was terrible. Uma Thurman auditioned, and Tom Hanks thought she was all wrong, despite being entirely wrong himself. He later fired his agent.

---

* Funnily enough, Chevy Chase was Tom Wolfe's first choice to play his craven main character, the bond trader Sherman McCoy.
† With Tom Hanks, Melanie Griffith, Bruce Willis, Morgan Freeman. Budget: $45m, domestic gross: a bruising $15.6m. Most of those careers bounced back, including De Palma's, but it began a run of damaging flops for both Griffith and Willis, who took another big knock when his own squawking vanity project, the $65m *Hudson Hawk*, went down in flames the next summer. While more profitable abroad, *Hawk* managed to beat *Nothing But Trouble* to Worst Picture at that year's Razzies. (It was typical of that doltish organisation that they gave Aykroyd Worst Supporting Actor, even though he's by far the best thing in his own film.)
‡ Originally published by the Houghton Mifflin Company in 1991, reissued often, and unputdownable. Salamon returned to the subject, digging out all her old tapes, for a seven-part podcast in 2021.

It's certainly possible to feel for WB's top brass in this Scylla-and-Charybdis predicament. While *Vanities* was stressing everyone out, they were under the naive impression *Valkenvania* (as it was then christened) would look after itself. They had huge comedy stars handling a comedy – what could go wrong? Periodically, they'd gaze over from the trials of *Vanities* and wonder why the sets on their own LA backlot kept expanding. 'You're our *little* picture!'

The crew didn't care. They were having a blast tossing out new ideas at Aykroyd, many of which he eagerly pounced on, such as the toy-train circuit sending condiments around the judge's table, for which the head of production reluctantly coughed up an extra $25,000. A spirit of reckless fun predominated. 'Boy, the things I'll do for a million bucks!' quipped the eternally good-natured Candy on first emerging in full drag, eliciting wolf whistles from all the men on set.

Before long, it dawned with horrible clarity on Warners just how deep their double trouble was. They'd agreed to everything – the 90-foot-tall mansion set, the rollercoaster, Mister Bonestripper, the judge's hydraulic chairs, the working drawbridge over an actual moat. They had no idea how grisly and far-out the film was getting. Emergency budget meetings were called week to week, with 'Stop the bleeding!' as the general imperative.

Chevy Chase, who must have seen the writing on the wall, had a habit of bullying the increasingly exhausted Aykroyd – who was admitted to St Joseph's Hospital for fatigue for half a day,* the result of having to do so many jobs at once. The crew hated Chase for such behaviour – one guy even threatened to drop a brick on his head if he kept it up. He'd brag about being the MVP, as if being on triple

---

* This was one of the two days with Digital Underground on set, which explains why most of the judge's shots are inserts.

Aykroyd's money gave him carte blanche. He also pissed off Moore*
by complaining behind her back that her costumes were too skimpy.
'I love Chevy,' Aykroyd would later say. 'We were great brothers and
collaborators. But there were times when it was like hauling ore up a
hill with a bad mule.'†

What ripped the guts out of the film in the end – literally – was
Warners' rising panic. No one was ever happy with the ending, and
no one's efforts to fix it worked. As the release neared, they vetoed
an R rating, and forced Aykroyd into a miserable round of recuts to
bring it down to PG-13, aiming to cut their losses by at least netting a family demographic. (Some of the film's extant sex references,
including to a 'pud collar' – cock ring – still make this feel like a
deeply weird thing to take your family along to.) Mister Bonestripper
would surely have been more of a splatterfest in Aykroyd's original
cut, rather than cleanly spitting out femurs without a droplet of gore.
Perhaps the production line for those disgusting-looking hot dogs
would have been shown.

People, and many critics, would undoubtedly still have hated
Valkenvania, but over time, more of them might have satisfied an
itch to see it, and – who knows? – it might have gained some kind of
Rocky-Horror-style cult status.

Bowdlerised and retitled by studio decree, *Nothing But Trouble*
was, to quote the *Washington Post*'s review, 'nothing but trouble and
agony and pain and suffering and obnoxious, toxically unfunny bad
taste'.[2] Much of this is naturally on purpose, but no one had time
for such nuances. Roger Ebert despised it so much that, after giving

---

* I must say, though zany screwball is plainly not her most natural mode, Demi
plunges into some of the filthy physical comedy like a trouper here.
† Quoted in '*Nothing But Trouble* is a Very Weird Movie', a passionately argued
2022 video essay by Zane Whitener.

it a supersized 'thumbs down' on his TV show, he refused even to write a review. He claimed he'd caught it one weeknight, with a few loud teenagers in the house, and apparently interrupted them, asking them to make *more* noise so he didn't have to hear the movie.

Trouble and *Vanities* – one film playing out almost like the sick-joke version of the other – would do a sad, jerky little *pas de deux* in and (quickly) out of those multiplexes. Aykroyd's film had been set for a 1990 Christmas slot, but all the recutting and remarketing shunted it back to 15 February 1991.* Not one of the topline talent, or producers, showed up for the cast and crew screening. Warners, meanwhile, inserted the equally troubled *Vanities* into that Christmas slot, then watched them both get dismally reviewed and die, one at a time.

Even the posters looked weirdly identical – three floating heads on one, four on the other, over a rosy sunset glow.† Salamon points out that the biggest billboard on Sunset Boulevard simply swapped one out for the other in mid-January, which might have prompted double-takes from passing drivers, wondering if they were suffering déjà vu.[3]

With their intertwined fates, these two films do rather sum up a kind of coke bloat at the tail end of 1980s excess: they have a 'last days of Rome' vibe. This was a theme in Wolfe's novel, but one that De Palma's film wound up illustrating better by falling on its puffy,

---

* Classically, February is a dumping ground of a release slot for poorly tracking studio fare. In this instance, *NBT* had the even worse fortune to be scheduled right up against two star-led thrillers audiences proved much keener to be scared by: *The Silence of the Lambs* and *Sleeping with the Enemy*.

† WB junked a far more eye-catching design for *NBT*, with cartoonish images of the leads on a mountain of bones, by Boris Vallejo, the Peruvian-American painter who'd done the art for Chase's *Vacation* movies. Instead: four floating heads, by who knows.

raddled face than it ever succeeded in exploring internally.

Aykroyd – this is relevant to his obsessions – had been a boy racer, and became a classic-car nut. He was the grand marshal of Toronto's Indy race for some years, and used to keep a half-dozen vintage models in his garage. In *The Blues Brothers*, he helped lay waste to all those police cruisers in Chicago, of which 103 were trashed for history's most expensive car chase.

Nothing But Trouble came into existence because of his speeding ticket. It ended – with all those written-off, clapped-out cars tossed in piles – as some kind of graveyard for its director's dreams. Aykroyd got virtually all the blame, and you can pinpoint this as the moment when his whole career swerved off the tracks. WB weren't going to throw him any more slack – they concentrated on making sure the terminally non-weird *Robin Hood: Prince of Thieves* (released that summer) was a four-quadrant megahit. Aykroyd's next vehicle as a writer and star, Paramount's *SNL* spin-off *Coneheads* (1993), tanked. It was effectively his last hurrah as a comedy lead.

It's said that he wrote to all involved in *Trouble*, taking all the flak for any harm to their reputations.* Candy was dead three years later, but had *Cool Runnings* (1993) to redeem him first; Moore managed to sandwich this embarrassment (and therefore forget all about it) between her two biggest hits, *Ghost* and *A Few Good Men* (1992). As for Chase, it does feel that the American public might have had just about enough of him – whether the rot had set in already or not, his pulling power would evaporate through the 1990s.

The film both is and isn't stupid; it has some feisty political undercurrents. The crazy judge hates anyone connected with finance, because of a raw deal his grandfather was 'hoglowsered and

---

* This speaks so well of him, and I hope it happened, but supporting player Bertila Damas doesn't actually remember receiving such a letter.

tubwangled' into accepting in 1917, when he was off fighting in the First World War. So he's deeply suspicious of Chase's hotshot, as well he might be. We're certainly not meant to *like* Chase in his part, but when comic friction's warranted, all we get is his not-even-veiled contempt for his surroundings.

He's plain lazy, doing the bare minimum of eye-widening. His scenes with Moore are tedious. I wonder if Bill Murray in his knowingly corrupt *Scrooged* (1988) mode might have fed more ideas into the mix. You get the impression Chase was just pocketing the cheque here and holding his nose. But then, this isn't *too* far from what his character is all about, a callous chancer only looking out for himself.

This pungent calamity gains odd flickers of purpose if you can bear to look back. Which some do quite regularly. Like all flops, it has a committed hardcore of surprisingly rabid fans, who generally caught it, like some pesky disease, while channel-hopping in the mid-1990s, and venture all sorts of arguments to defend it to the hilt. I'm a lot more sympathetic than I used to be, at least. While not *strictly* good, it's anything but ordinary.

THE HUDSUCKER PROXY (1994)

Director: Joel Coen
Studio: Warner Bros
Budget: $25m ($40m with marketing)
US gross: $2.8m

Critics are usually kinder to cheaper movies than to those they perceive to be big-budgeted Hollywood releases. A case in point is that of *Hudsucker*. Some of the bad reviews stated that the movie cost $40m. In fact, it cost $25m. It's true that a lot of money seems like a stick they want to beat you with. They cut you more slack if you spend less money, which makes no sense.[1]

Ethan Coen

In the output of the Coen brothers, *The Hudsucker Proxy* is a budgetary anomaly – a lavish blip. This pristine essay in executive screwball is about the fast rise and precipitous fall of a mail-room boy, Norville Barnes, at a 1950s manufacturing corporation called Hudsucker Industries. He's a rube, being manipulated by higher powers who certainly don't have the interests of the little guy at heart.

Being dopey, Norville's the last to figure out the dog-eat-dog imperatives of mid-century capitalism – he thinks it's a merry-go-round, and just wants his whirl like everyone else. To show him rolling in it, the Coens had to splash around a great deal of cash themselves. While it flaunts the gonzo eccentricity, along with the movie-movie-ness, typical of their work, the gamble was a riskily inflated cost that counted against them: they went all in, too early in their careers.

Does *Hudsucker* show us how flopping hard can be a kind of education? The upshot was by no means ruinous. In industry terms, you could call the film almost tragically inconsequential. But it was a formative mistake, in terms of shaping what we know the Coens can do and, in fact, do better, when they're making the most of slimmer resources.

If a $9m *Barton Fink* (1991) loses a few million, who even cares? That tale of a nebbishy playwright discovering scary truths in 1940s Hollywood won the Palme d'Or,* as well as Best Director and Best Actor for John Turturro in Cannes, and netted the first three Oscar nominations a Coen film had received (albeit in lesser categories).† This kind of esteem certainly offsets the trouble of marketing such a dank curio to the masses. It's a proudly eggheady object called *Barton Fink*, after all, which gives off a purposeful tang of being for cultists only. It doesn't *need* your tacky mainstream love.

A sadder case is the one before it. The Coens' gangster threnody *Miller's Crossing* (1990)‡ opened in America the very same day as *Goodfellas*, and was criminally overshadowed from the off. I'm no expert in marketing, but that feels like a misjudged launch strategy to me. *Raising Arizona* (1987) – the Coens' one *bona fide* hit till *Fargo* (1996) – had already proved their stylistic chops and dizzying comic dynamism. *Miller's Crossing* should have been the flipside: it shows how soulful, steeped in regret and melancholy, their investment in timeworn genre formulae can be. Yes, it also has Albert Finney in slippers and PJs on a tommy-gun rampage to the strains of 'Danny Boy'. I love it more on every pass.

The inverse, I have to confess, is probably true of *The Hudsucker*

---

* Completing a hat-trick of US Palmes, after *sex, lies and videotape* (1989) and *Wild at Heart* (1990).
† It was nominated for Art Direction, Costume Design, and Best Supporting Actor for the late Michael Lerner, whose death I weirdly learned about while writing this footnote.
‡ Budget $14m, domestic gross $5.1m.

Proxy, an art deco design bonanza that I'm sure I loved on VHS in 1995. Parts of it – the Hula-Hoop catching on, bang in the middle – are perfectly delightful. The sum is canned and hectic. It's not the big spend per se, or the story, that are sticking points. It's the knock-on effect you feel in your bones from the budget, in so many of the tonal choices. This is $25m (we'll go with Ethan) spent on skyscrapers and quotation marks. A dressy homage to Sturges, Capra and Hawks,* but one missing a heartbeat.

Instead, hollow laughter echoes through it. In no other Coen flick do a more daunting proportion of the characters keep cracking themselves up with their own jokes, from Jim True-Frost's perma-howling elevator boy to all the hard-bitten newshounds – even our dumb schmo Norville (Tim Robbins), once he gets his underhand promotion to the top. It's all a set-up to devalue the company's stock, so Sidney J. Mussburger (a pleasingly demonic Paul Newman) can take control. In one bound, goofy Norville from Muncie, Indiana, is suddenly the kind of fellow who chomps cigars and finds himself hilarious. We're served the American Dream, sped up, as parody.

With each gag come two chances to laugh, I guess – at the rat-a-tat quips themselves, then the vanity of these guys (and one gal, Jennifer Jason Leigh's thrusting journo) for thinking they're such ace comedians. If you find yourself failing on both counts, what exactly is going on? Does it deserve that gripe that's always been a critics' rod for the Coens' back, of simply being too clever by half? The carapace of irony can feel like reinforced steel. All too often, it's a dead weight.

————

* Todd McCarthy laid it out in his January 1994 *Variety* review: '*Hudsucker* plays like a Frank Capra film with a Preston Sturges hero and dialogue direction by Howard Hawks.'

Eagle-eyed viewers of *Raising Arizona* may note that Nicolas Cage's character goes to work for a company called Hudsucker Industries – a case of the Coens planting an Easter egg for a film they hadn't even made yet. Fully conceived before this, *Hudsucker* was one of the first scripts they ever wrote, together with Sam Raimi, who'd remain heavily involved in the production ten years on.

They'd been friends since Joel assistant-edited on Raimi's *The Evil Dead* (1981), and became housemates in LA who helped each other out through those early years. They all joined forces to write Raimi's ill-fated black comedy *Crimewave* (1985), while Joel's wife Frances McDormand would play the female lead in Raimi's nifty *Darkman* (1990), having debuted in the Coens' calling card, *Blood Simple* (1984).

You can tell what fun they all had writing and storyboarding *Hudsucker* together – there's a gee-whizzery to it on paper that's quite endearing. At the time, though, there was no cheap enough way of getting it made. It needed a high level of stylisation with the sets, and an army of extras, to come off, and no one was going to take that financial risk on such newbies.

Enter, of all people, Joel Silver. After the Coens' Palme win, they were keen to make a bigger splash, and it was the *Hudsucker* script they pulled out from a drawer. Silver, besotted with their craftsmanship* and wanting in, was at the peak of his powers as an action producer, with three killer franchises on the books: *Predator* (1987–), *Die Hard* (1988–), and the *Lethal Weapon* (1987–98) series.

Warner Bros were falling over themselves to keep him happy. He brought *Hudsucker* to them, brokering the deal so WB would take

---

* Silver also happens to be a fan of Frank Lloyd Wright, a huge influence on the *Hudsucker* production design: in 1984 he bought Wright's Storer House in the Hollywood Hills, and painstakingly had it restored.

the American rights and pay for half of it. Polygram and Working Title, desperate to work with the Coens but nowhere near as deep-pocketed, breathed a sigh of relief that they wouldn't be shouldering the entire cost.

The marriage of Coens + Silver, who produced this under his Silver Pictures banner but took no individual credit, is an odd alliance. He promised no interference – a blank cheque, pretty much – and the Coens have said he was true to his word. He wanted Tom Cruise to play Norville; the Coens preferred Robbins. Jennifer Jason Leigh 'came in and blew us away', according to Silver, which suggests he did have some level of involvement in the casting.

Clint Eastwood and Jack Nicholson were considered for Sidney, but you can't imagine anyone complaining when Newman took the part, in his return to films after a four-year hiatus. He's intimidatingly good.* The character is a ruthless corporate shark in tailored three-piece suits, whom we're meant to understand as an American fascist.

The cavernous sets at the top of Hudsucker HQ never seem more Albert Speer-esque than when Sidney's luxuriating in them, smoking his stogies in the dark. When Newman arrived to shoot his scenes, he was amazed by the immensity of Dennis Gassner's creations, remarking that he hadn't seen bigger sets for a film since the first he'd ever made, a creaking Roman epic called *The Silver Chalice* (1954).†

---

* When he holds up a newspaper with a headline about 'Hud stock', it feels like an in-joke about Newman's indelible role as a Texan cowboy in *Hud* (1963). He would claim all his best films began with 'H': *The Hustler* (1961), too, *Harper* (1966) and *Hombre* (1967).

† Newman had a terrible time on this turkey, a false start for his career that he would disparage repeatedly. When it was broadcast on TV in 1966, he took out a trade ad apologising for his performance. He also screened it for guests at home, handing out pots and whistles and encouraging everyone to lambast it.

No reviews at the time could help singling out the contribution of Gassner and his set dressers, a key reason why the film was so costly, but also its most eye-catching tour de force. Scale models of 14 miniature skyscrapers were made – buildings cherry-picked from the real New York skyline – to be clustered into a kind of stylised, Gotham-esque cityscape, then airbrushed to age them, with photo-realistic rust stains in the windows, say.

At DEG studios* in North Carolina, these models spent a lot of their time lying horizontally, while the effects shots for the tower-jump suicides were filmed on tracks. The first to plunge is Charles Durning as Waring Hudsucker at the start, who leaps to his death boisterously through the boardroom window. At the climax it's Norville who outdoes *It's a Wonderful Life* (1946), on the snowy New Year's Eve of 1958–9, by actually jumping, before being mystically rescued in mid-flight when time stands still.

The usual policy for struck sets at DEG studios was for them to be tipped into a pit, covered with petrol and incinerated. What saved these, which had cost some $400,000, was someone mentioning that James Cameron, who was planning his next film to be *Spider-Man*, might have a use for them.

While that film never happened, they were cannibalised for years on various blockbusters – *The Shadow* (1994), *Batman Forever* (1995), *Godzilla* (1998). Model-making supremo Ian Hunter remembers spying his babies for the last time, looking pretty tattered, in the background of a studio set for Nicole Kidman's *Bewitched* (2005) – now there's an undignified swansong.

Whatever tempers might have flared or disasters struck mid-shoot, we haven't heard tell of it – true enough for everything the Coens have made to date. Without evidence to the contrary, it's entirely

---

* Owned by the De Laurentiis Entertainment Group.

possible this ran like clockwork. Not a whole lot of time was wasted improvising, that's for sure. It has a lockstep quality, planned out to the millisecond. On some jobs, actors mainly have to concentrate on hitting their elaborate marks, wiping off sweat between takes, and generally obeying orders.

Take Leigh. Clearly riffing on Rosalind Russell in *His Girl Friday* (1940) – the wise-cracking dynamo of a lady reporter who falls for someone on the job – she's all mannered patter and 90-degree elbows, with enough Katharine Hepburn stirred in to let her goose up the accent. I have a hunch her performance is exactly what the Coens wanted.

And yet their conception of Amy Archer is a bust, a non-starter. She never gets to sparkle or gain our affection, victimised by a script that keeps insisting she must be miserable, being a high-flying career gal and all. Her love story with Robbins – strenuously doofus-y here, though he can be a nimble physical comedian – feels like the Coens are playing Cupid between a stick of chalk and a lump of cheese.

Sans star chemistry, all the swooning gets done by Roger Deakins's lighting, which is pretty magical, and Carter Burwell's swelling arrangements of Khachaturian's *Spartacus*. The vision of movie-Manhattan they help achieve is aglow with all the requisite starry-eyed romance – but it's strictly a romance for old films, with the people involved mere placeholders.

In the more frantic passages, the Coens seem to be copying a much more recent model, the bureaucratic nightmare of Gilliam's *Brazil* (1985), to whip up a pulse during *this* wimpy hero's induction to office chaos. Meanwhile, the celebrated Hula-Hoop montage, when inspired lift-off does occur, was in fact outsourced to Raimi, who obligingly came on board as first assistant director, this being the only film big enough so far for the Coens to need one.

Everyone remembers the Hula-Hoop. Norville ushers his bright idea to market – 'You know, for kids!' – while the Hudsucker machinery goes into overdrive. Camera dashing, and all dexterous cutting, the interlude is crafted like a standalone short. In form, it's pure Raimi, who makes a background cameo as one of the silhouetted guys in the 'creative bullpen', brainstorming brand names. To give the Coens *and* Raimi their due, the gag of making one runaway hoop collide with some random kid on the pavement, whose skills with it are instantly competition level, really does sing. It's a satisfyingly absurd pivot for the entire fortunes of Hudsucker Industries.

Would that the film's own fate had followed a similar trajectory. When *Hudsucker* hit the streets, what happened halfway through that sequence was as far as it got: the moment of unveiling to the sound of crickets, and an exasperated toyshop owner dumping all the unwanted hoops out back. There was no *deus ex machina*, no sudden craze turning it into a runaway success.

It premiered, mutedly, at Sundance in January 1994. Test screenings had been worryingly mixed; while Warner Bros felt reshoots were in order, the Coens exerted their final-cut privilege, standing their ground. The title? A mouthful, as the suits must have muttered, but so be it. Some minor pick-ups were done, tinkering with the ending.

Then the reviews out of Sundance confirmed everyone's fears. Even critics who lavished praise on the technical elements of pastiche found a vacuum inside – 'a wizardly but artificial synthesis', reckoned Todd McCarthy in *Variety*. Come May, it would open the Cannes Film Festival, where the Coens were already darlings, but *Pulp Fiction* ate up all the hype.

It's an atypical move for Cannes to save a high-profile slot for anything a rival festival has premiered – yet more so for a film that has had its entire stateside theatrical run already. The only explanation is that the Coens got a free pass as recent Palme winners.

For *Hudsucker* had already been treated, if that's the word, to a boutique release strategy on 11 March that caved in even more than *Miller's Crossing* had done. Opening at five sites, it needed double the screen average it got; by April, after a marginal effort to widen, it was toast. All the while, Polygram's *Four Weddings and a Funeral*, which soft-launched that very same weekend, just kept bouncing merrily up the charts. Costing an eighth of *Hudsucker*, it did 20 times the business.

I talked to one person involved with *Hudsucker*'s international marketing who described it as a 'feathered fish' – hard to sell because it's not quite one thing, not quite another. The fact that it was a Coen film with a Silver-boosted budget – and name stars – might have struck Warner Bros initially as a bumper scenario, but the vexing result, when they came to promote it, was how the elements actually subtracted from one another.

The figures (a truly grim $2.8m) tell a tale of WB's distribution team politely applauding while simply hoping it would go away. It did much better abroad: $12m is nowhere near profit-turning, but that's still wildly impressive in comparison, a sign of more nurturing treatment from smaller European players who didn't have the likes of *Major League II* to fret about.

The Coens' failed Hula-Hoop might have cost them dearly – it was their third flop running, after all, and much the priciest. I'd posit that the strained maximalism of *Hudsucker* taught them unignorable lessons, which we saw absorbed right away. They sprinted away from Norville Barnes and his busy fortunes towards a kind of solace in negative space. It was their own Eureka moment.

Fargo – 'a homespun murder story', as the embroidered poster art had it – wasn't just sensibly downscaled, with a production budget all the way back down to $6.5m, but visually *Hudsucker*'s exact opposite. While they'd started the script beforehand, the Coens' style choices were circumscribed by what they'd just been through. 'It's true that we were pressured in this direction,' Joel admitted in 1996, about forsaking theatrical dazzle for this new emphasis on bleak authenticity.[2]

Hudsucker remains their most vertical piece of film-making, with its fussy head stuck in the clouds – all *trompe l'œil* fakery and overreaching spires. *Fargo* instead presents white skies over a white horizon, featureless and flat, as far as the eye can see.

There's not much on screen that isn't real, bar the blood spraying from a wood chipper. All that wordy Hawksian patter gives way to affectless monosyllables, sometimes barely more than grunts. And it mesmerises. The desperation of these people counts for so much more with 'just snow' as the backdrop, levelling that Coen impulse to overdesign. The brothers needed *Fargo* like crazy, as did we. But they needed to get it right, too – and *Hudsucker's* towering failure had schooled them in how not to do it.

CUTTHROAT ISLAND (1995)

Director: Renny Harlin
Studio: Carolco/MGM
Budget: $98–115m
Worldwide gross: $18.5m

Cutthroat Island could only dream of being *Waterworld*.

That *other*, oddly notorious 1995 piratical romp* was lavishly, but inaccurately, reported as a megaflop. Knives were out in the press for *Waterworld* – indecently sharpened. The budget, much speculated on as filming dragged on, may even have rounded $175m. All that pre-release *Schadenfreude* translated to limp enthusiasm when it opened in the USA. And yet it scraped back a profit from foreign markets (less deterred by the anti-hype) and healthy rentals (curious, after all).†

Waterworld survived (if barely) a set that sank and the collision of Kevins: Reynolds quit before he'd finished directing, after one too many attempts by Costner to seize creative control. The nightmares of a complex shoot on open water had pretty much doubled the budget and schedule – exactly as Steven Spielberg had warned Reynolds was bound to happen.

But it was no *Cutthroat Island*. This was an epic failure for the books, one of the unluckiest films ever to crawl ashore. Dollar for dollar, notching up an inflation-adjusted loss of some $190m, it's

---

* The reunion of Kevin Costner and Kevin Reynolds, after 1991's very dumb, very successful *Robin Hood: Prince of Thieves*.
† Final worldwide gross was $264.2m, of which the US gross amounted to a mere $88.2m.

on a par with the worst financial write-offs of recent times.* Forget prints and advertising – nearly 90 per cent of *Cutthroat*'s production budget sank to the bottom of the sea. *The Guinness Book of Records* installed it for some years as the biggest flop ever made.

There's something pure about a catastrophe this cut and dried. You don't even need to calculate what they spent marketing it, which was practically zilch, because the company that made it, Carolco, had already filed for Chapter 11 bankruptcy by the time it opened, and the distributor, MGM, was in the process of being sold. The film was a sinking galleon before it even tried to set sail, and would take several careers down with it.

———

Geena Davis and Renny Harlin got married in September 1993. Their weekend involved a hoedown, hot-air balloons, and a sunset ceremony in the ruins of an old Napa winery. They'd met just six months before, because Davis wanted to find an action vehicle to supercharge the next phase of her career, and her agents effected an introduction to the Finnish director, which clearly went well.

Davis had divorced Jeff Goldblum in 1991. She already had an Oscar under her belt for *The Accidental Tourist* (1988), and had established herself as a viable lead with the one–two of *Thelma and Louise* (1991) and *A League of Their Own* (1992). But there was a slight danger of this slipping away unless she buckled up for something brasher.

* For example, *John Carter* (2012), *The Lone Ranger* (2013), *Mortal Engines* (2018). See p. 280. I've concentrated on films that didn't come close to recouping their production budgets – the purest kind of flop. These are rarer, these days.

She'd just fought to star in a rival pirate film, *Mistress of the Seas* – billed as '*Dangerous Liaisons* on ships' – which was developed then dumped by Columbia in 1993. Harrison Ford was involved for a hot minute. Paul Verhoeven was going to direct, then briefly Harlin, then Verhoeven again, then no one.

Harlin may have been a good notch below the James Cameron stratosphere, but he'd just climbed some peaks with *Die Hard 2* (1990),[1] then the banger that is *Cliffhanger* (1993)[2] – essentially *Die High*, with Stallone foiling thieves while dangling off mountains. (I could watch it all day.)

Cliffhanger had been the baby of Carolco, the independent hit factory whose Lebanese chief, Mario Kassar, was an industry titan, without whose bankrolling power the action-blockbuster scene of the early 1990s would have been in much poorer shape. From their early days peddling B-movies mainly used as tax shelters, Carolco had been boosted up to major league by Stallone's *Rambo* trilogy in the 1980s. They had a reputation for risky outlays on R-rated projects with massive stars, to whom they offered paydays bigger than any traditional studio.

'I have to go for it,' Kassar told the *Los Angeles Times* in 1990.[3] 'His attitude is that of a gambler,' chimed in Oliver Stone, who was then directing *The Doors* (1991) for him. Arnold Schwarzenegger, and all the other big boys, respected Kassar for his split-second autocratic instincts: 'You never see a bureaucracy or an entourage,' as Stone put it.

Carolco had just had back-to-back megahits with Paul Verhoeven, *Total Recall* (1990) and *Basic Instinct* (1992), which thrust a hungry Sharon Stone into the limelight.* Kassar had no end of trouble

---

* Stone was paid a mere $500,000 for that, whereas Michael Douglas would pocket $14m.

striking the various deals to make *Terminator 2: Judgment Day* (1991) happen, but the splurge was worth it. From its record-breaking $102m budget, it would become the third-highest-grossing film ever made at that time, behind only *E. T.* and *Star Wars*.[4]

Carolco's business plan was top heavy, in that they needed only one of these whoppers each year to fund any number of smaller efforts.* But they ploughed eye-watering sums into fixing up the big deals. No one could figure out whether the private jet Arnie got for *T2*, a $14m Gulfstream G-III, was on top of his $15m salary, or what, but it would have been very much Kassar's style to throw that in. His company had a fleet of stretch limos with Carolco plates constantly on the prowl around Bel-Air, and they threw Cannes parties at the Hotel du Cap that went down in legend.

They were haemorrhaging fast. In 1989, Kassar had parted ways with his founding partner, the more cautious Andrew G. Vajna, who'd been paid $100m for his share in the company.[†] In 1991 alone, Carolco posted a loss of $265m; it restructured in 1992 and sold off shares in 1993. The deal on *Cliffhanger* had been a gruelling mess, with TriStar and others stepping in to co-finance because of their existing debts.[‡]

---

* Those latter being the likes of *Angel Heart* (1987), *Jacob's Ladder* (1990) or Richard Attenborough's *Chaplin* (1992).

† The duo remained ultra-competitive to the point of yacht envy. The following summer, Kassar made sure his vessel in Cannes was longer than the old Carolco yacht, which Vajna had to make do with.

‡ Before that, they'd spent millions preparing a hurricane flick called *Gale Force*, which was the first idea for a Harlin–Stallone joint, and for which Harlin was paid a then record-breaking fee of $3m. Carolco cancelled it two weeks before production, switching bets to the twice-as-costly *Cliffhanger*, which still didn't get them out of the hole. The shoot was halted twice because Carolco ran out of money to pay the crew, and the film went at least $26m over budget, per *Variety* ('Budget tale a *Cliffhanger*', November 1992).

Things were getting desperate. Carolco *had* to have a money-spinner ready for the summer of 1995. Paul Verhoeven came to them in early 1994 with his next big Arnie pitch, a $100m historical epic called *Crusade*, billed as *Spartacus* meets *Conan*. The script was by our old pal Walon (*Sorcerer*) Green. It would be thunderous, bloody, relentless. It was Verhoeven.

Carolco was excited enough to sink $13m into pre-production. But then panic struck. Kassar and associates wanted guarantees from Verhoeven that the overall budget would climb no higher. Throwing an infamous wobbly at a last-ditch meeting, he refused to make the promise, and walked. The film never got made.

Carolco now threw all its eggs into the only remaining basket: *Cutthroat Island*, a rough-and-ready script that Kassar had optioned in 1990.

This was not conceived as a vehicle for Davis at first, who didn't even rate her role that highly, but an equal-billing enterprise in which Carolco's real commercial hopes centred (fatally, as it would prove) on Michael Douglas. The salaries told the story: he'd be receiving $13m, while Harlin and Davis got $5.5m apiece.

Davis was happy playing Morgan Adams, a swashbuckling pirate's daughter hunting for part of a treasure map in 1668 Jamaica, so long as Douglas, angling for a lighter romp after his post-*Basic-Instinct* hot streak, would be William Shaw, a roguish, Errol-Flynn-alike con artist who steals her heart. Much derring-do, in their quest for unimaginable riches, would ensue. Would it do? Pirate films hadn't been in vogue for years,* but Harlin was gambling on a *Captain Blood* (1935) revival with wild stunts. Douglas wanted it to be *Romancing the Stone* (1984) all over again.

---

* The crashing failure of Roman Polanski's $40m *Pirates* (1985) would have given them pause, and even Spielberg's $70m *Hook* (1991) hadn't been the megahit everyone wanted.

No one could get the script to work. Filming was meant to start in January 1994, then June, then September, weeks after Douglas would be done shooting that year's *Disclosure*. That didn't give the fifty-year-old much time to learn fencing and get in physical shape. The clock was ticking before his next commitment, on *The American President* (1995) in January.

Meanwhile, he became antsy about rewrites of the barely functional script, which was being endlessly redrafted to Harlin's specifications. Douglas wanted the male part beefed up; instead, Davis's role was the one that kept growing. On 11 July, citing dismay at all these developments, he bailed.

The list of names who were sought, in mounting desperation, to fill his shoes is a who's who of (all-white) A-list talent from the mid-1990s. Tom Cruise, Mel Gibson, Keanu Reeves, Liam Neeson, Jeff Bridges, Ralph Fiennes, Charlie Sheen, Michael Keaton, Tim Robbins, Daniel Day-Lewis, Kurt Russell and Gabriel Byrne were all offered it. No one took the bait. The script was becoming notorious around town as Harlin's wedding gift to his new wife, not a boon to any leading man who wanted to keep his edge or pulling power.

At long last, they secured Matthew Modine. Fifteen years Douglas's junior, Modine was still best known for his leading role as Joker in Kubrick's *Full Metal Jacket* (1987), but hadn't exactly set box offices alight in the years since. Ominously, his most recent big-budget effort, which few had seen, was a fairly inert yacht-racing epic called *Wind* (1992).* He could at least *look* credibly like a pirate, with California-beach-boy locks that gave him the right kind of matinee-idol glow. His fee was a fraction of Douglas's, and he had

* Directed by Carroll (*The Black Stallion*) Ballard, with lovely John Toll cinematography.

some experience fencing. But everyone knew it was non-star casting, dictated by Carolco's ever-worsening state of emergency.

As was his wont, Kassar had bullishly presold foreign rights to the film, so the lavish location shoots (in Malta and Thailand) could go ahead. This meant Carolco had been paid $50–60m by an assortment of distributors already, and needed a film to show for it. 'We knew from that point that if we lost *Cutthroat Island* as well, bankruptcy would be inevitable,' said a former executive to the *Independent* in 1996. 'If we made the film, there was at least some chance we could survive.'[5]

The situation this put Harlin and Davis in was unenviable. 'Everyone knew that, one way or another, this was [Carolco's] last movie,' Davis explained the following year. 'The ludicrous thing was that the only reason I was there was because of Michael. I never wanted to carry [it].'[6] Davis and Harlin both assumed Douglas's departure would sink the production but, unlike him, they had a legal obligation to carry on regardless.

'We *begged* to be let go,' Harlin put it in a 2011 radio interview. 'Geena was scared mindless about headlining this film. We felt that a pirate movie with a female lead was suicidal, but we were contractually obligated. And we were so concerned about the script at that point that I personally spent $1m of my own money [to hire] Mark Norman.'[7] This American screenwriter was a future Oscar-winner for *Shakespeare in Love* (1998), not that *Cutthroat's* cod-period dialogue – its weakest element – would have had anyone placing bets on this. The director had him doctoring the script on a day-to-day basis in Malta.

Harlin was unrestrained about spending Carolco's money, too, as if positively goading Kassar to yell 'Avast!' and cut him loose. There's a story that Harlin spent some $15,000 to break quarantine and get his dog through Maltese customs.[8] Per such gossipy reports, his *Cliffhanger* security team and Mercedes were also on the rider. Modine remembers dozens of cases of V8 vegetable juice being shipped in before Davis's and Harlin's arrival, most of which remained unopened in a storeroom.

Harlin had been so sidetracked by all the rewrites, not to mention recasting his male lead, that he'd taken his eye off the set-building, which was proceeding apace without him. 'If we build it, will he come?' became the crew's credo. A thousand feet of buildings along the quayside in Malta needed new facades erected to double as Port Royal in 1668. The director didn't appreciate what he eventually saw, and insisted much of it was ripped down and started again.

The film's two pirate ships, the *Morning Star* and the *Reaper*, had 20 working cannons on each side – full-sized replicas of seventeenth-century craft that cost $1m each. If Harlin was going to be forced to do this thing, he wasn't going to do it by halves. 'Our imagination and sense of invention cannot be limited by mundane reality,' he'd written to his crew in a July 1994 staff memo, which later got leaked to the press. 'I don't want big, I want huge. I don't want fast, I want explosive. I don't want accidents, I want disasters.'[9] (He sounds rather like Sean Connery upping the ante in *The Untouchables*: 'They pull a knife, you pull a gun . . .')

Even though they used giant tanks in Malta to avoid the perils of the open sea, the shoot was a perfect storm. The cinematographer, Oliver Wood, fell off a crane into one of the tanks in the first week, breaking his leg, and had to be replaced by Peter Levy. Harlin squabbled a lot, including with the producer David Nichols, who quit, as did the art director, Wolf Kroeger. He tussled with the chief camera operator, Nicola Pecorini, then fired him, causing more than two dozen other crew to walk out in sympathy.

Modine had a rough time even before the damning reviews. The back of his head was ripped open when a piece of timber came loose during a storm scene. The day the stitches came out, a barrel then thwacked him on the head. A wastepipe burst, too, causing raw sewage to flow into the tank where actors were meant to be swimming.

Davis did many of her own splendid stunts, and suffered for it. She swings from chandeliers and rigging, rides horses, jumps off cliffs. In one amazingly seamless-looking shot, she jumps out of a window in Port Royal, rolls off a roof and lands upright in the seat of a carriage. During one take the timing was off, meaning she rolled under the vehicle, narrowly escaping permanent spinal damage.

Oliver Reed (uh-oh*) was originally meant to appear as a grizzled old buccaneer called Mordechai Fingers. After getting in a bar fight on his first night and supposedly showing Davis the eagle-claw tattoo on his penis, he was given the heave-ho.

One person who doesn't think Reed deserved to walk the plank, for essentially behaving like a Method pirate? Modine. These days, the actor whose career took the biggest hit also comes to the film's defence. It *is* unfairly maligned. But Modine has admitted to on-set frustrations, after those reviews squelched his hopes of ever having an A-lister's career.

'I felt like I had my stomach cut open and my guts spread all over the United States,'[10] he said on reading them. The script he'd signed up to had been the one Douglas had okayed, not the new one 'about a girl and her journey'. 'It's the first movie I've worked on where the director never really spoke to me,' he shrugged a year later. 'Renny spent a lot of his time just finding new ways to blow things up. He likes to blow things up.'[11]

When the shoot finished in Thailand, with a wrap party on April Fools' Day, Davis and Harlin had already run for the hills. Kassar had wheedled an extra $40m out of a European banking syndicate just so

---

* See pp. 115–6 for his *Munchausen* misdeeds.

the film could cross the finish line. The release date had to be shunted from summer 1995 to a much more competitive slot in December. During those few short months, Carolco's number was up.

With the IRS on its case, the company filed for bankruptcy in November 1995, Kassar resigned, and Canal+ bought its film library. The pre-release press around *Cutthroat Island*, especially in the wake of *Waterworld*, was so hostile that no one had much enthusiasm, let alone money, for promotion come Christmas. It opened in 11th place at the US box office, with a shudder-worthy screen average of $1,464, while the likes of *Toy Story*, *Jumanji* and the debuting *Waiting to Exhale* got everyone's four bucks instead. Within two weeks, it had disappeared.

The wrong assumption for years was that *Cutthroat Island* ruined Carolco. It was costly, slow to make, feebly written and lopsidedly cast, but these were only the final nails in a long-assembled coffin. If anything, it was the other way round: the company's dire straits doomed the film at birth.

There's plenty about it that's hugely silly. We have to go along with Shaw, an enslaved peasant scamp, being a dab hand at Latin, or Morgan would have no reason to buy him at auction to decipher the portion of the treasure map she has cut from the scalp of her own dying father. She knows full well that Shaw is fraudulently claiming to be a doctor, yet lets him extract a bullet from her hip, in the most intimate scene? Sure.

The fact that various writers bagged $4m devising this malarkey is daylight robbery. But it's hard to blame the actors, or not as much as reviews did. The *idea* of chemistry between Davis and Modine is quite appealing – it's just that the script keeps bungling their chances, never landing on the right jokes or gender-flipping the usual pirate–damsel dynamic successfully.

The film still cuts a dash. John Debney's score, popping up in trailers for years afterwards, lends a hearty bombast. Some of the location shooting has a magic lost to us these days – take Morgan's sumptuous horseback gallop along sandbanks to rescue her dad, or that reckless carriage chase along Port Royal's harbourfront.

So we get galleons firing cannons at the leads for literally no reason, and cannonballs that explode, with Harlin filming about half the action in slow motion?* All part of the fun. The same could be said of Frank Langella spontaneously bellowing, 'I love this! *I love it!!*' through the blasts as Morgan's conniving, sweat-drenched uncle. Better yet is the brilliantly bone-dry Patrick Malahide, keeping it together.† He's a powdered dandy of a governor, tormenting Angus Wright's hapless deputy for the hell of it.

When Disney executives agreed to the first *Pirates of the Caribbean* (2003), they were biting their nails from the memory of this capsizing. There's *far* less separating the two than people like to argue, other than Johnny Depp pulling off a polysexual one-man show, to wizardly effect, in the middle of one of them. The Disney one! It speaks to the crapshoot of blockbuster economics that Depp's franchise spun off to four sequels and $4.5bn worldwide, while this cursed pearl gets brought up every time Harlin so much as steps out of the house.

The couple got to make one more film together, which was already locked to shoot just weeks after *Cutthroat* bombed. *The Long Kiss*

---

* We also hear tell of 'riflemen' (rifles didn't come in until the nineteenth century) and glimpse a few Union Jacks in Port Royal, even though the flag wasn't flown anywhere until 1801.

† His exit from the flick is sadly unceremonious, lost in a vague flash of cannonfire; Harlin explains in his director's commentary that he had planned an elaborate sword duel for Ainslee's demise, but had to drop this.

Goodnight (1996), from one of Shane Black's better scripts, was a winking thriller about an amnesiac assassin. Though a minor cult classic, it only broke even at the time – undoubtedly dented by Davis and Harlin's previous collaboration.

Their marriage didn't last much longer. Davis found out that Harlin was fathering a child with her personal assistant, and they divorced in 1998. After getting back to business by giving sharks bigger brains in the gleefully idiotic *Deep Blue Sea* (1999), Harlin's had only one palpable hit since, a Jackie Chan–Johnny Knoxville buddy-cop comedy called *Skiptrace* (2016), which was huge in China* and nowhere else. Davis retreated from films to a muted second act on TV,[†] while Modine reverted to the peculiar little indies he clearly prefers, before a comeback in *Stranger Things*.

Cutthroat held them all at knifepoint, in the end. It's very daft, childishly engaging, and there are far worse films – even pirate flicks starring Johnny Depp – that have piled up glittering fortunes. Scrape off the barnacles, shoot some rum, and it does have the blurry allure of sunken treasure.

It also represents the demise of something valuable – an old-school way of making blockbusters, to which we might feel quite a lot of nostalgic attachment. I do. I've heard it referred to as 'practical magic': real stunts, real locations, everything done on camera. Blowing up your own sets, when it comes to it. As the CGI revolution beckoned, those *Sorcerer*s and *Munchausen*s may already have been on borrowed time but, in 1995, *Waterworld* and *Cutthroat Island* were like twilight voyages.

---

* Chinese gross: $129m. Total worldwide: $136.6m.

† She won a Golden Globe for playing the US President in ABC's *Commander in Chief* (2005–6), and gave a wonderful speech, but it struggled in the ratings. To her lasting dismay, it ran for one season only.

SPEED 2: CRUISE CONTROL (1997)

Director: Jan de Bont
Studio: 20th Century Fox
Budget: $145m–165m
US gross: $48m

I feel sorry for Jim Cameron.

Jan de Bont, in February 1997

The only way to make sense of *Speed 2* is to pop your eyes out on stalks, bare your top row of gnashers in a grin no stable person would attempt, and adopt the point of view of Willem Dafoe's character, a boat-obsessed fruit loop named John Geiger.

So let's say you are John Geiger. You used to work aboard this cruise ship, *Seabourn Legend*, but got copper poisoning from sitting at the controls too long, something that has famously happened to no one, ever. You're now hellbent on revenge against the company that both stunted your lifespan and had the atrocious nerve to sack you afterwards.

You covet diamonds, which are handily stashed in the ship's vault. Your deadly masterplan, then, is to hack the controls, confuse everyone on board with smoke, steal the diamonds, escape by speedboat, and destroy the ship, by setting it on a collision course with an oil tanker. You're completely insane, which becomes an escalating disadvantage. But assuming the identity of an only lightly deranged golfing enthusiast at least gets you a ticket aboard.

You're no ordinary golfer, either. Exploding balls are stashed in your bag, and your clubs are smoke bombs. You've packed your pet leeches, too – you call these 'my nurses' – which are meant to be sucking the copper out of your blood, a last recourse which even you might admit looks . . . insane.

What could go wrong? Not doing your homework, that's what. You make a schoolboy error in one of your earliest scenes, by not paying the slightest attention to a major golf tournament that's playing on TV in the bar, while UB40 are up on stage doing tragic cabaret duties.

From this point on, another holidaymaker has your number, and unfortunately – for absolutely everyone – he's an LAPD SWAT officer called Alex Shaw, played by Jason Patric. Aiming to propose, he's booked this cruise as a surprise for his girlfriend Annie (Sandra Bullock), who has proved already that she can do a lot better. (Romantically, *and* in her script choices.) This new guy just cannot seem to relax, or switch off his boring, robocop brain for a second. He will be your nemesis. Annie will be your hostage, because she might as well have *some* function.

The truth is, *Speed 2: Cruise Control* is not really a sequel to *Speed* at all if you're John Geiger, who knows nothing of a bus, a bomb, Keanu Reeves, $350m worldwide, or any of that jazz. This one man is blissfully unaware of the existence, let alone entertainment value, of *Speed* (1994) – and that's the only hope of scratching out even shreds of enjoyment from the franchise killer here before us. He may be a delirious mess of a character, but he's also the only one enjoying himself.

For everyone else, it is, and was, pretty much a wholesale disaster. *Speed* – let's address the basics – had speed. That bus couldn't go below 50 mph, or it would blow. *Seabourn Legend*, at full pelt, gets up to 19 knots, which is roughly 20 mph. So for 90 per cent of its running time, *Speed 2* is stuck on a huge boat that might as well be obeying the traffic laws outside a kindergarten.

'Cruise Control'? One wonders if someone at Fox got a promotion for that pun – *riiight*, it's a cruise, that someone is controlling.

Might anyone have dared point out that 'licence to take your foot off the accelerator, and just kick back' doesn't sound very James Bond? Sandra Bullock would have killed for cruise control on that bus.

Just ask her, the veteran of both flicks, for her opinion of this one. 'Slow boat. Slowly going towards an island.' It's one of only two films she's vocally embarrassed to have appeared in across her whole career, the other being *Miss Congeniality 2: Armed and Fabulous* (2005). ('I've done two sequels. They were horrible. I'll never do a sequel again,' she confirmed, at the premiere of *The Heat* in 2013.)

There was really no excuse for *Speed 2*, but plenty were given. It came into being only for two reasons: the automatic 1990s necessity that a hit action flick must yield another instalment, however moronic, plus the fact that Jan de Bont had a dream about a cruise liner crashing into a tropical island settlement.

History does not record how many of this Dutchman's other pictures were dream-derived. Before *Speed*, his directing debut, he'd become one of the most sought-after cinematographers in the business – especially thanks to the blood and tinsel of *Die Hard* (1988), with its glittering nightscapes, that plummeting sense of vertigo.

What *Die Hard* managed for Bruce Willis at 20th Century Fox, *Speed* did for Keanu Reeves, making it the same studio's favourite kind of dumb hit. It didn't cost much (a snip at $30m), made a megastar of its established leading man, catapulted his co-star to the A-list too, and had long legs throughout the summer holidays. If you were a teenager in the 1990s, almost anywhere, you saw *Speed*.

You probably saw de Bont's next film, *Twister* (1996), too, whipping up its destruction at that midway point in the 1990s when the effects jamboree took over. (*Independence Day* and *Twister* were the No. 1 and 2 hits of that year, establishing the pattern whereby extinction-level events and/or natural disasters had to be threatened at least twice per summer.)

De Bont's work may sound synonymous with that onslaught of late-1990s CGI – just wait for the ghosts poured like syrupy ecto-plasm over his laughable remake of *The Haunting* (1999). But that wouldn't be *entirely* fair. He'd chivvied a reluctant Reeves into doing a lot of his own stunts on *Speed*, and had Bullock actually driving the bus in many shots.

De Bont had wanted to do *Godzilla* with 'a guy in a suit', before TriStar rejected his ideas, eventually going with Roland Emmerich for the crummy, rain-drenched 1998 CGI-fest. De Bont was also the one who pushed for as much of *Twister* as possible to be shot on the road in Oklahoma, reasoning that it could be 'the last great action movie not shot on a soundstage'.[1] OK, real tornadoes couldn't be coaxed into showing up, nor cows into flying through the air. But the amount of practical effects stuff in *Twister* is underrated. Combine harvesters *were* literally dropped from the sky, and ice cubes blown by wind machines at Bill Paxton's head.

A decade before the conception of the Marvel Cinematic Universe, a year before Sony's slick-ass *Men in Black* (1997), de Bont knew where we were headed. 'It was a transitional period,' he said to *Vulture* in 2020, '[when] we were all desperate to add a new layer of life to the movies'.

This was the same Jan de Bont who had been literally scalped by a lion on the set of *Roar* (1981), an infamous action comedy set on a Tanzanian nature preserve. The savaging he got, sustained while hiding under a tarpaulin to take close-ups, needed 220 stitches to patch up. Like Renny Harlin, then, he'd gained a reputation as a crazy-stunts sort of journeyman, with the scars to prove it.

His actors would find themselves wishing for *more* green screen, not less – definitely true of *Speed 2*, and *Twister* before it. 'We had flying debris in every scene,' de Bont insists of the latter.[2] Both leads were blinded by lamps, needing eye drops and shades to speed their recovery. Helen Hunt also had her head slammed by a truck's door while speeding through a cornfield. 'She can be a little bit . . . clumsy,' was de Bont's recollection during the promo tour. 'Clumsy?!' Hunt shot back. 'The guy burned my retinas! I thought I was a good sport.'[3]

Seen in this light, *Speed 2* was just de Bont's latest attempt to – as it were – push the boat out. The contract he'd signed with Fox on *Speed* obliged him to make another if they so desired, which they certainly did, expecting Reeves and Bullock to sign up in a shot. But even de Bont was agnostic about how a sequel could work. How do you actually follow *Speed*, with its incredibly specific, lightning-in-a-bottle premise? Hundreds of ideas were submitted, including a couple by original screenwriter Graham Yost: there was a warship carrying ammo that might explode if it got wet, or a plane that had to fly through the Andes without ever exceeding 10,000 feet in altitude.

De Bont rejected all that, in favour of putting his dream on screen: a five-star cruise ship coming to rest in the middle of a hotel, in what he envisaged as a grinding, scraping humdinger of a climax with extensive practical effects. Using CGI only for long shots, that sequence required an entire jetty to be built, over the course of four and a half months, on the island of St Martin, with 35 buildings for the ship to crash into. A 150-foot-long replica of the *Seabourn Legend*'s prow was built, which weighed 300 tonnes, powered by four diesel engines along a 1,000-foot track just below the water's surface.

As extras ran and screamed, this huge, fake front third of a boat would rip its way through the resort set. This was the kind of demolition derby that would be an all-computer-generated affair now. But the production designer, Joseph Nemec, claimed it would have been way too expensive with 1997's digital technology. The mainly-in-camera method cost $25m for that five-minute sequence alone: that's about $83,000 per second.

Speed 2 was gaining quite a price tag for a film that had an ending (really, all it still has) before it boasted a beginning, a middle, a script of any description, or either of *Speed*'s stars on board. A writer called Randall McCormick, to whom we owe the existence of John Geiger, was given the job of reverse-engineering a story to get us to this point.

Unlike de Bont, the actors had no legal mandate to come back. Bullock was keen at the time for Fox to fund her passion project, *Hope Floats* (1998). She let herself be roped in, with a $10.5m salary sweetening the deal. But Keanu, who was offered $12m, just couldn't get enthused.

Back then, he was much pilloried in the US press for ducking this payday – he packed his guitar, went touring with his band, Dogstar, and wound up playing Hamlet in Winnipeg* instead. Fox were livid that he wouldn't step up for a sequel, so much so that Reeves claims he was blacklisted from making any films for them until *The Day the Earth Stood Still* (2008).

In hindsight, this now looks like one of the sagest decisions Reeves ever made. 'Movies that are set on water are the kiss of death,' he reasoned later that year, possibly recalling the brief moment when he was in talks to do *Cutthroat Island*, too. 'I mean, just how fast can an ocean liner go?'[4]

'I was totally fine with doing a sequel,' he clarified in 2014. 'I loved working with Sandra, I loved Jan. Fundamentally, I thought a film called *Speed* on an ocean liner was counter-intuitive.'[5] He'd also just been running around in the cold for months during a particularly freezing Chicago winter, to make another action thriller, the utterly middling *Chain Reaction* (1996). He'd clearly had enough. 'I was physically exhausted. And the script . . . I just didn't think it was quite there. So I couldn't get on the boat.'

---

* A piece of casting that helped inspire an entire TV series, the cult-classic Canadian show *Slings and Arrows* (2003–6).

With Reeves out, it was Matthew-Modine-gate* all over again. The entire character of Jack Traven had to go. In came Alex Shaw,† via a hasty rewrite, as not only Bullock's new love interest but an entirely new Ken-doll action hero, built to do everything Traven might have done in a given situation.

'The moment Keanu wasn't going to be in the movie, I became very worried,'6 de Bont would later admit. For Fox, though, it was full steam ahead at all costs, with the brooding Patric, who announced he had no intention of watching the first film, a famously awkward fit in Reeves's shoes. Jon Bon Jovi, Christian Slater, and Billy Zane (!!?!) were first considered, with Bullock chipping in the idea of her then other half, Matthew McConaughey, who politely declined.

Patric did have a major role in *Sleepers* (1996), a forthcoming, star-laden drama for Warners that was generating buzz at the time. Anyone old enough in the 1980s might have remembered him for *The Lost Boys* (1987), too. But there was very little on his résumé to suggest he'd be comfortable – or *fun* – fronting a bombastic summer blockbuster. If anything, he was more famous around Hollywood for the roles he'd turned down – Tom Cruise's character in *The Firm* (1993), for instance – than the string of gritty indies and downbeat flops he'd actually been persuaded to star in.‡

No one involved in shooting *Speed 2* has delightful memories of the experience. 'Being wet for five months sucked,' Patric told *Entertainment Weekly*, pledging never again to be seen in water on screen. 'Not even in a shower.'

---

* See *Cutthroat Island*, pp. 146–7.
† Even sharing a surname with Modine's *Cutthroat Island* character.
‡ The likes of James Foley's *After Dark, My Sweet* (1990), Roger Corman's *Frankenstein Unbound* (1990), Walter Hill's *Geronimo: An American Legend* (1993), and his career-best performance as an undercover narcotics cop opposite Jennifer Jason Leigh, in Lili Fini Zanuck's *Rush* (1991).

De Bont was still a stickler for getting his actors to do their own stunts, but the travails of *Twister* were nothing next to this. On the second day of filming, during the ho-hum prologue when he has to chase after stolen goods on dry land, Patric's Ducati motorbike flew thirty feet off a cliff. He was sent flying through the air, and avoided killing himself, according to Bullock, only by landing 'on the only bush on the entire hill'.[7]

Bullock had to overcome her lifelong fear of water – a tough ask, given that *Seabourn Legend* doubled as cast-and-crew accommodation for much of the shoot. Matters did not improve when Hurricane Lili made a very non-computer-generated beeline for the ship in week two, causing the Coast Guard to order *Seabourn Legend* out of port to outrun twenty-foot swells, and wrecking the St Martin jetty set before the money shots had been executed. 'We were thrown about quite a bit,' de Bont said in the run-up to release. 'I had to give the actors time to go out, throw up and come back in before each scene.'[8]

In one underwater sequence, Patric saved Bullock from being very nearly decapitated by the ship's rudder. Meanwhile, a stunt woman needed reconstructive surgery after being struck in the face by a boat cable. 'We had twelve cameras going, and the stuff that Jason and I did, we should be dead,' Bullock told *Movieline* in 1998.

Trumpeting how near-lethal and constantly rough your shoot was, in the name of verisimilitude, is a classic way to drum up pre-release hype: boy, did we hear endless tales of Leonardo DiCaprio's hardships on *The Revenant* (2015), for instance. The trouble for *Speed 2* is that shockingly little of the death-defying stuff the actors went through actually translates into tangible thrills on screen. The entire storyline is a clattering shambles, especially when you compare the near-real-time suspense of *Speed*. Wait – the sun sets on this cruise, we get a full hour of turgid cat-and-mouse below deck with Geiger and his golf clubs, then clamber out to fresh *daylight*?

Speed 2 is some kind of temporal Tardis, killing time that turns out to be practically an entire minibreak, before the extortionate pay-off of that jetty collision, which all the trailers duly spoiled anyway. By the same logic that bad science is 'not even wrong', here's a *Speed* film that isn't even slow: hefty chunks of it are so set-bound and stuck that we're given no sense of forward motion whatsoever. Are we even *on* a ship? Where did UB40 go?

That old W. C. Fields quote, 'Never work with animals or children', probably deserves the addendum 'especially not at sea', so numerous are the off-putting precedents, from Lew Grade's *Raise the Titanic* (1980) to Barry Levinson's *Sphere* (1998). *Jaws* had nearly destroyed Spielberg, before turning out to be the rare exception commercially – before *Titanic* – to Hollywood's aquatic curse.

Somehow, Fox assumed *Speed 2* would sail through, according to the safe-bet law of lazy sequels. They were very wrong. They were equally wrong, in the other direction, about *Titanic*, which was in the midst of an even-more-waterlogged, twice-as-tough shoot at exactly the same time, and widely predicted to be a disaster waiting to happen. *Titanic*'s budget went north of $200m, it took half a year to shoot and finished a month late, with oppressive amounts of post-production ahead. Fox saw an iceberg looming, and sold the domestic distribution rights to Paramount for $65m, so they wouldn't be caught carrying the whole bag if it failed.

There was no way James Cameron was going to have *Titanic* finished for the original release date, in July 1997, so it was pushed back to Christmas. Everyone was very, very nervous – it only narrowly topped its first weekend's box office chart, with a mediocre $28.6m domestically. But then it gained miraculously in week two, an instant testament to once-in-a-generation word of mouth, and remained No. 1 for a staggering fifteen weeks, seeing off everything that came near it.

Meanwhile, because Fox had nothing else to ring the tills that summer, *Speed 2* was shunted precipitately into existence, with no time to pause, work out the wrinkles, or think through every aspect of it that was plain stupid. The only thing fast about it was the headlong race to shove it through production. That, and the rapidity of its tumble down the charts, dying a painful death at the mercy of *Con Air*, *Face/Off* and *Batman and Robin*.

Bullock was lucky to pull clear of the wreck, retrenching with a string of romcoms and scripts she actually liked. De Bont, who vowed, 'I'll never make another ship movie', received a critical drubbing for *The Haunting*, then, it's said, got so bossed around by Paramount on the *Tomb Raider* sequel (2003) that he would never make another movie at all. And Patric, whose every interview for this implied it was a grim job he would never wish to repeat, instantly turned his back on the stardom he never wanted anyway.

What of Willem Dafoe, whose career has never seemed remotely affected by what's a hit and what's not? He just carried on Willem Dafoeing, which seems as good a policy as any.

BABE: PIG IN THE CITY (1998)

Director: George Miller
Studio: Universal
Budget: $90m
US gross: $18.3m

But fate turns on a moment, dear ones, and the pig was about to learn the
meaning of those two cruel words of regret: 'if only' . . .

Roscoe Lee Browne as the Narrator

Farmer Hoggett (James Cromwell) gets maimed three minutes into
Babe: Pig in the City, in a scene of horrifying physical trauma which
tosses him to the bottom of a well, 6 foot 7 inches of kindly, shattered
bones. So rapidly are the bucolic charms of the first *Babe* (1995)
overridden by a base note of 'harrowing nightmare' that my radar
pings immediately for a pet favourite genre – 'family films that might
require therapy even for the adults watching' (see also *Return to Oz*,*
and Nicolas Roeg's 1990 version of *The Witches*).

It is instantly, threateningly clear that we're in for a George Miller
movie, rather than a cosy sequel to Chris Noonan's adorable sleeper
hit, which Miller co-wrote and produced. Thanks to the creative
freedom Universal semi-accidentally gave Miller from the other side
of the world, this one was likely to be at least 50 per cent a *Mad Max*
film revolving around a talking pig. It was going to be savage.

I paid to see it twice as an undergraduate in December 1998, agog
at the film's spine-tingling perversity, Miller's frequently astonishing
staging, and the blunt homage midway to the ghetto raid from

* See p. 108.

Schindler's List. I took friends. The way I remember it, seats clattering as entire families fled the movie formed an integral part of the soundtrack. I remain in awe of many things about it.

That mishap in the well serves notice: this film is going to be about mortality and happenstance, the cruel quirks of being alive, and trying to stay that way. (The *Mad Max: Fury Road* slave bride played by Rosie Huntingdon-Whiteley, who loses her foothold for that one irreversible moment, can surely relate.) Short of hanging 'Beware!' signs around Babe's neck with barbed wire, *Pig in the City* could hardly forewarn us more directly that it's heading to some dark places.

Audiences, unfortunately, felt very much forewarned – in most cases, before they'd even bought a ticket. People tend to sound surprised when I tell them it flopped. In the US, it performed so dreadfully that Universal's top-tier management was gone by Christmas. However badly they muffed up the release, and despite the emergency cuts it suffered, we owe them a debt of gratitude that the film even exists, in its trippy, rebellious, admittedly uneven form.

What seems hard to believe is that Universal had no idea what they'd paid for – at triple the cost of the first film, to boot. Noonan's adaptation of Dick King-Smith's beloved 1983 novel *The Sheep-Pig* was a runaway hit of rare perfection, which absolutely no one had a bad word for. *Babe* remains one of very few family-targeted films ever to score a Best Picture nomination, rightly won the Best VFX Oscar, and was nominated for five others, including Best Director for Noonan and Supporting Actor for Cromwell.

The next year, Universal commissioned a sequel, which Miller set to writing from scratch, with the eventual help of Judy Morris and Mark Lamprell. Noonan was out – amid something of a feud with Miller over who deserved creative credit for the first one. 'The vision was handed to Chris on a plate,'[1] Miller griped, while Noonan felt his own contribution had been undervalued. Cromwell even had to step in during *Babe*'s shoot to cool down an altercation. 'Chris's humanity and his heart and his sweetness, his vision, was really imprinted on the way he shot that picture,' the actor would recall 25 years later. 'George thought there should be more edge [to *Babe*]. What he wanted was more like *It's a Wonderful Life*. [And it got] darker, and darker, and darker.'[2]

Universal kept faith, blindly, that Miller would deliver something they could promote. The whole production was outsourced once again to Sydney, on sound stages at what was then called Fox Studios Australia;[3] Hoggett's farm had to be built anew, because no one had expected *Babe* to be such a hit. 'We won't tear it down so quickly this time,'[4] remarked the production designer Roger Ford, rather tragically. (There has never been a *Babe 3*.)

Forget the 1,200 extras, 600 crew members and 50 animal trainers. Getting 799 animals to work together, in close quarters, for ten months was always going to be the hard part. These included 80 pigeons, 100 pigs, 130 cats and 120 dogs, more than half of which came from dog shelters around Sydney, and were subsequently rehoused by members of the crew. (Miller took home a chihuahua.) The half-dozen mice who serve as a Greek chorus, trilling out Edith Piaf's 'Are You Lonesome Tonight?', kept breeding like crazy – there were more than a hundred within weeks, until their friskier tendencies were somehow curbed. No one had any idea whether chimps could get along with pigs, until they gave it a whirl.

Mutterings later from the high-ups at Universal, that Miller had swanned off with a small fortune and taken them for a ride, make them come across as somewhat myopic – or just poor readers. Merely to describe the plot undoes their case. According to Miller, the shooting script had everything in it that would later cause conniptions. There's the near-drowning of a bull terrier (voiced like a Brooklyn hoodlum by Stanley Ralph Ross), the flapping distress of a goldfish flung from its smashed bowl, and the pushing-up-daisies experience of a disabled Jack Russell named Flealick (Adam Goldberg), a chatty fellow with his own little wheelchair, who has a dangerous obsession with clinging onto mudguards by his teeth.

These and many other non-farmyard animals are met by Babe (voiced this time by squeaky-croaky E. G. Daily) when he finds himself stranded in the big city at a woebegone boarding house beside a neon-lit canal. With Arthur Hoggett bedbound, his wife Esme (Magda Szubanski) has hatched a desperate plan to save their farm from foreclosure with 'the wee pig' in tow. But a sniffer dog at the airport raises a ruckus; Esme is humiliatingly strip-searched before being thrown in jail; in all these ways, their money-raising scheme comes unstuck. In the scary urban jungle, Babe gets bed and board only thanks to the charity of pencil-like, jittery landlady Miss Floom (the Modigliani-esque Mary Stein, who's delightful – her every utterance a question squeezed out between adenoids).

In this one-size-fits-all metropolis, we espy the Sydney Opera House, Big Ben, Christ the Redeemer and the Eiffel Tower all poking out of the same cramped skyline. 'This is all cities,' as Roger Ebert put it in his rave review. (Ford's maximalist set design has hints of *Brazil*, *Blade Runner*, and Jeunet–Caro's *The City of Lost Children* (1995), mashed together into a composite J. G. Ballard might have cherished.) While the curtains of snooty opera fans twitch from facing houses, Miss Floom has been a Samaritan on the down-low, taking in the city's starving strays out of the kindness of her heart.

To be fair to Universal's execs, there's a great deal in Miller's vision that the script alone could never have betrayed, including a level of characterisation that's disturbingly brilliant – funny and poignant at the same time, owing not just to the animal casting (and nonpareil wrangling), but the voice casting, too.

There's a homeless pink poodle (Russi Taylor, wondrous) whose every line is a Blanche DuBois sob story: 'Please, sir. Please. I know you're different from the others. Those that had their way with me make their empty promises, but they're all lies – *lies*!' The family of chimps indoors, with their string vests, hair ties and bubblegum, are typed in their turn as salt-of-the-earth slum lodgers. That's the late Glenne Headly as warm-hearted Zootie ('You gotta praablem, sweetie?') and stand-up comic Steven Wright as her lugubrious bloke Bob, a shady customer given to philosophical musings on life ('It's all illusory: it's ill and it's for losers . . .').

As for Miss Floom's Uncle Fugly, played with zero dialogue and unkempt clothes you can practically smell by a then-76-year-old Mickey Rooney, he's fugly, all right. If you found him hanging around the festering apartment complex in David Lynch's Tinseltown death-dream *Mulholland Drive* (2001), he'd be right at home. In the non-Lynch context of a family blockbuster sequel, he's all the more hellish as a joyless clown, genuinely grotesque in his full get-up for 'the Fabulous Flooms', with a giant egg-like dome and pink candy-floss hair poking out.

We don't get a lot of Rooney at all – his scenes became especially vulnerable at the cutting stage, when executives finally clapped eyes on what Miller had put in the can. Still, what's left of him is distressing enough. His butler, the still centre of this vortex, is a very special Bornean orangutan named Thelonius* (laconically voiced by a Scotsman, James Cosmo), who gravely looks down on the madness from a stained-glass clerestory,† passing silent judgement. The camera is mesmerised by his doleful, unblinking face.

---

* [*sic*].

† In a rhapsodic capsule review for the *Chicago Reader*, Pat Graham compares him to the Phantom of the Opera and the Hunchback of Notre-Dame, both of which feel apt.

You can't stop trying to intuit what he's feeling – say, when Babe trips Fugly up by mistake, causing havoc during the Flooms' circus act in a children's cancer ward. This is not what you'd call slapstick havoc. A fire breaks out, the traumatised chimps run for cover, the sprinkler system kicks in, and Uncle Fugly's life's work collapses in tatters. He and Thelonius stare back, shellshocked, at the aftermath, in a slow-mo reaction shot that has a godforsaken poetry.

It's amazing, gratifying, and kind of hilarious that as much of this survived as it did. Clearly, Miller provided so little cuddly stuff for the studio to fold in, they simply had to put up with much of what they were given – that is, once they'd finally persuaded him to show it to them and their families. A focus-group screening in Anaheim Hills, on 8 November 1998, went horribly with children – as you can well imagine – and the Motion Picture Association of America (MPAA) also came back with a PG certificate, which seems positively mild when you hear about what Miller's original cut had in it.

Viewers of this even-darker version would have been treated, for instance, to a full scene of Esme being strip-searched – reduced, in the end, to the sound of a latex glove being snapped on by her tormentor. Ferdinand the duck barely escaped a chef's cleaver turning him into Chinese takeaway. Rooney had a deathbed scene and numerous others too disturbing to see the light of day.

It could have been much worse. In early drafts of the script, Farmer Hoggett was actually supposed to *die* at the bottom of that well. One of the nosy neighbours was originally *murdered* by Esme and Miss Floom as comeuppance for being a snitch – a beyond-dark punchline they actually shot, but sensibly jettisoned early on.

Plenty more had to go, though. Babe nearly got pushed into the fire during the hospital inferno, until that scene was rejigged; he was also sadistically tricked by the chimps into clambering up a pyramid of junk and tumbling into the canal – yet another scene featuring

Rooney that was binned outright. When the animals are impounded, there were rabbits smoking cigarettes, hair products being tested on cats, and all sorts. 'That's a vivisection laboratory,' as Cromwell recalls. 'There [were] animals with posts drilled into their skulls and sores, cancers, it was – oh my God.'[5]

It shouldn't be funny. Imagine the faces of Casey Silver, then chairman of Universal Pictures, and his boss Frank Biondi Jr, when they beheld Babe's entire life flashing before his eyes in near-subliminal flickers, as the narrator asks us to ponder his relentless pursuit by scrapyard dogs and, by extension, the senseless cruelty of the universe. 'Something broke through the terror – flickerings, fragments of his short life, the random events that delivered him to this, his moment of annihilation.'

That bull terrier, dangling off a bridge by his studded collar, jerking out his last breaths. The goldfish, flapping and helpless. These are moments that actually made the final cut – the drowning of the dog, per Cromwell, was shot using an animatronic puppet and massively cut down, but as he rightly says, 'It's still pretty harrowing.' Just before Flealick goes to heaven, one wheel on his overturned chair squeaks out a final few rotations, before grinding to a pitiful halt.

That might be Miller's most profound image – his answer to life's brief candle sputtering out. But it's soul-scarring. Did *no one* spot that his film's whole middle act was an immigration parable, Dickensian in its pathos, crossed with *Animal Farm*? The excluded, the outcast, all find shelter in a sanctuary that's a long way from utopian – the only food's jelly beans. Cats and dogs are on the verge of hostilities. And then it's round-up time. The Gestapo-like raid on the boarding house (after a tip-off from the neighbours) also had to be trimmed down into less harrowing form, so the film could at least *look* like wholesome family fare.

The MPAA did finally come back with a G rating* – heaven knows how. But the alley cat was out of the bag. The schedule for recuts was worsened by a sound glitch: the entire film was 'an assault on the ears',† according to Miller, because of an overly loud mix that had somehow passed muster in Australia. To fix the problem, Universal's dubbers supposedly had to work 20-hour days against the clock. They had no choice but to cancel a benefit premiere, scheduled for 15 November, while the work was done – and after this announcement reports started to leak out far and wide that the film was a problem child undergoing a severe remedial programme. (This was, surely, partly true.)

Days before this, Universal's parent company Seagram fired Biondi, the overall head of its entertainment division. *Babe*'s unfinished state and a string of other underperforming films were factors, but the most obvious trigger for his departure was the brand-new failure of *Meet Joe Black*‡ – the three-hour long, $90m romantic drama starring Brad Pitt as Death, which had just opened to baffled reviews and a dud, third-place opening weekend. Pressure only intensified on *Babe*, and on Silver, who was hanging on to his own position by a thread.

By the end of the month, he was gone too. *Pig in the City*'s Thanksgiving release slot might have looked like prime real estate a year before, but November had since filled up with the most brutal competition possible (except *Meet Joe Black*, of course). Delaying the release wouldn't work, because the trailers, ad spots and cross-promotional tie-ins were all cued up.

---

* The equivalent of a U in the UK.
† 'Work on *Babe* Stretches Well into the 11th Hour', *Los Angeles Times*, 20 November 1998. The official line on what caused all the delays has the telltale ring of damage limitation.
‡ See also p. 211.

Pixar's *A Bug's Life* went on wide release right at the same time, and was instantly massive, grossing nearly triple in a week what *Babe* would achieve over its entire stateside run. Coming in second was Paramount's *The Rugrats Movie*, out a week already, and gobbling up even more of *Babe*'s core audience. *Babe* crawled in fifth – a miserable result Silver couldn't escape from, and very much the kind of high-profile flop that makes studio regime change a foregone conclusion.

———

I still love the film. (So does Tom Waits.) If we're picking holes, I've never been wild about Miller's climax at a hospital ballroom gala, with Esme strapped into the late Fugly's clown suit and swinging about on a chandelier – it's a descent into boisterous Roald Dahl slapstick that doesn't give Babe himself nearly enough to do. It's hard to know how a film as perverse as this could have ended satisfyingly in a way that keeps faith with its themes, but this is too much of an abdication towards generic hoopla.

'That'll do, Pig' from Farmer Hoggett was the first film's motto, but when it's trotted out at the end here, with Babe safely back at the farm, it plainly doesn't work. Our pig's various acts of kindness, such as saving the bull terrier and goldfish from near-certain death, have gone without human notice at any stage. If *Babe*'s a round hole, with its human-porcine teamwork, *Pig in the City* is far too square a peg to get away with the pretence that it's about the same things. It's about other things instead – mainly, the heroism of lending a hand when there's no one watching.

None of these considerations caused it to flop, though. Beyond the poorly planned release and too-late flurries of studio panic – over legitimate issues that ought to have been addressed far sooner – it conveys so little desire to mollify its intended audience that they blatantly smelled a rat. Particularly in the US, newspaper reports raising eyebrows at lofty ambitions ('Fellini-esque', 'much darker in tone') rarely fail to put off wary consumers, who paid more attention to the bad press hounding the film than the decent clutch of impassioned reviews.* It fared better abroad† – but not nearly well enough to erase the taint of a serious failure.

Miller has barely talked about it ever since. Further setbacks stalled him – the planned shoot of a fourth *Mad Max* in 2003 was aborted by Warner Bros, because the US dollar had collapsed after the Iraq War, and security concerns made shooting in Namibia too dicey. In the meantime, Mel Gibson went down his own fury road and was written out of the franchise. Miller pivoted to *Happy Feet* (2006) – the one about dancing animated penguins – thereby regaining faith that he could be trusted again with family entertainment. But that film's 2011 sequel repeated *Babe's* pattern by, yet again, flopping; he would be stung again by the underperformance of *Furiosa* in 2024.

Sequels are expensive: everyone involved demands more money, and you need an airtight vision to stop audiences feeling jaded. Miller had an astonishingly clear one for *Mad Max: Fury Road* (2015) by the time that got off the ground, but the production was still chaos, and could easily have resulted in a ruinous turkey with cult appeal only. His next one, *Three Thousand Years of Longing* (2022),‡ landed in that terrain – an archetypal passion project cum folly that essentially set fire to $60m on an auteur's whim and took a bow. Even *Fury Road* wound up costing so much it barely broke even, but it staked

---

* Roger Ebert's partner in thumbs-up, Gene Siskel, even called it the best movie of 1998.

† Overall worldwide gross was $69.1m.

‡ Miller's disappointing *Arabian Nights*-esque fantasy romance, with Tilda Swinton and Idris Elba. Budget: $60m. Worldwide gross: $20.3m.

its rightful claim as the action blockbuster of the decade, and the fan worship more than compensated.

Miller keeps charging on, in pretty fearless pursuit of doing things his own way. He reminds me less of Babe than the intimidating bull terrier, who openly admits, 'A murderous shadow lies hard across my soul.' Feel free to commiserate with the execs dishing out such foolhardy blank cheques, but when the films soar – and scald – like this one, there's almost no budget I'd wish to deny him.

SUPERNOVA (2000)

Director: 'Thomas Lee'
Studio: MGM/UA
Budget: $70m
Worldwide gross: $14.8m

James Spader as Nick Vanzant:
'How do we put out a fire that can burn up the stars?'

Sweetie, the ship's computer: 'Data . . . unavailable.'

*Supernova** is a textbook shambles – peak shambles so far – with a half-digested mess of a plot that could roughly be summarised thus: everyone gets naked in deep space, some mutate, then most of them die. First, the crew on board *Nightingale 229*, a twenty-second-century medical ship, take time out from various dimension-jumping hiccups to shed clothes and get laid – and here's where it gets very bizarre indeed.

Basically, the sex scene that was shot did double duty in the finished film. We have to unpick this particular knot, because it is an all-time instance of editorial WTF, decided long after various directors had already quit.

At some stage during principal photography in the summer of 1998, a sequence of what was meant to look like zero-gravity shagging was filmed between *The Craft* star Robin Tunney and *Nurse Jackie's*

---

* This is not, in any way, *Supernova* (2020), the lovely two-hander written and directed by Harry Macqueen, with Colin Firth and Stanley Tucci as a long-married couple facing up to the latter's dementia.

Peter Facinelli. This was meant for the middle act of the film, before Facinelli's villain, who is a super-hench, sexually voracious psycho not unlike Billy Zane in *Dead Calm* (1989),* sets about taking charge of the ship and killing everybody.

Sitting down to watch *Supernova*, which I can't say I wholly recommend, you'll be treated to this copulation twice – but, in the first instance, it's not those two actors we're led to believe are getting busy. Look, instead, for a fly-by shot of a couple floating around nude in the ship's bowels, with the heads of top-line stars James Spader and Angela Bassett spliced in.

Now, eagle-eyed observers of Robin Tunney and Angela Bassett may be starting to grasp what added headache this decision caused – one they tried solving with a VFX fix that can only be described as insane. Tunney is white, Bassett is Black. So, somewhere around the September mark in 1999, at the fifth director's post-production facility in San Francisco, one or more computer artists were tasked with 'digitally darkening' Tunney's skin tone for the shot in question, so that her body could get away with looking like Bassett's.

That may take a moment to sink in. Imagine *doing* it. The concatenation of crises leading Francis Ford Coppola (for it was he) to give that steer to his technicians at American Zoetrope is involved, to say the least: 'pure chaos' may be the only legitimate explanation. Not only is the credited director, Thomas Lee, *not* one of the five (!!?!) hired at various phases of production to take the tiller, but he doesn't even exist. Lee is a pseudonym – the one recommended by the DGA (Directors Guild of America) when Walter Hill, director No. 3 and the man who put in the longest shift, did not wish to have his real name attached to the finished result.

---

* Phillip Noyce's crackerjack boat-based suspense thriller, with Nicole Kidman and Sam Neill fighting for their lives.

Why was that pseudonym not 'Alan Smithee', the name coined in 1968 and credited on some 40 films when directors walked out? The reason is that Smithee was discontinued in 2000 as the preferred moniker, after becoming quite recently notorious. While no one paid to see it, plenty of atrocious reviews were filed for Arthur Hiller's in-jokey satire *An Alan Smithee Film: Burn Hollywood Burn* (1997), about a first-time director (Eric Idle) who has the misfortune actually to be named Alan Smithee, and runs off with the negatives of his own film. Hiller even refused credit for the multiple-Razzie-winning final cut of *An Alan Smithee Film*, meaning that it wound up as, literally, an Alan Smithee film.

Let's rewind to *Supernova* director No. 1 – though his involvement was aborted long before. This was William Malone,* a UCLA graduate later responsible for the humdrum remake of William Castle's *House on Haunted Hill* (1999) and the unanimously reviled *FeardotCom* (2002).† At some point in the 1980s, he was shopping around a script called *Dead Star*, the latest in a run of *Alien* knock-offs he aimed to direct, with H. R. Giger handling the creature design. The idea was roughly *Hellraiser* in space.

It came to naught, and Malone moved on. Meanwhile, his script got redrafted as *Supernova* by one Daniel Chuba, an LA-based special effects producer, who put together a short promo reel and successfully sold it to MGM/UA in 1995. The idea was still supremely familiar – a space ambulance in the twenty-second century picks up a distress signal and finds something in the cold reaches of the void (initially, a portal to hell) that wipes them out, one by one. It would flaunt all the other staples of the genre, and,

---

* It was Malone, as a young make-up designer, who sculpted a cast of William Shatner's face into the mask Michael Myers would wear for *Halloween* (1978).

† See also p. 246.

to the very day of its release, barely managed to drum up a USP anyone could identify.

'A halfway house disguised as a studio.'[1] So latter-day MGM has been described, with the disguise only getting tattier in the decades since. The glory days of the roaring lion – the home of *Gone with the Wind* (1939), *Singin' in the Rain* (1952), *North by Northwest* (1959), *2001: A Space Odyssey* (1968) – were far behind it in the late 1990s, when it was clinging on as a production entity mainly thanks to the Brosnan-era James Bond films.* A by-and-large dismal slew of co-funded releases marked time between those. It was typical of MGM to land a surprise hit with *Species* (1995), then follow it up with the kinky-trashy absurdity of the godawful *Species II* (1998),† a film that feels in its earthbound fashion like *Supernova*'s unstable older brother.

Now for director No. 2. He would never make it to the start of photography, but was put in charge while sets were getting built, and had a major say in casting – enter Spader as the hard-bitten pilot, Bassett as chief medical officer. This person was Geoffrey Wright, an Australian wild card whose main achievement had been launching Russell Crowe's career with the neo-Nazi drama *Romper Stomper* (1992).

Hollywood hadn't quite figured out what to do with Wright since then. Having signed on with MGM, he'd been sitting around for three years waiting for something to happen. Why not try him out on *Supernova*? We can only detect glimmers of the vision he hoped to impart, since 'creative differences' with MGM's chairman Frank Mancuso led him to step away five weeks before the shoot.

---

* And only just: the hiatus between *Licence to Kill* (1989) and *GoldenEye* (1995), which might have been terminal, came about because the company kept being bankrupted, then repeatedly bought out by different European funding bodies mainly interested in flogging its back catalogue.

† *Species* drummed up $113.3m worldwide from a $35m budget. *Species II* made $26.8m from . . . the same budget.

The final straw, supposedly, was Wright demanding major chunks of the film be shot aboard NASA's zero-gravity training aircraft – the so-called 'Vomit Comet', which had been used for parts of Ron Howard's *Apollo 13* (1995). With a budget that was already spiralling out of control, this was an added indulgence to which MGM refused to stretch, no matter how much weightless cast nudity they were sacrificing.

If anyone could have performed a successful rescue mission at this point, Walter Hill ought to have been the man to do so. After all, he'd done about eight rewrites with David Giler to beat *Alien* into shape, while in transition from his tough, cult-spawning early work (*The Driver*, *The Warriors*) to mainstream paydays in the 1980s (*48 Hours*, *Red Heat*). Despite passing the reins over to Ridley Scott while he instead developed *Southern Comfort* (1981), he'd doggedly stayed put as a producer on every subsequent film in the *Alien* franchise. He knew his way around steel-grate walkways and smoke machines, in other words, and tended to do well with cynical, wisecracking ensembles in situations of extreme peril.

Moving away from the *Hellraiser* paradigm, as soon as someone muttered the words '*Dead Calm* in space, instead!' it at least helped pin down the *source* of the peril in David C. Wilson's script – Facinelli's frat-boy fugitive Karl, the sole survivor of an ice-mining disaster on the moon Titan 37. He comes on board packing something pink, glowing and predictably phallic – a retrieved artefact made of ninth-dimensional matter, which softly moans whenever it's touched. ('Maybe it's an alien sex object?' ventures Tunney's Danika, with a hilariously straight face.)

Whatever Karl is up to with this cosmic vibrator, tracking that business through the story was the script's chronic weak point. Watching the truly wacky theatrical trailer, there are shots hinting at whole scenes and subplots that were subsequently abandoned, like amputated tentacles lopped off a flailing mutant organism.

That trailer has a claim to be one of the most ridiculous ever cut, shamelessly misselling the film as a good-time interstellar romp for horny teens. It commits the obviously desperate crime of spoiling half the crew's death scenes in abbreviated form – witness Facinelli retaliating to a blow on the head from Tunney by simply booting her out of an airlock. This was the heyday of Trailer Voice Man, made to perform a deranged tonal pivot when Three Dog Night's 'Mama Told Me (Not to Come)' serenades a final flurry of chaos, all at the whim of Karl: 'He's about to turn the heavens . . . into *hell!*'

We also glimpse an unidentifiable actor* in glutinous, melty-face prosthetics, begging for mercy. This character, cut from the release print but preserved in a charmingly stupid deleted scene, is a fellow miner who's been screwed over by Karl, later to be found by Spader's Vanzant on his one-man mission to extract fuel supplies from the moon base. The squeaky voice they tried giving this overgrown foetus makes him come across as a Munchkin on steroids. Had the scene been kept in, it would have brought the house down.

Separately, in a fate that *Supernova*'s, shall we say, select audience did get to witness when it came out, Robert Forster's captain makes an icky exit near the start when a dimension-hop goes horribly wrong. 'We do a space-jump . . . and my chamber was cracked,' he recalled in a slightly fatigued interview for the Blu-ray. 'When we get to the other side I had become decorporealised . . . or something, and I'm stuck to the inside of the shield.' The prosthetics glued to Forster's face for this swansong moment were stifling, uncomfortable, and generally gross, but on the plus side, he was spared the purgatory of being dragged back for reshoots.

The uncredited mastermind of these was director No. 4: Jack Sholder, best known for the accidentally gay horror sequel *A Nightmare*

---

* IMDb says: Knox Grantham White, with the voice of Kerrigan Mahan.

on Elm Street 2: Freddy's Revenge (1985). That film has queer overtones so unusually blatant, Sholder's sincere claim to have been blind to them throughout the shoot has always been quite staggering to horror fiends. MGM hired him when Hill's version of *Supernova* got some of the all-time worst test scores the industry had ever seen. This was partly because they insisted on testing Hill's initial cut before he'd been allowed to do his own reshoots, leading him to breach contract in a fit of pique by simply walking away. The two directors, inevitably, have rather different accounts of how it all went down.

According to Hill:

> There was a desperate political situation with a failing administration, and I foolishly got into helping a movie that I thought could turn into something. But I then discovered I didn't have as free a hand as I had been led to believe . . . So we had a rather angry breach, and the movie was recut by two or three directors . . . The ending's much different, and much of the set-up is different. Mine was a much darker vision. I can honestly tell you that I have yet to have seen it, but it's on cable a lot, and sometimes I'll be surfing about and I'll sit there and watch about four minutes just to see what they've fucked up.[2]

And now Sholder, on the version that was dumped in his lap:

> I have to tell you, it was awful. It was really bad. Basically, you hated everybody in the film; there was not a shred of humour. Every time [Bassett] talked to [Spader] or looked at him, she acted like she hated his guts. It was very hard to figure anything out. We tested [Hill's] version and the audience absolutely despised it. Twenty per cent walked out, and of the 80 per cent that were left, it got a 25/100.
>
> This is when you, like, jump off a bridge. That is the lowest number that anything has ever gotten. If the 20 per cent had stayed,

it would have gotten even lower . . . My opinion, personally, is that [Hill] needed a payday, he did the movie, and he never really cared about it. I know he said he never liked the sets or the costumes.

I threw out the soundtrack, I completely recut the movie, I threw out the drug sub-plot, and I changed a bunch of things around. Streamlined it, changed the voice of the computer, cut out most of the lines, and ended up getting about a 70 with nobody walking out. Frank Mancuso said, 'Jack, you saved the studio, we're erecting your statue in front of the studio. What do you want to do next?' And then, about two weeks later, he was out. Then the head of United Artists was out, then they disbanded UA, a whole bunch of new people came in, and they said, 'Gee, why is this movie only getting a 70?' And then I found out that Francis Coppola was taking over the movie.[3]

The fifth and final surgeon to attempt multiple transplants on this cadaver, Coppola was creatively and financially at a low ebb around this time. Huge debts accruing from his Napa Valley vineyard had only partly been offset by his only major success in 20 years, *Bram Stoker's Dracula* (1992), and he'd had to file for bankruptcy multiple times.

He spent large chunks of the 1990s embroiled in various extortionate legal battles, including two suits against Warner Brothers for projects he'd tried to develop – one of these being the idea that would turn into Robert Zemeckis's *Contact* (1997), the other an unmade version of *Pinocchio*. Coppola was awarded a princely $80m for the loss of that project, until WB appealed and the decision was countermanded.

With all this going on, the $1m his company, American Zoetrope, would reap for an emergency re-edit of *Supernova* was chump change, but he did it anyway. And so it is that the film reached its bastardised final form, shorn of much of the gloopy weirdness – the gateway-to-hell stuff – that Hill had wanted to contribute with the make-up designer Patrick Tatopoulos.

No doubt, MGM's bean-counters would have been anxious about the fate of another expensive cosmic horror flick while this was in pre-production. Paramount's *Event Horizon*, a big flop in the summer of 1997,* had already tried dimension-hopping to some pain-filled circle of hell, where Sam Neill's designer of the Lovecraftian title vessel becomes possessed, before he gouges out his own eyes and starts looking like one of Clive Barker's minor Cenobites.

Paul W. S. Anderson delivered a legendarily gruesome 130-minute director's cut, including an orgy scene that used real-life amputees. Paramount baulked, hacked the whole thing down to 90 minutes, and it died. The lost footage, packed away in a Transylvanian salt mine, corroded so badly it can never be restored, much to the chagrin of the film's significant fan following.

'Make this as little like *Event Horizon* as possible' appears to have been the instruction to Sholder, then Coppola, and then whoever cut that berserk trailer together. Out, among many other things, went a gory autopsy – *Event Horizon* had done that, too – the crushing of Lou Diamond Phillips's eyes into his skull by Facinelli, and Hill's bleak ending with multiple star systems being obliterated by the doomsday device (or whatever it is) that Karl has smuggled on board.

Leaning into the fact that every cast member except Forster gets naked, the decision was made to go down the sex-party-in-space route (no terrifying orgies though, please!), and just retrofit the rest of the story limply together. No wonder it produced a baffling tonal mishmash, but it also left little for the likes of Tunney to do except expose her breasts for dimension jumps, gawp at the gym-bunny

---

* It grossed $42m worldwide off a budget of $60m.

physique of Facinelli as if they've just collided on Venice Beach, and then roll around naked, unbeknownst to her, as *both* of the main female characters. (The fact that the MPAA didn't bestow the hoped-for PG-13 certificate, despite most of the violence being cut, surely had something to do with the laughable gratuitousness of absolutely all of this.)

The crew member who gets the shortest straw of the lot is a technician called Benjamin, sweetly played by the gay Puerto Rican actor Wilson Cruz. Amid all the other canoodling, his love interest is essentially the on-board computer, voiced by someone called Vanessa Marshall, which wakes him up to play flirtatious chess games – and that's it?!

It's a pity no one grasped *Supernova*'s untapped potential to be not only *Hellraiser* in space, or *Dead Calm* in space, which are perfectly decent foundational ideas – but maybe something along the lines of Pasolini's *Theorem* (1968) in space. Karl could have been Terence Stamp, seducing his way omnivorously right down the running order, sowing pansexual chaos. If it was always going to be bewildering trash, at least it could have stepped out of the closet and gone for broke.

ROLLERBALL (2002)

Director: John McTiernan
Studio: MGM
Budget: $85m
Worldwide gross: $25.9m

Whatever happened to John McTiernan? Not just an indefinite stretch in directors' prison, but, in point of fact, federal prison, where he served ten months beginning in April 2013. We'll get to that in due course, since it was only thanks to his amazingly botched remake of *Rollerball*, a decade earlier, that it came about. The quality of the film itself was in no way relevant to the conviction, or he might have been sent down for life.

Despite this abrupt curtailing of a major career, we should never forget the glory days. The Juilliard-educated film-maker who once helmed *Predator* and *Die Hard* was a certified action maestro in the VHS era – not infallible, but vigorous as hell, and one of mainstream cinema's bright sparks.

The muscular craft of those two films alone could be studied over and over. Thermal imaging not only as visual gimmick but genuine suspense-heightener. The dizzy-making rooftop swings of *Die Hard* (shot by future *Speed 2* culprit Jan de Bont). A knack for getting urgent, propulsive work out of his composers (Alan Silvestri, Michael Kamen).

McTiernan's most underrated gift, though, was his wrangling of movie stars, egos and all. He knew exactly how to make Bruce

Willis's cockiness heroic rather than merely annoying;* and no other film (give or take James Cameron's first *Terminator*) ever made better sense of Schwarzenegger.

Following those up with one Sean Connery banger (*The Hunt for Red October*) in 1990 and one clanger (*Medicine Man*) in 1992, McTiernan stumbled into his first truly dicey setback with *Last Action Hero* (1993), an overpromoted, over-facetious Humvee of an $85m Arnie vehicle that suffered a grisly fate in the maw of a T-Rex. It was pushed into cinemas, barely ready, in June 1993, after a rough cut had already played so poorly that Sony destroyed the test cards.[1] Then Universal, sniffing blood in the water, moved up the release of *Jurassic Park* to a week before it.[†] Unused to such crushing failure, Schwarzenegger would describe it as the beginning of the end of his film career.[‡]

Generally a straight shooter in his interviews, McTiernan was quizzed about that one in 2001, and paused to weigh his words for a long time. 'It was so overwhelmed with baggage. And then it was whipped out unedited, practically assembled right out of the camera . . . It was kamikaze, stupid, no good reason for it. And then to open the week after *Jurassic Park* – God! To get to the depth of bad judgement involved in that you'd need a snorkel.'[2]

---

* McTiernan added a great insight about Willis playing John McClane in a 2020 interview with Nick de Semlyen, for his book *The Last Action Heroes* (p. 153): 'The secret is that [McClane] doesn't like himself. He thinks he's a loser. His wife thinks he's a loser. And he's just doing the best he can. He's being a smartarse to rise above the pain. And Bruce being a smartarse in that circumstance becomes an act of heroism.'

† Even in its second week of release, *Jurassic Park* grossed two and a half times the measly $15.3m opening weekend that *Last Action Hero* would score.

‡ 'To be rejected so soundly – it sort of broke his heart.' McTiernan interviewed by de Semlyen, p. 274.

The director might turn his hand to an eye-opening memoir about the industry, one day. He showed a knack for pulling himself out of scrapes, but also the courage of his political convictions. Having convinced his producer, Joel Silver, to make Alan Rickman's gang in *Die Hard* robbers, rather than terrorists – 'I don't like the idea of movies about terrorism,'[3] he explained in 2022 – he was equally queasy about *Patriot Games* (1992), with its IRA baddies, as the next Jack Ryan picture after *Red October.**

McTiernan hadn't fancied *Die Hard 2*, either – 'It just felt like it was repeating the same thing.'[4] But he pounced on a third one, based on a script called *Simon Says* that was retooled to centre on John McClane. That was how *Die Hard with a Vengeance* (1995) saved McTiernan's bacon, presenting a specific logistical challenge he quite relished: 'OK, I need to make New York City seem like you're in one building.'

Even before his massively troubled Viking epic *The 13th Warrior* (1999), a blood-drenched adaptation of Michael Crichton's *Eaters of the Dead*, was going through its final re-edit without him, he found a crafty way to pull clear. Crichton, who also produced, had taken over reshoots, tacking an extra battle sequence on at the end that makes no real sense, while the budget went through the roof.† That film cooks up a fervent, Hadean atmosphere and looks pretty amazing, but it was chopped to ribbons, eventually coming out a year after McTiernan delivered his cut.

While everyone else waded through that mire, he got busy post-haste on his remake of Norman Jewison's *The Thomas Crown Affair*

---

* The fact that both he and Alec Baldwin had Irish ancestry also deterred them from getting involved, and Harrison Ford took over the role instead.
† With production and marketing costs, it might even have gone as high as $160m.

(1968), which used a between-Bonds Pierce Brosnan to outfox Rene Russo, in a career peak performance for her that McTiernan managed very dexterously. That suave art-heist caper succeeded in beating *The 13th Warrior* into cinemas by three weeks in August 1999, and stuck around well into the autumn with stellar word of mouth – the kind of sexily romantic, grown-up entertainment we hardly see any more. McTiernan timed it perfectly: there's no better way to get ahead of a flop than by sitting pretty in the box office charts before it even lands.

Hero of the hour for that MGM remake, he immediately plucked another from their back catalogue – weirdly enough, another update of a vintage Norman Jewison picture, *Rollerball* (1975). It would not pan out nearly so well.

———

'A jumble of footage in search of plot, meaning, rhythm and sense,' Roger Ebert wrote in his bang-on review of McTiernan's *Rollerball*, to which he bestowed his second-worst possible rating: half a star.* He's not kidding.

Rollerball is more incomprehensible than it is objectionable, but deciding on what level it fails most completely is a high-stakes game. Ebert quite reasonably wonders whether the negatives were put through an MRI scan before the editor (or many, many editors) got hold of them. Barely one sequence knows what it's doing with

---

* What kept it from a flat zero is seemingly hard to discern, though Ebert tended to reserve those for films that caused him outright moral offence, such as *Wolf Creek* (2005) (where I happen to agree), Ken Russell's *The Devils* (1971) (where I firmly do not) and Alan Parker's dreadful *The Life of David Gale* (2003), which thinks the best rebuttal to the death penalty is to have Kevin Spacey deviously submit to it, while hiding the worst, smirkiest twist in film history up his sleeve.

space, emphasis or tempo, and there are cuts, line readings and entire stretches of action that leave you gawping in disbelief at their ineptitude.

Stepping into the skates vacated by James Caan in Jewison's dystopian satire, Chris Klein plays Jonathan, an NHL hopeful in 2005 or so, who starts the film sledding on his back down the steep hills of San Francisco, while seemingly (?!?) in flight from traffic police. Being a thrill junkie, he's an easy mark when his best pal Marcus (LL Cool J) dangles the lure to come to Kazakhstan and make his name in the titular sport – a brutal extension of roller derby involving (in this iteration) a seemingly random bevy of motorbikes, skaters and a metal ball that has to be thwacked, Quidditch-style, into an elevated iron bowl.

Rollerball's litany of problems begins, straight up, with the casting – a down-the-line list of poor choices that could have been made only in the year 2000, topped by a head-slappingly dumb use of its leading man. Klein, twenty-one at the time, was practically brand new (he'd just done *Election* and *American Pie*), and his wholesome affability is so foreign to the entire assignment, you wonder how the usually shrewd McTiernan landed him with such a unplayable gig.

He's so sweet, and so wrong. The second he starts high-fiving with LL Cool J, they act like two guys playing nice who've just met, struggling horribly through the kind of cringeworthy banter in which this screenplay majors. (Kazakhstan: 'A place in which even a doofus-ass white boy like you can get laid!')

In place of Caan's rugged brand of couldn't-give-a-toss machismo, this version treats us to endless shots of Klein trying to scowl (actors often talk about how tricky it is to smile on camera; he has the inverse problem). When they give him a five o'clock shadow, it looks like something he's been sculpting for weeks. The overall effect is like watching an angelic choirboy determined to prove himself as a really badass Herod in the school Nativity play.

We need barely concern ourselves with how good a time anyone had shooting this, but there was no single version anyone considered redeemable. No one, except McTiernan and his producers, knew how badly it was going until around April 2001, when they test-screened it in Las Vegas, still hoping for a May release that year.

The cards came back with scathing reviews. MGM pushed it back to July for emergency re-edits, then August. Meanwhile, McTiernan decided to invite Harry Knowles, the much-courted supremo of the entertainment website *Ain't It Cool News*, to come and view a work-print of the film at another preview in Long Island on 4 June, heavily manned by MGM's top brass. The hope was to win back round segments of the fanboy community by wooing Knowles, who got to fly there on a private jet from Austin, and spent four hours powwowing on the plane with McTiernan, one of his film-making idols.

This was deep into Knowles's absurd dominion* as an influential force in Hollywood, a man whose take on a leaked script had the power to scupper whole marketing campaigns. He'd already come out against *Rollerball*, speculating that it might be one of the worst films of 2001, because McTiernan had junked an early draft of the script, which Knowles had raved about, in favour of one he hated. Still, he was prepared to admit he was wrong, and perhaps they thought they could butter him up enough to say so.

The report he would file[5] on this super-sneak preview bends over backwards to describe McTiernan as a mensch, a gracious anecdotalist, and so on. Naturally, you have to wade through the usual bloviating Knowles prose ('Dear god this blew . . .'), and credibility is at a premium: when singling out one supporting turn in the film

---

* Very much behind him by 2017, when he was thrown out of the Austin Film Critics' Association after multiple allegations of sexual assault. (He denied sexual assault, but later posted an apology to 'the women I hurt'.)

as redemptively charming, he doesn't bother establishing the actor's name (Naveen Andrews), instead describing him as 'Jean Reno's Number 2 man . . . He looked like he was from India.' Still, once you reach his point-by-point slamming of everything this initial cut did badly, it's pretty clear that *Rollerball* was beyond rescue.

Just about the only aspects Knowles liked, except the Indian chap, were the hard-R violence, with blood and teeth being knocked out of faces, and the full-frontal nudity, including a much perved-about locker-room sex scene featuring *X-Men*'s Rebecca Romijn-Stamos up against Klein. 'This isn't a pansy film, this is mean and cruel and hard,' the no-longer-popular blogger added.

It wouldn't stay that way. General enthusiasm for the film was nowhere near encouraging enough for MGM to keep faith with McTiernan's R. So the bad but violent/sexy film was about to become, if anything, an even worse one with the violence and sex gone. In June 2001, the studio appointed a new head of marketing, Bob Levin, who came in on a lucky break, weeks before the smash hit *Legally Blonde* was opening. Levin, who had previously done well at Disney and Sony, had an otherwise unenviable slate of forthcoming films to oversee, including John Woo's Second World War epic *Windtalkers*, Barry Levinson's crime comedy *Bandits*, the dreary PoW drama *Hart's War*, and the laughably dire Angelina Jolie–Antonio Banderas bodice-ripper *Original Sin*.

Every one of those flopped, but none would flop as badly as *Rollerball*, which limped third into the US charts and tumbled to 13th by week two. It had been pushed all the way back to a graveyard slot in February 2002, to give McTiernan time to reshape it as a PG-13, shoot a brand new ending, and lop out half an hour. These changes inflicted further deaths by a thousand cuts, even after it was dead on arrival. To say that the finished film bears the scars of all this post-mortem surgery is an understatement. It's nothing *but* scars.

With moments of impact strewn all over the cutting-room floor, players of the sport suffer major injuries on the track out of nowhere. You watch the film sabotage itself in real time, slicing away all hope of even basic commentary about extreme sports or corporate control. When Reno's character, the game's Machiavellian promoter, gives his underlings the nod to make something shady happen, we hop right over the very bloodlust that is supposed to be getting everyone so jazzed up. Then the 'Global Instant Rating' on a digital readout spikes excitedly, and we're like, 'Huh?'

The movie overuses an obnoxious commentator (played by a fixture in the world of wrestling, Paul Heyman), whose sporadic efforts to explain the rules do absolutely nothing to help us understand who's winning or why. 'There's unbelievable tension in this arena!' he trumpets before the concluding bout, when the opposite is true, with a lot of minor characters not knowing where to look. Asinine plot holes abound: the chin strap on Klein's helmet flaps about freely, which would be fine, if the script hadn't laboured the point earlier of another character having their strap deliberately and fatally cut.

Klein drawls a reply in slow motion because they obviously didn't have enough coverage; plenty of other desperate jump cuts litter the movie, with punishing thrash metal overlaid to obliterate our attention. The film's so broken it beggars belief, but no one shard bespeaks its ruin better than an infamous eight-minute stretch at the one-hour mark, when Klein and LL Cool J try to flee by truck, then motorbike, to the Russian border.

For reasons only the post-production team would be in a position to explain, this whole part is presented in green night-vision – murky, bewildering, insanely unmotivated. Was this a reshoot they never got to process properly? A budget-conscious gamble on a key sequence they just lit terribly? We may never know, until those McTiernan memoirs.

However it landed on this form, the chase climaxes with LL Cool J's murder by a sniper, and then a wretched reaction shot to his death, courtesy of Klein, whose character has zero sight line on his friend's demise, and certainly doesn't look to be acting out any pertinent emotion so much as pausing in mild dismay. If you could teach *Predator* or *Die Hard* for their mastery of high-octane action geography, you could teach this scene as a corresponding example of how to screw it all up royally.

I doubt there are many people out there who have voluntarily sat through *Rollerball* twice. Returning to it was one of the more depressing tasks for this book, because, step by step, it means watching McTiernan give up on everything we used to rely on him for.

This ear-pummelling trainwreck sent him off the rails for good. He would squeeze in just one more film – the grim-faced, barely decipherable military whodunit *Basic* (2003), with John Travolta and Samuel L. Jackson – before becoming *persona non grata* with a felony conviction. It transpired, you see, that McTiernan was on such different pages from fellow producer Charles Roven about what sort of film *Rollerball* should even be, that he went to the Watergate extremes of wiretapping the man's phone calls.

For two weeks in the summer of 2000, the director hired an undercover investigator named Anthony Pellicano to wiretap Roven. A wealthy financier and the widower of Columbia production chief Dawn Steel,* Roven went on to flourish as the producer of Christopher Nolan's *Dark Knight* trilogy (2005–12), along with several other lucrative DC superhero flicks, and won the Best Picture Oscar for Nolan's *Oppenheimer* (2023).

The FBI had been sniffing around Pellicano, a Jake-Gittes-in-*Chinatown* figure once nicknamed 'the private eye to the stars',

---

* One of the sworn enemies of *Baron Munchausen* (see p. 114).

for 110 counts* of racketeering and conspiracy, among which this mysterious episode counted as only one. McTiernan initially denied his involvement, which is why he was convicted for perjury, sent to a minimum-security prison in Yankton, South Dakota, and served ten months of a twelve-month sentence. Though he continues to argue that his treatment was overzealous,† he has not got a film off the ground since his release in 2014.

In a tape of Pellicano's and McTiernan's phone conversations, the court heard them mutually despairing about the endemic corruption of the film business, and the millions shelled out on major productions for shifty reasons – such as possible arson on *Rollerball*'s set, which meant they had to pay off a fire department in Canada. 'Everybody has their hands out,'[6] McTiernan sighed. Pellicano also bragged about his insider knowledge, specifically about then MGM President Michael Nathanson:‡ 'I saved his fucking career. There was a whole lot of shit with him and prostitutes and cocaine. I saved him. This fucking guy loves me. Now if I ever called him up and said to him, [McTiernan] is my guy, leave him the fuck alone, that would be the end of that.'[7]

The precise details of why McTiernan thought that Roven, in particular, was bad-mouthing him have never been publicised. No one testified to any particular animus between them; even contemporary reporting on the trial is head-scratchingly thin on what the actual beef was. It's been speculated[8] that McTiernan's paranoia had been rife ever since *Last Action Hero*, alert to the malicious early buzz that

---

* Pellicano would be convicted on seventy-eight of those charges, and sentenced to fifteen years' prison in 2008.
† He called himself 'just roadkill' in the case, in a 2023 interview for the *Guardian*.
‡ The following allegations were denied by Nathanson.

can spread like wildfire across Hollywood, stoked by rival studios with a dog (or dinosaur) in the fight.

But how would Roven – his film's own producer – have gained from undermining *Rollerball* in this way? What seems likelier is that McTiernan, with a history of having films ripped from his grasp, already sensed a production going awry, and wanted to know what contingency plans Roven and MGM were discussing if the worst came to the worst.

Hideous buzz certainly put paid to *Rollerball*, not just when Harry Knowles delivered his verdict. But a mess this absolute doesn't come to pass without a whole load of people failing to see eye to eye. Perhaps they couldn't agree which script to use; maybe it was casting, or the decision to blunt the satire entirely. Or else the money was just disappearing faster than anyone could understand. To endure *Rollerball* is to grasp quite viscerally that no one knew, ever, what it was aiming to deliver. To paraphrase McTiernan himself, you could get to the depth of bad judgement involved, but you might find yourself tickling the floor of the Mariana Trench.

THE ADVENTURES OF
PLUTO NASH (2002)

Director: Ron Underwood
Studio: Castle Rock/Warner Bros
Budget: $100m
Worldwide gross: $7.1m

We have to buckle up around now, hold our noses, and continue rifling through the stinkiest binbags dumped outside the studios 20 years ago – an era when flops really did flop hard, spending ludicrous sums to repair unfixable problems.

There are several sagas so well trodden in Internet coverage that I couldn't face recapitulating their woes, such as John Travolta's *Battlefield Earth* (2000),[1] an infamous bid to get Scientology out to the masses through the medium of a panto-shonky space opera. There was also *Town and Country* (2001),[2] an intolerably smug oldsters' sex comedy hopping about between Park Avenue, the Hamptons, and a ski resort in Idaho, which came out three years late, after nearly as many changes of release date as Warren Beatty has had . . . well, you get the idea.

Even more of a cliff dive than either of these was the fate of Eddie Murphy's moon-based action-comedy *The Adventures of Pluto Nash*, a staggering misfire that opened tenth at the US box office on a $100m budget. Murphy's salary alone on this film – $20m, at his earning plateau around the turn of the 2000s – was nearly three times the amount it grossed worldwide. Especially if you're among the minuscule faction of people who've seen it, it's impossible to understand how anyone was capable of *spending* that budget on *The Adventures of Pluto Nash*. Even harder is deducing why.

Some version of a script (by Neil Cuthbert) had been hanging around in development hell since at least 1983, in the hands of producer Martin Bregman (*Serpico*, *Dog Day Afternoon*, *Scarface*). Harrison Ford was briefly interested, but evidently snapped out of it. *Crocodile Dundee*'s director, Peter Faiman, was announced as Bregman's choice to handle it in 1989, but that didn't happen, either.

During the script's circuitous voyage around town, it coalesced into a comedy about a nightclub owner on a lunar colony, who must save his business from the hands of the Mafia. There would be gadgets, robots, possibly aliens and plenty of neon streetlife. Think *Casablanca* meets *Total Recall*, but funny. Hopefully. 'Supply jokes here' might have been the instruction rubber-stamped on every page.

The production company Castle Rock, thriving in the early 1990s thanks to smash hits with *City Slickers* (1991) and *A Few Good Men* (1992), were the ones who first presented it to Murphy as a potential star vehicle. He was undergoing a mid-career transformation at the time: after a string of disappointments, the R-rated Murphy of *Beverly Hills Cop** (1984) was being phased out, successfully, in favour of PG-13 Murphy for family-friendly consumption, with the likes of *The Nutty Professor* (1996) and *Dr Dolittle* (1998) – the only film of that name, by the way, that's ever turned a profit.

Murphy liked *Pluto Nash*'s concept but not the screenplay, an attitude he would retain through four entire years of making the damn thing, with a revolving door of script doctors brought in on a more or less monthly basis. It *never* got funny. The director Castle Rock plucked was Ron (*Tremors*) Underwood, who'd done *City Slickers* for them, and just spent three years on the complex, CGI-laden production of *Mighty Joe Young* (1998), a so-so giant gorilla flick for Warner Bros, which he'd largely found a positive experience. He was up to

* See also p. 105.

speed on working with VFX, and a proven hand at comedy, though had never yet dealt with a star of Murphy's magnitude.

Through all the troubles that followed, the person you have to feel for most is Ron Underwood. He certainly wasn't pocketing $20m for *Pluto Nash*, just sincerely trying to make it work, long after it became grindingly obvious that he was manacled to a sinking ship. He's always spoken rather kindly of Murphy, despite the agonisingly drawn-out (and failed) process of trying to make his star comfortable enough to perform well.

Interviewed about the film in 2020,[3] Underwood had this to say about his leading man's chronic dissatisfaction with the material:

Eddie was always very pleasant and easy to work with in some regards. But he didn't like the scripts we were writing. He kept rejecting the scripts. And we'd bring on a new writer and try again; and we'd bring on a new writer and try again. And it just . . . he wasn't responding. I mean, maybe we should have stopped at that point. I don't know. He said that his best work was: a film written for [say] Sylvester Stallone* or Harrison Ford, and he would bring the comedy. And so our last draft was fairly straight. Probably the straightest. And it's . . . I don't know. I feel like Eddie gave a lot. But he didn't . . . I mean, he wasn't feeling that funny, I don't think.

Underwood could have pulled out of the ordeal at several points, but stuck with it through a sense of fair play. Reading between the lines, it's clear he was at loggerheads with Martin Bregman, who yanked the film away from pre-production in London, arguing that it would be too expensive, and moved it to Montreal – shades of Thomas Schühly† ruinously dislodging *Munchausen* from Pinewood

---

* The star, in fact, for whom *Beverly Hills Cop* was originally written.
† See p. 109.

to Cinecittà. A film this big had never been shot in the Canadian city's facilities, so Castle Rock built an entirely new studio to house *Pluto Nash*'s moon sets – rarely a solution which ends up saving anyone cash.

'I was getting other offers during this time,' Underwood admitted, 'because this seemed to just be going on and on. But I felt an obligation to go through with it just because we'd been spending all this money.'[4]

For a heartbeat in mid-1999, Jennifer Lopez was close to signing on as Murphy's romantic interest, a tag-along aspiring singer named Dina Lake. Red hot after *Out of Sight* (1998), J.Lo would have bagged $5m, easily her biggest payday at that point, but managed to veer clear, opting instead to make Tarsem Singh's *The Cell* (yay!) and Adam Shankman's *The Wedding Planner* (puke emoji). The Dina part, which is thin, demeaning and generally thankless, went to poor, lovely Rosario Dawson instead.

How this situation escalated to the level of a nine-figure catastrophe is an even costlier redux of *Rollerball* – a case of rising panic, jittery delays, ceaseless readjustments, and throwing good money after bad. Bizarrely, even in John McTiernan's trial,* the giant mess of *Pluto Nash*, which he had nothing to do with, gets mentioned in the transcripts. McTiernan offers the titbit that principal photography went $23m over budget when it overran by just two days, a figure that would climb way higher with the following year's reshoots. '[It] translates to just graft,' McTiernan's heard saying about how such overages can possibly be explained – as in, the lining of pockets with dubiously allocated studio funds. 'Nobody budgets wrong that much.'

Pluto Nash was another victim, too, of merciless pre-release scrutiny from *Ain't It Cool News*, this time from a nameless scribe

* See p. 194.

who managed to sneak into a test screening in January 2001, then published a review[5] of this unfinished cut – the kind of scenario that would now have Hollywood's publicists screaming down their phones and threatening savagery. 'In space, no one can hear you laugh,' ran the item's sub-head. Even after that, a whole eighteen months of damage limitation stretched grotesquely ahead, with the actors dragged back to those sets in mid-2001, before the film finally landed on its ultimate, humiliating berth in August 2002, and took just $2.2m in its opening weekend.

———

In most respects, *Pluto Nash* is dead, flat and endlessly inert, a lunar desert of mediocrity. Murphy achieves not one laugh in it – nor does anybody else. It hardly bothers to flaunt a particular style so much as hang around waiting for a reason to exist.

Hillary Clinton appears on a banknote, in a rare attempt at satire. There's a quick glimpse of George Méliès's *A Trip to the Moon* (1902) playing on a digital hoarding as scenic art, to place this tragic flick in its proper cinematic lineage. Occasionally the camera will pan around to get a look at some of the sets, which are uninspired rehashes of familiar cyberpunk razzle-dazzle from *The Fifth Element* (1997), *Total Recall* and *Blade Runner*.

Your mind may stray (heaven knows, it has the time) to the man-hours involved in building these, and how long they sat there while the cast shuffled about, trying out brand new scenes a year or even two after they first hit their marks. *Futurama* was already on the air, managing 1000x the entertainment value with zero carpentry, and no folk waiting in trailers. Now we have *Rick and Morty*. I can't help thinking of all the live-action sitcoms that managed three-year runs in the time they spent making this. Imagine visiting it for a day. Any day.

A few scenes of video-calling can hardly help but stand out for their stunningly feeble graphics, which announce factoids in a surrounding scroll, such as the number of meteorites making up the weather report. These shots look like loading screens from a 16-bit computer game circa 1993, and not one of the good ones. Honestly, if this is the best a lunar colony in 2087 can devise, our species is toast.

It wouldn't be fair to call the film plotless, quite – it arranges a string of scenes that just about lead from one incident to the next. Murphy's Pluto hires Dina to be a waitress in his club, then refuses to sell it to some kind of Mob syndicate and goes on the run with Dina and his security robot Bruno (Randy Quaid). They get chased around the moon by various goons wishing them dead, then eventually make their way back to figure out what's what. It's not that none of this makes sense. It's just that we have literally no idea why we're meant to be watching it.

All I remembered from reviewing *Pluto Nash* the first time around* was the indelible creepiness of Randy Quaid. Going back in was like facing up to long-buried trauma from half a lifetime ago – hooboy, does he make a malign impression. In a silver suit with rivets down the arms, affecting a jerky, I'm-an-android gait, and speaking through permanently clenched teeth, he's instantaneously the stuff of nightmares.†

The idea is that Bruno is a cranky old model – a '63 Deluxe' – before they really got to grips with emulating human speech patterns or movements very well. But for some reason, he's also a sex predator.

---

* 'Randy Quaid's catastrophic performance as a creepy robot bodyguard': from a baffled 90-word capsule review it took me some while to dig up using a newspaper archive search.

† He reminds me a lot of the 'Working Joe' robots that come after you relentlessly in Sega's beyond-scary survival horror game *Alien: Isolation.*

(Quaid, to put it another way, has never been Randier.) Whenever a female droid crosses his path, which they do quite often, he pivots with terrifying lasciviousness in their direction.

He even spanks one – a French-waitress number named Babette (Jacynthe René) who's been programmed to do only one thing: drop her feather duster, lean down to pick it up with a 'whoops!', and expose her frilly knickers. Whoever programmed Babette either had a lot of affection for the *Carry On* series, or perhaps Colleen Camp's Yvette role in *Clue* (1985). To extend those technicians the greatest possible benefit of the doubt, perhaps things are meant to be so boring on this crummy populated moon that people had to find some way of getting their kicks, even if that means forms of self-parodic sex farce with expiry dates more than a century behind them.

Still, whoever programmed Bruno, a security android, to *lust* after these pleasure bots is a straight-up psychopath. You genuinely worry for Rosario Dawson when she's left alone with him – she's not playing a replicant, which seemingly gets her off the hook, but it's impossible to know whose rules we're actually following. Quaid's performance is so insane there's no safe haven, even in the context of a PG-13-rated Eddie Murphy comedy that, presumably, had some intention of entertaining families without making everyone feel physically ill.

Later, Bruno is himself stalked by a mobile, gender-neutral slot machine, whose overtures he must briskly fend off. Maybe *this* is the closest thing to a functioning joke in the film, but then again, it hinges on the deranged premise of tables being turned on non-consensual robo-seduction. Our trusty bodyguard breaks off the culprit's arm-lever to disable it, and that's that.

Murphy was still yo-yoing at the time between mildly frisky romps with family appeal, and bouts of the old aggression (like the R-rated *Showtime*, a grim buddy-cop pairing with Robert De Niro which came out that spring). If *Pluto Nash* holds a unique place in his oeuvre for anything but fiscal reasons, it's because it's the only film with absolutely no idea which version of Murphy it's pimping out from one scenario to the next. He's got no truck with Jay Mohr's lounge singer wearing a kilt, that's for sure, as we laboriously establish in the first scene. (Too much like cross-dressing.) The most bizarre element, though, is the film's sleaze factor, which is off-the-charts icky for something Warner Bros were surely hoping to market to the *Shrek* brigade.

It's hardly worth explaining why Murphy's and Dawson's characters must pose as a married couple to interrogate a cosmetic surgeon (played by a surprisingly sprightly Illeana Douglas) about her connection to the plot. But beware, it's heading somewhere: the scene climaxes with a holographic pre-visualisation of what 'anatomical enhancements' Pluto would choose, in his fantasies, to inflict on Dina, a woman he has just met. Cue a dizzyingly lewd VFX shot of Dawson's front and bottom ballooning to four times their existing voluptuousness, while Murphy smirks like a horndog.

What level of desperation led to these routines – or during what phase they were scripted – is information lost somewhere in the deepest vaults of *Pluto Nash* lore. I hate to tell you, such lore does not really exist (unlike *Casablanca* lore, or even *Clue* lore), because of everyone's understandable desire to forget the whole thing ever happened.

Confronting the film itself is therefore like picking over an unusually well-preserved archaeological dig, to find chunks of physical evidence from which we can only make rogue guesses at what led to what. How well did it test when they gave Dawson boobs the size of space hoppers? What possessed Underwood to cast his own daughter, Lana, in the walk-on role of Sexy Robot? Did they ever consider making an action figure out of Bruno?

Instead of successfully ending, *Pluto Nash* is one of those films that just stops. Top of the ensuing credits, by a cruel quirk of fate, is Frank Capra III – grandson of the legendary auteur – who is named and shamed as first assistant director. What an assignment. Bregman, who was already 76, soon retired. Underwood, traumatised by his own admission, slunk into helming TV movies and series episodes, where he now dabbles across a miscellany of genres, after turning in just one more film-directing credit, on a 2005 vehicle for the singer Usher, *In the Mix*. (It still grossed more than *Pluto Nash*.) He has never ducked responsibility for all that went wrong. 'I mean, it is the film I made. That was me at that time making a movie.'[6]

For Murphy, who has turned in more than his share of shockers amid semi-regular comebacks – including an Oscar nomination four years later for *Dreamgirls* (2006) – this film represents an almost unarguable career low. True, there are films of his that got even more kicked around by critics, such as the poo-fixated *Daddy Day Care* (2003) and the generally gruesome *Norbit* (2007), which is widely thought to have cost him that Oscar. But the gross-out comedy of those still enabled them to clean up (probably not quite the right phrase) at the box office.

Pluto Nash isn't even gross, just barren, wrong, and disconcerting. Perhaps only *Meet Dave* (2008), in which Murphy played two roles – an alien spaceship manned by tiny humanoids, and the captain of said ship – rivals it for making you wonder if you're on a bad trip, and if there's a button somewhere for an ejector seat.

GIGLI (2003)

Director: Martin Brest
Studio: Sony/Revolution Studios
Budget: $75.6m
Worldwide gross: $7.3m

Let's start with pronouncing it. *Gigli*. Surely not 'Giggly'? The phonetics are so troublesome that Ben Affleck's Larry Gigli, a low-end Mob enforcer no one likes, must give a crash course in saying his name to strangers. 'Rhymes with "really",' he keeps trying, with a long-suffering air. So, 'Jeely'. Toy with that on the tongue. Pucker up to it. See if you can dimly remember what made it the most notorious bomb of its day.

It's a solid rule of thumb, when releasing a $75m crime romcom aimed at broad international audiences, to pick a title that won't prove entirely unpronounceable for a wide majority of punters. Imagine a couple of Scottish teenagers at the ticket counter. 'Two for . . . Gigg . . . Jiggly?'

If anyone even made it that far. Sony, who released the movie with a sinking feeling in August 2003, had reasons to be jittery. The film had been subject to a lavish crescendo of bad press. Jennifer Lopez wouldn't commit early on when she was courted to play Ricki, a lesbian gangster, and was nearly replaced by Halle Berry, who can be forever grateful (well, until the next chapter) that scheduling conflicts on *X2* gave her the opt-out.

Lopez was lured back after a planned thriller called *Tick Tock*, about terrorist bombings, was cancelled in the wake of 9/11. There was also the money. Her $12m salary, just $0.5m shy of what Affleck got, propelled her near the top end of Hollywood's highest-paid actresses.* Plus, she was given the sweetener of a back-end deal in the high single digits – that's to say, a percentage of the profits. Nobody yet surmised that these were going to add up to a long way less than zero.

Instead of being a film, *Gigli* was a package, designed to provide juicy pay-outs for everyone in town – a cork-popping moment for whole teams of agents. It exemplifies the inflated deal-making of the early 2000s, much as *Last Action Hero*† (not coincidentally, another Sony release) did of the 1990s. After this film's failure, an entire business model came under scrutiny, and the course correction gave Hollywood whiplash.

Most of the money for this exasperating mess came from Revolution Studios, the company launched in 2000 by high-flying executive Joe Roth, who'd done chairing stints at Fox and Disney in the 1990s. He'd nurtured good relationships with stars, especially Julia Roberts, and had a plan: Revolution would produce a half-dozen mid-budget films each year, and release them through an arrangement with Sony.‡

Roth pledged to keep these in the under-$50m bracket, and managed this at first, with such elementary vehicles as Rob Schneider's *The Animal* (2001) and the all-star, cost-cutting romcom *America's Sweethearts* (also 2001), which was written by Billy Crystal, fronted by Roberts, and directed (badly) by none other than Roth himself. That

---

* Julia Roberts had broken the $20m ceiling – previously a male-only threshold – when she received that (and deserved every cent, dammit!) on *Erin Brockovich* (2000). Cameron Diaz matched the figure for *Charlie's Angels: Full Throttle* (2003). (No comment.) Sandra Bullock was paid $15m for *Murder by Numbers* (2002); Angelina Jolie would get $12m for *Lara Croft: Tomb Raider – The Cradle of Life* (2003).

† See p. 186.

‡ Sony would handle 42.5 per cent of the financing for each one, and 100 per cent of the marketing budget.

was a rare money-maker, despite being, like almost all Revolution's product, lousy entertainment. (It must never be forgotten that we have these guys to thank for the godawful *xXx* franchise.)

Sony needed a boost around then, because their in-house film division (Columbia Pictures, as was) had drifted into the doldrums, with a market share that sank below 9 per cent from 1999 to 2001. But then along came *Spider-Man* (2002), sending them soaring back up to 17 per cent in 2002. With more cash in the parental coffers and more pressure for his own films to compete, Roth rolled the dice, and green-lit a slate of costlier films for 2003. To quote Roberts in *Pretty Woman*: big mistake. Huge. She should know – obliterating her own pay record, she got $25m right off the bat for the simpering inspirational-teacher drama *Mona Lisa Smile*.

Roth's worst gambles were the dud action-comedy *Hollywood Homicide** ($75m); the eye-wateringly pricey co-production *Peter Pan*† ($130m); and the Bruce Willis war-in-Nigeria rescue thriller *Tears of the Sun*.‡ All of those lost a king's ransom, but *Gigli*, seen by the fewest, would lose the most. After Roth's annus horribilis in 2003, Revolution had to stamp on the brakes – meaning lowered budgets, no more back-end deals, party time's over, folks. With a staff soon halved, it would limp on as a production entity for only another three years.

---

* Directed by Ron Shelton, starring Harrison Ford and Josh Hartnett. Worldwide gross: $51.1m.

† Directed by P. J. Hogan – the one everyone has forgotten, with a rather good Jason Isaacs as Captain Hook and Rachel Hurd-Wood wonderful as Wendy. It took $122m worldwide.

‡ Directed by Antoine Fuqua, starring Monica Bellucci opposite Willis. It was initially listed with a conservative budget of $75m, which would mysteriously rise to $100.5m when Revolution put their library up for sale. Worldwide gross: $86.5m.

While this expenditure ballooned, all tabloid eyes were on Affleck and Lopez, who were rumoured to be getting close on the *Gigli* shoot, even though Lopez had been married for mere months to Cris Judd, a Filipino dancer she'd met around the time of her break-up from Puff Daddy. Make no mistake, the Lopez early-2000s relationship timeline is stuffed with far more drama than anything that actually occurs in *Gigli*, which was half the problem.

As the shoot wrapped in April 2002, Affleck took out a full-page trade ad complimenting Lopez as a co-star, which was either supremely gentlemanly of him, or a shameless case of flashing the cash. They were all cuddles at a surprise party for her thirty-second birthday that July, just two days before she filed for divorce from Judd.

A summer of love followed – and we have evergreen evidence, the 'Jenny from the Block' video, which premiered on MTV in November 2002. As they sunbathe on a luxury yacht in the manner of absolutely everybody from the block, Affleck pats Lopez, smooches her on the behind, and undoes a string from her bikini. Engagement followed swiftly, with Affleck whipping out a much-gawped-at 6.1-carat pink diamond ring that set him back around one-sixth of his *Gigli* salary.

Just as the film's marketing campaign needed to ramp up, these two became the first celebrity couple of the day to find themselves with a portmanteau nickname – Bennifer – thereby pre-dating red-top obsessions with the likes of TomKat and Brangelina.* The over-exposure of its stars became the film's worst enemy, other than the film itself. It was shaping up as *Bennifer: The Movie*, and already had the look of something hubristic and smug – a supercouple love-in.

---

* Historically, this sort of thing started with Pickfair, the name coined by the press for the estate Mary Pickford and Douglas Fairbanks owned in the 1920s. Then there was Desilu, as Desi Arnaz and Lucille Ball named their TV production company in the 1950s.

The ghastly first poster didn't help. It showed a rapt Bennifer gazing into each other's eyes and looking conspicuously Photoshopped, right down to Lopez's buns in tight low-rise denim. But the real architect of this catastrophe, thus far unnamed, was the man who wrote, directed, and produced it: Martin Brest.

———

In the 1980s, the Bronx-born, NYU-educated Brest had made his name with a pair of star-led action comedies, *Beverly Hills Cop* (1984) and *Midnight Run* (1988). He'd increased his cachet by directing Al Pacino to the Best Actor Oscar for one of his phoniest performances, as hoo-hahhing blind army vet Frank Slade in *Scent of a Woman* (1992). While the film was a surprising hit, critics griped about its excessive length, windy script, and indulgence of that mega-hammy star turn.

It was long, slow, and looked calculated to win awards. But in all those regards, it had nothing on Brest's next one, *Meet Joe Black* (1998).* A three-hour romantic drama starring Brad Pitt as Death? What was anyone thinking? Dressed to the nines and shot with wasteful splendour by Emmanuel Lubezki, this was opulent, $90m prestige bait that didn't reap a single Oscar nomination, and recouped only half its budget in the USA.

By any sane studio accounting of risk and reward, Brest should have been in trouble. This was the moment to retrench into something cheap and cheerful, or at the very least commercially fail-safe. Instead, on *Gigli*, he was given enough rope to hang himself several times over. You could start, because someone should have, with his script – a hard-to-swallow confection, guilty of trying too hard when it's not causing active, jaw-dropping offence.

* See also p. 170.

The plot's almost by the by. The callow Larry and sultry Ricki, previously unacquainted, are thrown together on a criminal assignment that turns this flick into something like *Get Shorty* meets *Rain Man*. A New York Mob boss named Starkman (played, for delayed impact, in a ranty one-scene cameo by Al Pacino) is in trouble with a federal prosecutor, so he wants the latter's young brother kidnapped to use him as leverage. Played by then twenty-four-year-old unknown Justin Bartha, this is Brian, who has learning difficulties and lives in a care facility.

Ever present if increasingly a third wheel, Brian is obsessed with what he calls 'the *Baywatch*' and talks about his penis sneezing while watching it. He's described in the film's press notes as 'Brian, the guileless innocent, who changes the destinies of Ricki and Gigli'. A pick 'n' mix buffet of developmental issues, he demonstrates symptoms of autism, brain damage and Tourette's, seemingly depending on what Brest finds cutest or most novel for any particular scene.

Having worked at Bronx State Hospital while going through college, Brest claimed to have been 'intrigued by the variety of behaviours, disorders and pathologies he encountered'.[1] It's a boon to us all that this wealth of diverse human experience got funnelled into one absolutely terrible character. Brian gained little in specificity when Bartha (who goes full Dustin Hoffman) went about his research. 'Most of the disabled men and women I encountered are honest, optimistic, and live in the moment,'[2] he said at the time. The net result of their findings is a patronisingly twee take on intellectual disability, to say the least.

Then there's the question of Ricki's sexuality. She's a lesbian, a fact elided in the trailer and marketing. (Mustn't frighten the horses.) In one especially toxic monologue, the thwarted, unlovable Larry moans to her face that she's 'a stone-cold dyke. A fucking untouchable, unhaveable, unattainable brick wall fucking dyke-a-saurus rexi.'

Followers of Affleck's career as a leading man might wonder for how long this dyke-a-saurus remains one, especially if they've seen Kevin Smith's *Chasing Amy* (1997), in which his character single-handedly converts the lesbian played by Joey Lauren Adams into someone who prefers sex with men. And yep, before we know it, J.Lo's Ricki is an untouchable, unhaveable, unattainable brick wall whom Larry has managed to touch, have and indeed attain. Is there no lesbian on movie Earth who wouldn't 'hop the fence' (his phrase) after a vigorous Afflecking?

Before this can all be fully consummated, there's the infamous 'turkey time' scene – an invitation for Larry to go down on Ricki, which ends with J.Lo beckoning him in with the fateful words 'gobble gobble'. Larry's closest thing to a character arc, then, is learning to perform oral sex as a pre-condition of pulling lesbians. That, and encouraging Brian to face his fears and chat up busty blondes on the beach.

Reading *Gigli*'s production notes now, you get no indication that anyone thought things might be going a little off-piste. A lost classic of the PR-puffery genre, they conjure a delusional halcyon era, after the wrap, when *Gigli* was about to be enshrined as a future classic.

'Marty [Brest] would jump up and down and dance around and scream when a take was particularly good,' said Lopez to the press kit. 'He does more takes than anyone I've ever worked with,' added Affleck, which begs an entirely different set of questions, mainly what the bejeezus ended up on the cutting-room floor.

There's something so intently embarrassing about *Gigli* that – here's the plot twist – it's almost interesting. Those few critics who stuck their necks out with semi-positive reviews* tended to focus on the

---

* They included Roger Ebert in the *Chicago Sun-Times*, who gave it a tempered two and a half stars out of four, and Charles Taylor for Salon.com.

film's frank discussion of sex as an unusual virtue for a Hollywood star vehicle. Sure, 'gobble gobble' was justifiably mocked – low-hanging fruit for the vast majority of the press coverage, which competed for attention by seizing on the script's worst excesses.

But that scene comes after a far more ambitious one, in which Lopez, who's magnetic in it, performs a long yoga routine, patiently listening to a peroration of Larry's about the penis – an emblem of thrusting progress, no less – and then, while doing downward dog and all sorts, luxuriantly rebuts it with her own paean to the charms of the vagina.

This scene is amazingly unafraid of everything it was guaranteed to be accused of. Above all, it's pretentiously overwritten, because Brest has always loved the sound of his own writing. But couldn't the same be said of Tarantino? Here, and in the good, first half of Al Pacino's scene, you sense Brest's desire to spin an Elmore Leonard-ish yarn with the same hang-out vibe that QT achieved in *Jackie Brown* (1997). The two film-makers share a taste for these show-offy monologues, gifts to actors even when they wind up being poisoned chalices.

What almost saves Affleck's performance is how good he is at embarrassment. He and Brest are trying to get to the bottom of Larry's dickishness, by way of therapy. The trouble is his cynical posturing, which is both way too much like Tom Cruise's in *Rain Man* (1988), and rings false in its writerliness. When Ricki intrudes on a scene with his mother (Lainie Kazan), it's a step in the right direction, because he seems so boyishly ashamed, so seen by them both.

I've never been able to square all the problems with *Gigli* with how stunning and warm Lopez is in it. It's a weird conundrum that one of her most appealing performances, somehow, is in *Gigli*;

what's less weird is that she took home a Golden Raspberry* for it, because the knee-jerk decision-making of that awards body is legendarily undiscerning.

Ricki, most of the way, is a delight. She sees through Larry's BS immediately and keeps the upper hand, but gently; she oscillates between toying with him and pitying him, and simply observing him, like an amateur shrink. They don't have romantic chemistry, as the reviews griped – but this is partly on purpose, because he's idiotically smitten, and she finds him a sad specimen. It's not as though they're equally matched.

This makes it all the more galling that Brest had to Go There and make this pair hook up, tarring the film with hopelessly gungy gender politics. With these characters as presented, *Gigli* simply shouldn't have been a romcom. It's not funny, has a half-disaster making Larry relatable, and a total one making Brian scan as a credible human being. Scads of errors wash up in the last 20 minutes, with a finale meandering somewhere up the Pacific Coast by car. As they stumble across the literal shoot for *Baywatch*, Brian is mesmerised, and his minders can't bring themselves to go their separate ways. It all sinks, with sudsy music, into absolute mush.

This was not Brest's plan for the ending, which was meant to be both mystical and tragic. The final moments, which they shot, had Larry bleeding to death on this beach, after a showdown with the cop played by Christopher Walken (who gets only one, flatly hostile, scene in the released cut). Ricki also revealed herself to have been posing as a contractor the whole time, which makes a lot more sense of everything she's doing (if hardly her decision to bed Larry).

* The film swept, of course, 'winning' six out of its nine nominations, including for Worst Picture, Director, Actor and Screenplay.

Joe Roth, who was alarmed at how poorly this all tested, leaned on Brest to do five weeks of reshoots and recut much of the last section, compressing the criminal intrigue while boosting the romance.* This cost a lot more and still didn't help. 'The movie didn't work,' Affleck admitted to *Variety* the very Monday after it came out. 'We tried to fix it. But it was like putting a fish's tail on a donkey's head.'3

The blame must rest, then, not only with the ever-overreaching Brest, but a faithless producer who promised him final cut, was freaked out by bad test screenings, then strong-armed him into softening his film's whole tone for a facile happy ending. Even after this, Sony's desperate marketing division made a late swerve away from lovey-dovey Bennifer – consumers were done – and back towards the dark-crime-comedy angle that Brest, ironically, had filleted out. Given that about half the film is spent mooching about in Larry's boring apartment, and a quarter of it cruising in no particular haste around LA's boulevards, it stood no chance of being hailed as much of a thriller.

When *Gigli* opened to a lamentable $3.8m in August 2003,† Affleck and Brest nursed each other's wounds. 'I was like, it's just spectacular, it's a tsunami, it couldn't be worse. This is as bad as it gets,'4 Affleck now recalls. It actually did get worse: by the third weekend, the film had been dropped in disgust from a record 97 per cent of the screens it opened on.‡

The shower of unkind publicity attending all this sure seems to have tarnished the Bennifer engagement, which was called off by January.§ Meanwhile, the pair fitted in one other, obviously doomed,

---

* The critic Michael Dequina caught an early screening and unveiled the differences at *TheMovieReport.com*.
† It came eighth at the US box office; *American Weekend* (the third in the *American Pie* series) topped the weekend with $33.4m.
‡ 2,215 cinemas in the first weekend, dropping to 73 by the third.
§ By June, Lopez had tied the knot with Marc Anthony instead, and Affleck

A set photo of the thirty-foot 'white elephants' D. W. Griffith had made for *Intolerance*. There was no evidence they'd ever featured in Babylonian iconography, but Griffith couldn't care less.

Fuming Ruritanian queen Regina V (Seena Owen) whips Gloria Swanson's convent lass, dubbed *Queen Kelly* in her African exile. This saucy epic was overtaken in the rush to make talkies.

The circus troupe in *Freaks* welcome the so-called 'normal' bride, Cleopatra (off-screen), for the famed banquet. When she responds with cackling disgust, they close ranks to get even.

Katharine Hepburn in her fizzy element was no draw; instead, her cross-dressing romcom became notorious. Her next few vehicles would bomb, but none as badly as *Sylvia Scarlett*.

An army of Egyptian extras herald Pharaoh Khufu (Jack Hawkins) in *Land of the Pharaohs*. Warner Bros put the local workforce through hell, with minimal pay for back-breaking labour.

Taming Rex Harrison on *Doctor Dolittle* was hard enough, let alone his four-legged co-stars. This accident-prone giraffe scarcely made the cut – an emblem of the elusive fun being missold.

Sumptuous craft in *Dune*: Tony Masters' jade-floored throne room; a few of Bob Ringwood's 8,000+ costumes; and Carlo Rambaldi's Guild Navigator, which so blindsided customs officials.

Eschewing the likes of Sean Connery, Terry Gilliam's casting idea for *The Adventures of Baron Munchausen* was to pick 'a great actor who'd been forgotten': sixty-two-year-old John Neville.

Chevy Chase and Demi Moore take a plunge into the booby-trapped Gothic funhouse that was *Nothing But Trouble*. Behind Moore's back, Chase griped that her costume was 'too revealing'.

Geena Davis and Matthew Modine brave *Cutthroat Island*'s carriage chase – cue exploding cannonballs. 'He likes to blow things up,' Modine remarked of her husband, Renny Harlin.

Same pig, new friends: the waifs and strays who look to him as the moral centre of *Babe: Pig in the City*. More than half the 120-strong canine cast came from dog shelters around Sydney.

If it worked at Agincourt? *Alexander* (Colin Farrell) peps up his band of brothers before the battle of Gaugamela in 331 BC. The speechwriting, not by Shakespeare, visibly lets the side down.

Prepare for *Catwoman*'s boss battle between black widow Laurel Hedare (Sharon Stone) and once-meek Patience Phillips (Halle Berry), who's seen into the wicked heart of Big Make-Up.

Ben Kingsley's Time Safari CEO gives marching orders to peeved Edward Burns in *A Sound of Thunder*: a scene shot roughly three years before the film hobbled broken into cinemas.

'Genius' playwright Caden Cotard takes five in *Synecdoche, New York* – letting Philip Seymour Hoffman catch his breath, too. It was a punishingly hot shoot under heavy latex in Bed-Stuy.

Taylor Swift's one scene in *Cats* before she prudently scrammed. Belting out 'Macavity' as flirtatious cabaret puss Bombalurina, she got away with the only kind mentions in reviews.

collaboration – Kevin Smith's sentimental dramedy *Jersey Girl* (2004).* Only after the *Gigli* fiasco did Miramax and Smith decide to eliminate Lopez almost outright from that film's marketing, trimming her already small role, and letting the cat out of the bag that her character dies of an aneurysm during childbirth, thereby sparing everyone *Gigli 2*.

And yet there *has* been a sequel. Come 2021, Bennifer were back on. Come 2022, they went through with the nuptials that *Gigli* may or may not have scuppered the first time. Perhaps it took that long to banish the whiff of the movie from collective memory. While both stars succeeded in taking stock to reposition themselves – Affleck with a canny pivot to directing and an ultimately unhappy stint as Batman; Lopez by concentrating on her music, before *Hustlers* (2019) and the Super Bowl – the same cannot be said for Martin Brest, who has yet to be let out of the Hollywood sin bin even now.

Fifty-one at the time, he has vanished practically without trace, give or take a hasty namecheck when Affleck's *Argo* (2012) won the Best Picture Oscar. Brest's silence on the film's failure has been total. Then and now, *Gigli*'s touchingly loyal leading man is the one forever saying he believes in the director – who evidently failed here to make the film he wanted to make, capitulated reluctantly to a studio-dictated overhaul, and got career-destroying reviews for the mutant result. After this experience, you can hardly blame Brest for turning his back on the industry: the only thing anyone truly loved about *Gigli* was eviscerating it.

---

briskly rebounded by dating, then marrying, his *Daredevil* co-star, Jennifer Garner.

* Smith not only took credit for coining 'Bennifer' on *Jersey Girl*'s set (in a 2021 tweet) but has repeatedly blamed *Gigli* for killing that film, and sometimes just says the word 'Gigli' to wind up Affleck.

CATWOMAN (2004)

Director: Pitof
Studio: Warner Bros
Budget: ~$100m
US gross: $40.2m

Everybody around me said, 'Girl, don't do it.
It's going to be the death of you. It's going to end your career.'

Halle Berry in 2018

Over time, Halle Berry stopped regretting *Catwoman*, or found ways to bulwark herself against the chronic mockery. Her career outlived it, though it did take a nasty hit; and the notion of a female-centred superhero flick would eventually find favour again, though not for at least a decade.

The problem was not that a *Catwoman* film of any kind was a terrible idea in 2004. The problem was the particular terribleness of this one. It's easily among the most bungled efforts in this book, from script to lighting, acting to soundtrack, angles to edits, soup to nuts. Not until *Cats* (2019) – get ready – would cats, themselves, have such a pressing reason to stay out of cinemas.

It was also a classic example of the Best Actress Oscar curse in action. Two years earlier, Berry had won for *Monster's Ball* (2001) – becoming the first Black actress to prevail in the leading category, and dedicating her award to every 'nameless, faceless woman of colour' who might find doors opened because of it. The trouble for Berry herself was that the door that swung wide – for a juicy $14m salary – turned out to be a cat-flap.

Before and after her Oscar-winning walk on the wild side, which was not without inbuilt controversy,* Berry was having a mixed time in the blockbuster arena. She'd done two stints as Storm in Bryan Singer's *X-Men* series, but found herself boxed in by the story-telling, and got bullied by fans for failing to do her character justice. Overshadowed especially by Hugh Jackman's runaway success as Wolverine, she mainly stood around summoning bad weather and worse dialogue:† all Singer's fault,‡ hardly hers.

There was much tabloid noise about Berry going topless for the low-IQ cyber-hacker thriller *Swordfish* (2001) – even the rumour she'd been paid $500,000 extra for doing so, which she laughed off as a fake-news publicity grab. Her role as Jinx in *Die Another Day* (2002) was in the can before the Oscar win, making her a rare Bond actress to boast one.§ The unorthodox A-list casting (she was paid $4m) certainly helped that ridiculous film make the most money of the Brosnan Bonds, invisible car and all.

There was even a cancelled spin-off vehicle for Jinx,¶ with the suggestion that Berry take over 007 duties from Brosnan, making her a forerunner to Lashana Lynch's Nomi in *No Time to Die*.

---

* Berry's uninhibited sex scenes with Billy Bob Thornton, who played a racist prison guard, ignited debate in the Black community over the virtues of her role. Angela Bassett claimed to have turned it down, labelling it 'a stereotype about Black women and sexuality' that she couldn't have slept with at night. (Interviewed by Allison Samuels, *Newsweek*, 30 June 2002.)

† Most notoriously, 'You know what happens to a toad when it's struck by lightning? The same thing that happens to everything else.' Apparently we have Joss Whedon to thank for that.

‡ 'Bryan's not the easiest dude to work with,' Berry recalled euphemistically in an interview for *Variety*, September 2020.

§ The others, as Alan Partridge would surely know, are Kim Basinger, Michelle Yeoh and, of course, Judi Dench.

¶ Neil Purvis and Robert Wade were set to work on the script, with Stephen Frears due to direct.

According to Berry, this idea was 'ahead of its time', and got scuppered because 'nobody was ready to sink that kind of money into a Black female action star. They just weren't sure of its value. That's where we were then'.[1]

The final leading role Berry took pre-*Catwoman* was in the asylum thriller *Gothika* (2003), a one-way trip to hokumville which did decent business despite reviews that couldn't help laughing at it – a trade-off Berry might not have adored, but which she'd have taken in a heartbeat over the all-round humiliation about to be inflicted.

Commercially, there's a real argument that *Catwoman* might have been made to work if smarter thinking had been involved. Fox's first two *X-Men* (2000, 2003) and Sony's megahit *Spider-Man* had kickstarted the superhero craze, paving the way for the rise of Marvel. In *Blade* (1998) and the superior *Blade II* (2002) – Marvel-derived, in fact – Wesley Snipes also proved that a Black star could command his own franchise as a comic-book antihero. While women of any skin colour had yet to seize that mantle, there were encouraging precedents for female butt-kicking in the adjacent realm of video-game adaptations – most notably Angelina Jolie in *Lara Croft: Tomb Raider* (2001) and Milla Jovovich in *Resident Evil* (2002).

Meanwhile, Warner Bros were in the midst of a drastic rethink, mulling ways to resuscitate the terminally uncool DC brand, which meant pulling clear of the campy fiasco that was *Batman and Robin* (1997). They'd already hired Christopher Nolan to direct *Batman Begins* (2005), the gloomily impressive first part of what we might call his why-so-serious trilogy. David S. Goyer (*Blade, Dark City*) was co-writing, and it was envisaged as a straight-up antidote to Joel Schumacher's garish panto silliness.

They wouldn't be rushed, mind. As that film took shape, a proposed *Batman vs Superman*, which had gone through various drafts around 2002, was prudently scrapped.* This left Warners with a window to think fast in 2004 – the year when Sony had *Spider-Man 2* ready to pop, but WB's own DC slate was still blank.

In fact, they'd announced plans for a standalone *Catwoman* a decade earlier, after the field day enjoyed by a miaowing, latex-clad Michelle Pfeiffer in Tim Burton's *Batman Returns* (1992). She boarded the idea with Burton, as did that film's producer, Denise Di Novi, and screenwriter Daniel Waters, who turned in his script to WB on the same day *Batman Forever* was released in July 1995.

In retrospect, Waters rued his timing. His scabrous vision for a Batman-free *Catwoman* clashed with the studio's current style directives (per Waters, it was 'definitely not a fun-for-the-whole-family script'†). Burton and Pfeiffer slunk off in other directions, while attempts to revive it with Sarah Michelle Gellar, then Ashley Judd, then Nicole Kidman, proved abortive.

The new race to get it off the ground with Berry meant scrounging bits and bobs from various earlier scripts and simply hoping, on a wing and a prayer, that they'd harmonise. It was first decided that Pfeiffer's character, Selina Kyle, died after all at the end of *Batman Returns*, and an entirely new Catwoman, Patience Phillips, was dreamed up.

In a 2000 script by Kate Kondell, she was a vengeful pet groomer, referred to as 'Robin Hood with PMS'. By 2002, in a rewrite by John Rogers that would be green-lit, she'd become a veterinary scientist

---

* By Goyer's logic, '*Batman vs. Superman* is where you go when you admit to yourself that you've exhausted all possibilities . . . somewhat of an admission that this franchise is on its last gasp.' (*LA Times*, May 8 2005.)

† Daniel Waters interview, *Film Review*, August 1995. The script which so appalled Warner Bros, was leaked online a few years later: it involves Selina Kyle fending off sex pests at a desert casino, and exposing a fraudulent gang of alleged superheroes called The Cult of Good.

working for a biotech firm. Rogers retained a credit on the finished film, even though he would describe *Catwoman* in 2018, around the time of *Black Panther*'s release, as 'very, very bad' – 'a shit movie dumped at the end of a style cycle' that had 'zero cultural relevance either in front of or behind the camera'.[2] Ouch.

Rogers, who said he was fired for pushing back against the increasing stupidity of the notes he was receiving, also clarified that 'an insane rights issue' ruled out the name Selina Kyle from being used. Come the final rewrite, by regular collaborators John Brancato and Michael Ferris (*Terminator 3*), Patience was still Patience, but in this iteration she became a frazzled graphic designer, now working for a cosmetics firm called Hedare Beauty, owned by seething nightmare boss George Hedare (Lambert Wilson, in a performance that's woeful even by *Catwoman*'s standards).

George's wife Laurel (a beyond bitchy Sharon Stone) used to be the iconic face of the company, but having just rounded forty, she's been replaced by a younger model, with whom her husband is also sleeping. Stone may look like the Cruella de Vil of this outfit, right down to her black-and-white fur coat, but her entire role as the villain of the piece is essentially 'bitter ex-model put out to pasture'.* Three men, funnily enough, were ultimately credited for writing *Catwoman*, and another directed it.

The person hired for this last job, now remembered for little else, was a Frenchman dubbed Pitof (full name Jean-Christophe Comar), whose main field of experience was as a visual-effects supervisor on French blockbusters. He was the go-to guy for

---

* We were living through a bad moment for female sex symbols of the 1990s being repurposed as sour-faced baddies – see also Demi Moore's depressing comeback in the previous year's *Charlie's Angels* sequel, as 'ex-Angel gone rogue' Madison Lee.

Marc Caro and Jean-Pierre Jeunet when they made their zany black comedy *Delicatessen* (1991) and fantasy folly *The City of Lost Children* (1995); he'd also done second-unit work in Hollywood on Jeunet's *Alien: Resurrection* (1997).

But he had, to date, only one feature directing credit to his name, on a below-the-radar curio called *Vidocq* (2001), starring a sweat-soaked Gérard Depardieu as the titular figure, a real-life criminal turned detective who inspired Poe's 'The Murders in the Rue Morgue'. It was notable as an early instance of HD digital cinematography, a not-insignificant budget of €23m, and having 800 effects shots. Honestly, the trailer alone looks batshit, and not in a way that would have me, if I were a discerning studio exec, desperate to quadruple Pitof's budget and set him loose.

Warner Bros saw something in him, though.

Excitedly signing on, Pitof never got round to picking a colour scheme. (Watching the finished film is often like staring at a ran-domised splatter of Dulux paint testers.) He also didn't elect to turn to the Catwoman of the DC comics for inspiration. While there's a certain logic there, as Patience is meant to be an entirely new char-acter with a clean-slate mythos, it's not as though the film has a host of new ideas dangling from its sleeves. It's just extraordinarily feeble. And sexist. And bad.

Much like Pfeiffer's character, Berry's is a chaotic dogsbody – again, nothing to do with the Catwoman of the comics – who's thrown under a bus by corporate interests and left for dead. Flushed out of the waste pipes of Hedare's R&D lab and drowned, she's resurrected on a garbage island, after a single miaow in the mouth from a grey, randomly magical Egyptian Mau cat named Midnight, and gains the usual feline superpowers.

What to use these for? The screenplay has even less of an idea than she does. Before we can question it, her first hobby is cat burglary, because you know, *cat* burglary. She demands milk at nightclubs by ordering white Russians, without the vodka, Kahlúa or ice. She craves sushi, hates rain, slinks around on her own bookshelves, and doesn't *appear* to use a litter tray, unless that was a deleted scene.

Berry's styling – pure leather fetish bar, with a shiny black bustier, ripped-up trousers, high heels and rhinestone-encrusted nails – was all anyone wanted to talk about. What else was there? She got in incredible shape, learning capoeira to tone up for the role.

But sexualising the character this brazenly wound up being a hostage to fortune, because the dominatrix attitude foisted on Patience (at PG-13 level!) was such a ridiculous put-on. They were aiming, to quote costume designer Angus Strathie, for 'the sensual awakening of a sexy warrior goddess'. Yikes. Her red lipstick and cat helmet may have been instantly dated lad-mag fantasy material, but the hair beneath was worse: a snip-snip pixie cut trying way too hard.

The overall transformation from malcoordinated office frump to kinky feline vigilante had the forced quality of Olivia Newton-John's makeover at the end of *Grease*: a hard no. We were better off with klutzy Berry. It didn't increase her comfort levels with her own stranded performance. 'You're in a suit like that,' she would admit, 'and you're doing backflips and cartwheels . . . things are bound to happen. I can't tell you how many times my pants split right open.'³ The frequency of 'Janet Jackson moments' kept turning the set into *Swordfish II*.

Patience's other accoutrements include a remorselessly vanilla love interest, in the shape of Benjamin Bratt's cop Tom Lone, who first catches her trying to rescue Midnight from a fire escape, and assumes, because he's such a gentleman, that she must be trying to jump to her death. (Women simply cannot be trusted in this film not to want to kill themselves.)

Next up, to be hip, she flaunts some new-found basketball skills. A frantic sequence ensues (set, with an overconfidence bordering on insanity, to Mis-Teeq's 'Scandalous'), which has such show-offy cutting you wonder how many energy drinks Pitof and his editor sank while crafting it, or what substances they were laced with. Did they put the camera *in* a basketball? It's hard to say. When Patience takes to scampering up and down the walls of a jewel emporium, or doing parkour on rooftops, the CGI, not to put too fine a point on it, shits the bed. This isn't Spidey in action, where we go along with a leap into cartoonishness, but a hideously blurred replica of Berry's actual physique doing 'gritty' acrobatics.

The worst aspect of *Catwoman*'s plot is, roughly, the entire plot. Patience's fateful discovery in Hedare's lab concerns the side effects of a skin-cream called Beau-line, which is meant to reverse the effects of ageing. In fact, per Laurel, this stuff makes a woman's skin like 'living marble . . . and you can't feel a thing!' When she gets into a domestic with her ghastly husband, he almost breaks his hand slapping her face.

Stone's Laurel is psychotically invested in bringing this goop to market, knowing full well that it's evil, toxic and ruinously addictive. 'I don't care that the FDA never saw the headaches,' Laurel shrugs, 'and the nausea and the fainting spells.' Other effects missed by the Food and Drug Administration include your entire face necrotising if you try to phase it out, but never mind. 'It's a disease in a jar – I wouldn't caulk a sink with it,' hisses Patience, who sets about doing women everywhere a favour: taking on Big Make-Up by sabotaging the supply chain. Caulking a sink with this stuff actually sounds better than most of her ideas, or many of Gwyneth Paltrow's.

Drag Race parodies could quote this entire script and never hope to capture the singular idiocy with which it lands. In the slap-down *mano a mano* between Patience and Laurel that ends it (which has much the same stakes as a lip-sync battle), those diamantine nails of Catwoman's are the only thing that can crack the face of her nemesis, instantly turning it to crumbled chalk. When Lauren sees her ruined visage in the reflection of a window she's dangling from, the glacially perfect bitter ex-model – who has reached game over at forty, poor thing – lets go in horror and dies. Shantay, Catwoman stays.

———

No one was stunned when Pitof's film was eaten alive at the box office, opening against an all-time banger (*The Bourne Supremacy*) and doing less than a third of the business. (It barely outgrossed weekend 4 of *Spider-Man 2*.) There was simply no hiding from the film's absurd tattiness – the publicity shots, the trailers, the savage reviews,* all telling the same story.

Conspiracy theorists have sometimes hypothesised that *Catwoman* was set up to fail. It was certainly made with none of the care or savvy that carved out bright futures for male superhero franchises at that time. Instead, it was brutally sloppy and half-baked. Warner Bros wiped their hands of it and hastily moved on, much as 20th Century Fox did when the following year's *Elektra* – Jennifer Garner's spin-off from the minor hit that was *Daredevil* (2003) – also failed.

Marketing divisions could, and did, point to these extremely bad films bombing, then use them as scapegoats for keeping femme superheroes in their place – usually as sidekicks lucky to get gigs beside the boys. So, the next time Catwoman (aka Selina Kyle, back to canon) made a film appearance, it was in the second-fiddle form of Anne Hathaway in Nolan's nadir, *The Dark Knight Rises* (2012). The time after that, it was Zoë Kravitz, who teased her role in *The Lego*

---

* It stands with a frankly generous score of 8 per cent on Rotten Tomatoes.

Batman Movie (2017) before playing Selina as Robert Pattinson's helpmeet in *The Batman* (2022).

You have to wait until *Wonder Woman* (2017), *Captain Marvel* (2019) and *Birds of Prey* (2020) before the studios were ready to throw their clout back behind women as the protagonists – and, gosh, directors – of a comic-book blockbuster. Naturally, all had white leads. This wasn't *all* the *Catwoman* effect, but some of it was – and the consequence was men establishing a chokehold for the entire first decade of the Marvel Cinematic Universe.

Pitof might not have literally been hired to kill off *Catwoman* as a solo film prospect, but no one given that assignment could have done a more comprehensive job. In terms of studio employment, it was an instant career-ender. His only other directing gig came on a fantasy TV movie for the Sci Fi Channel called *Fire and Ice: The Dragon Chronicles* (2008), in which he's credited as Jean C. Comar – perfectly heeding the advice of Roger Ebert's review, which was never to be associated with that Pitof guy ever again.

The one silver lining in this whole debacle was Berry showing up at the Razzies to collect Worst Actress. (*Catwoman* won Worst Film, too, of course.) Talk about spinning gold from straw. Berry – holding her *Monster's Ball* Oscar aloft in one hand, and the freshly engraved Golden Raspberry in the other – found the one way to make such an appearance funny, which is to faux-gush and fake-cry exactly as if you're receiving the industry's highest accolade.

It was a rare instance of that ceremony being worth watching. She had many, many people to thank – no one earns a Razzie single-handedly. She warmly praised Pitof, while admitting she could never understand a word he said. She was, above all, in Warner Bros' debt, for doing her the huge honour of putting her 'in a piece-of-shit, godawful movie. It was exactly what my career needed! I was at the top! And *Catwoman* just plummeted me to the bottom.'

ALEXANDER (2004)

Director: Oliver Stone
Studio: Warner Bros/Intermedia
Budget: $155m
US gross: $34.3m

Of all the glib, back-row-of-the-classroom theories Oliver Stone was determined to peddle in his film about Alexander the Great, perhaps the goofiest is this: that the Macedonian conqueror never produced an heir because he was too busy being emasculated by his mother and making bedroom eyes at Jared Leto.

There were, as history records, illegitimate sons with mistresses. Diodorus of Sicily might have been brown-nosing, but he claimed that Alexander had a different female concubine for every night of the year. Meanwhile, his wife Roxane (played in Stone's film as a wildcat slave bride by Rosario Dawson) was pregnant when he died in 323 BCE, and that child, Alexander IV, would indeed succeed him.

Stone doesn't care. The Alexander he wanted Colin Farrell to play is a die-hard man among men – clearly more gay than bisexual in Farrell's portrait, as is Leto's soft-spoken Hephaistion, his doting right hand. But Alexander is also a bafflingly puny protagonist who never manages to earn the epic treatment he's given.

He's a terminal worrywart, barely construable as virile, who gets presented with weird insistence as a much less successful rapist than his father, the deranged Philip II (Val Kilmer). That said, after childhood horrors with the latter chasing after his screaming consort Olympias (a full-tilt Angelina Jolie, baying on all fours), their boy has grown up with some fairly ingrained consent issues when it comes to female companionship. Plus – it's strongly implied – the hots for his own mother.* 'You're nineteen and the girls are already saying you don't like them,' Jolie's withering matriarch later scolds – as if he isn't busy enough learning to tame bucking broncos, skewer barbarians and give painfully try-hard *Henry V*-style pep talks.

Especially in the USA, where it was derided and destroyed, *Alexander's* failure pitted one form of homophobia against another. On the one hand, you've got the round rejection of the film by America's public, who'd been pre-warned about how same-sex-fond Farrell's character was, and blew raspberries in its general direction. (Many critics got in on the mockery.) On the other, though, you have the lumbering intent of Stone, who blamed the 'moral fundamentalism' in his homeland for the film flopping, but also made a pig's ear of a rare opportunity – a $155m classical blockbuster, centring queerness. It managed to backfire and cop out simultaneously, pleasing no one.

Stripping Alexander of all vigour and exposing him to knee-jerk ridicule, Stone might be the gay ally you'd least want pitching up on a Pride march. To cap things off, he gives this warrior king the feyest bleach job this side of Jon Heder's prattish figure-skater in *Blades of Glory* (2007). If this is Stone's praise song to a historical giant he actually reveres – whose idealism inspired him to spend 30 years developing the script – you'd hate to get on the director's *bad* side.

———

* 'If they are not a couple, they should be,' Stone coyly remarked about the on-set chemistry between Jolie and Farrell. 'Boy, did they hit it off.' (Interview in the *Sunday Telegraph*, 3 January 2005.)

Some time in the 1980s, *Alexander* was a faraway glint in two men's eyes. One was Stone, a name screenwriter after the Oscar he'd won for *Midnight Express* (1978), who turned in a draft of *Conan the Barbarian* (1982), then the script for *Scarface* (1983), while deep in the throes of cocaine addiction. Well before *Platoon* (1986) proved his directorial mettle, he harboured a fantasy about a psychedelic war epic, which he began writing in 1980, with guidance from the 1973 book *Alexander the Great* by Robin Lane Fox. In fits and starts, the obsession grew. In Stone's *The Doors*, Jim Morrison's face in the mirror cross-fades to a bust of Alexander, and it was that film's star, Val Kilmer, whom Stone originally saw as the lead.

The other progenitor of the film – according to him, at least – was Thomas Schühly, the soon-to-be-infamous German producer who ushered *The Adventures of Baron Munchausen* to its downfall.* In a tragically optimistic 2004 interview with the *New York Times*, headlined 'A Hopeless Idea for a Film about *Alexander* Is Finally Successful',[1] Schühly took credit for keeping the dream alive for two decades.

'A lot of people said I was finished in the industry,' he admitted, before detailing how he clung to an Alexander project to have any hope of a post-*Munchausen* future. It was he who sent Stone a 170-page pitch of his own in 1989, and spent $500,000 to design costumes, armour and sets for the as-yet-unscripted film in the early 1990s.

Much as both Schühly and Terry Gilliam got carried away with the mad quest of putting *Munchausen* up on screen, Schühly and Stone clearly saw some of themselves in Alexander the Great – the fearless warlord extending his resources to breaking point in 326 BCE as he pushed his armies from the Balkans over the Himalayas. While Francis

---

* For the whole saga of which, see pp. 109–113.

Ford Coppola was the only other director Schühly was willing to consider, no studio would go near the project – with Coppola, Stone, or anyone else – while sword-and-sandals epics, so popular in the days of *Ben-Hur* (1959) and *Spartacus* (1960), were so out of fashion.

All that changed with Ridley Scott's *Gladiator* (2000), the riskiest foray into the genre for a generation, and a meaty hit that grossed half a billion dollars and won the Best Picture Oscar. The bonanza of Peter Jackson's *Lord of the Rings* trilogy (2001–3) furthered a vogue for battle scenes on horseback. A slew of lavish, crashingly dull wannabe blockbusters were green-lit, including the likes of Tom Cruise's *The Last Samurai* (2003), Scott's own *Kingdom of Heaven* (2005), Jerry Bruckheimer's *King Arthur* (2005) and Wolfgang Petersen's *Troy* (2004) – a critically derided money-spinner* that, opening six months before *Alexander*, would steal much of its thunder.

Schühly and Stone felt in 2000 that it was time to strike, going to another Teutonic producer, Moritz Borman, whose company Intermedia used a German tax-break scheme to co-finance the likes of *Terminator 3* (2003) and Scorsese's *The Aviator* (2004). The budget was suddenly achievable, the cast set. But just as the shoot was being prepared, even more direct competition clattered across their path. With US troops preparing to invade Mesopotamia as part of George W. Bush's war on terror, a whole flurry of potential Alexander biopics was suddenly being pushed into development.[2] There was hardly any more currency, or controversy, that a take on ancient conquest in the Middle East could ask for.

Ridley Scott threw his hat into the ring, before opting to handle the Crusades instead, interminably, with Orlando Bloom. Mel Gibson was gearing up for a 10-part, $120m Alexander the Great series for HBO, abandoned in the autumn of 2002 as he pivoted to *The Passion*

---

* *Troy* did more than respectable box office – $497m worldwide.

of the Christ (2004). His version would have been based on Mary Renault's two historical novels, *Fire from Heaven* and *The Persian Boy*, but Gibson's comfort levels with their overt gayness will never, perhaps mercifully, be known. HBO switched to making *Rome* (2005–7).

The most lingering threat was a collaboration between Baz Luhrmann, Steven Spielberg and Dino De Laurentiis, as, respectively, director and co-producers, with Leonardo DiCaprio riding in on Bucephalus. The screenwriter was Ted Tally (*The Silence of the Lambs*), who based this on a trilogy of books by the Italian historian Valerio Massimo Manfredi.

The budget was $150m, and it got close to shooting in Morocco in the spring of 2003. De Laurentiis, in one of his classic deals, even persuaded King Mohammed VI to provide 5,000 soldiers and 1,000 horses for the battles, in return for building three new sound stages. Nicole Kidman was cast as Olympias. Luhrmann promised not to sanitise the conqueror's bedroom antics: 'He had sex from everyone and everything . . . he couldn't be loved enough,' he declared in Venice that year.

The race was on. Both sides were bullish about the market existing for two *Alexander* pictures at once. After all, recent years had seen competing films about planet-endangering asteroids (*Deep Impact* and *Armageddon* in 1998), deadly eruptions (*Volcano* and *Dante's Peak* in 1997) and animated insects (*Antz* and *A Bug's Life* in 1998) all successfully make it to release without especially cannibalising each other at the box office.*

---

* Sometimes called the 'twin film' phenomenon, when rival companies sprint to develop similar concepts. Future examples would include the biopics *Capote* and *Infamous* (2005/6), self-explanatory romcoms *Friends with Benefits* and *No Strings Attached* (both 2011), presidential action movies *Olympus Has Fallen* and *White House Down* (both 2013), and *Churchill* and *Darkest Hour* (both 2017).

With its cheap crew and ready supply of local extras, Morocco was to be the jumping-off site for both pictures, not least for all the combat footage needed in the desert. But the starting blocks were obliterated by the May 2003 suicide bombings that killed 43 people in Casablanca. Concerned that DiCaprio would be an obvious target, Team Luhrmann was forced to abandon the studio De Laurentiis had built, just south of Marrakech. They all heaved a big sigh, and decided to shift base to Australia, where that postponed shoot would never actually get re-started.

Fatefully, Team Stone gambled on staying put: Farrell, after all, was nowhere near DiCaprio's level of fame, even with his new-kid-on-the-block ubiquity shading into bad-boy notoriety. Here was their chance to gain a head start.

Filming was under way by late September 2003 in Marrakech. It instantly became bedlam. On the first day, three Moroccans fell off their horses and were hospitalised. Playing the lieutenant Cassander, the perma-pouting Jonathan Rhys Meyers had his mouth cut open when he aggravated his steed by pulling too hard on the reins. Scorpions, snakes and soaring temperatures bedevilled everyone's nerves.

Behind-the-scenes footage makes it hard to envy Farrell, or anyone, their marching orders. While dozens of extras hack away at each other with stunt weaponry, you espy Stone essentially hanging off the back of the camera operator as he swivels about, training it towards anything interesting going on. Beyond commanding his horse and lobbing spears where instructed, Farrell ends many of his shots unenviably close to the lens, scowling like a lunatic, declaiming cod-macho dialogue in his native accent: 'You can run to the ends of Earth – you caarward! – but you'll never run farrr 'nough!!'

Some of the hardships of *Alexander*'s shoot have been logged in the annals thanks to Robin Lane Fox, the Oxford don Stone brought in to safeguard historical accuracy as an on-set boffin. Rather than a fee, Fox had an unusual quid pro quo in mind. As he relayed to the *Guardian* in the run-up to release, he told Stone, 'I want to ride in the front ten of every major cavalry charge involving Alexander and the Macedonians. And when my name is in the credits, I want it to be preceded with the words "and introducing . . ."'[3]

The patrician academic – latterly a gardening writer, and father of Martha (the founder of lastminute.com) – had no concerns about falling off his horse, having been an expert equestrian since he was ten. Taken aback, Stone could only scoff and say yes – though not to the credit request, which would have had the entire Screen Actors Guild demanding their heads on pikes.

So it is that Robin Lane Fox, by his own account, was brought to tears in the Moroccan desert by war cries and sarissas, over several weeks spent re-enacting the battle charges of a Macedonian cavalry-man. 'One sequence might take five hours, with cameras filming boldly among our hooves,' he recounted with odd pride.

Fox survived the experience, perhaps by turning a blind eye to everything that was being turned to fiction. For instance, Alexander did not sustain a soon-to-be fatal arrow wound, as the film has it, while charging an elephant at the battle of Hydaspes in 326 BCE. To be sure, it's a sexier endgame than his real-life demise from a mystery illness in Babylon, which has been variously posited as malaria, typhoid fever, strychnine poisoning or alcoholic liver disease.

There wasn't much Fox could do about the Irish accents, either. Pick an accent, really, to play an ancient Macedonian commander barking orders in English, but maybe don't go mad, as Stone did. He chose to keep the relative newbie Farrell in his comfort zone, rationalising that Macedonian dialect was to Greek what Celtic strains are to English; but then took the further step of asking Kilmer, as Alexander's one-eyed shagger of a father, to speak in an identical brogue.

It's identical . . . -ish. When they're both screaming bloody murder at Philip's latest debauched wedding banquet, all you can think about is whether the event stretched to a free bar with Guinness on tap. For no particular reason, Jolie opted to go vaguely Russian, but such is the general campy-bizarro vibe of her best-in-show supporting turn – sleeping with a basket of snakes by her bed, bragging about nailing Zeus* – that it seems the least of her quirks.

'I do wish he'd listened to me about the wigs,' Kilmer would say of Farrell. It was probably that ludicrous barnet that first alerted media attention to the film's non-heterosexuality, and what a sitting target it would be to lambast from all sides. (As one gay critic's review would zing, 'It's full of brilliant highlights, and they're all in Colin Farrell's hair.'[4])

Anyone disposed to fret about goldilocks heroism could *just* about cope with Brad Pitt growing his tresses out for *Troy*: after all, that film's Patroclus was glumly downplayed as some kind of supportive cousin, for all the oiled-pecs homoeroticism flying around. Stone's script bangs on endlessly about Homeric man-love, so there's no doubt that Alexander and Leto's Hephaistion are (or at least have been) physically involved. Still, they never share so much as a kiss, just one awkward hug.

To be fair, the king's relationship with a submissive eunuch called Bagoas (Francisco Bosch) – the title character of Renault's *The Persian Boy*, and previously the secret lover of Alexander's enemy Darius III – was taken much further. Stone shot a softcore scene of heavy petting between Farrell and Bosch, after a candle's blown out. In Greece, a group of lawyers took umbrage before they'd even seen any of this and threatened to sue Warner Bros (the film's international distributor) for in some way denigrating their national hero as bisexual.

---

* All stuff backed up, as it happens, in Plutarch's *Life of Alexander*.

It's one of the more ridiculous attacks that came the film's way – an unwinnable suit, because no one owns Alexander's public image. But it fanned the flames of suspicion about the film's content in America's heartland, and the perturbed top brass took notice.

Postponing the release from early to late November, Warner Bros made Stone trim the film down by half an hour from his preferred cut. 'I don't know how people are going to respond,' WB's president of production Jeff Robinov had anxiously admitted to *Entertainment Weekly*, 'but I know Oliver didn't run away from who this guy was.'

They started to wish he had. Out, by executive edict, went the scene where Bagoas kisses Alexander's chest in bed; almost all their scenes, in fact, were cut back, and the entire relationship soft-pedalled. A long, romantic talk between Farrell and Leto, on a balcony in Babylon, was also heavily pruned. 'Alexander the Gay', as the headlines were calling him, was pushed halfway back into the closet by these excisions, with Roxane's nudity naturally unimperilled. But, like any closet case strenuously claiming to prefer boobs, this just made him even more susceptible to bullying.

'Queer Eye for the Macedonian Guy,' scoffed the *New York Post* in a pre-release feature, which also called Bagoas, now barely glimpsed, a 'hunky topless Persian castrato'.[5] Stone was caught between a rock and a hard place – pilloried by the mainstream press in all these ways, while also being accused of chickening out by the LGBTQ+ commentariat. As he put it in despair to the *Sunday Telegraph*, 'The gays lambasted me for not making Alexander openly homosexual, and in the Bible Belt pastors were up in the pulpit saying that to watch this film was to be tempted by Satan.'[6]

Not since Jonathan Demme's *Philadelphia* (1993) – where the lack of physical intimacy between Tom Hanks and Antonio Banderas, as boyfriends, aroused ire – had a film caught so much flak for not being gay enough, for all the protests of Stone, Farrell and Leto in interviews that the love between Alexander and Hephaistion was meant to go deeper than sex. 'Young boys,' as Stone further lamented, 'wanted a warrior and nothing else. [Not] a man with vulnerabilities.'[7]

Nothing, at this point, could quell the conservative outrage, which mobilised into a de facto boycott – and was reinforced by damning reviews across America. *Alexander* did vastly better overseas than it did in the USA, where it opened in miserable sixth place across the five-day Thanksgiving weekend. But it was still a flop everywhere, cobbling together $167.3m worldwide and only just squeaking past its production budget. (It would have needed at least $300m to come anywhere near breaking even.)

Stone's next move – an admission of defeat that made him an enemy of the gay blogosphere – was an even more sanitised recut for the DVD release. Ever since then, he has persisted in trying to fix *Alexander*, which has reared its head in more variants than Covid. There have, to date, been four versions endorsed by Stone – the 2004 theatrical cut; that 2005 'director's cut' (eight minutes shorter, and lying to itself); the longest one, a 214-minute, Bagoas-is-back extravaganza he entitled *Alexander Revisited: The Final Unrated Cut* (2007), and then, at 206 minutes, the *final* final, honestly, swear on my *life* final cut, *Alexander: The Ultimate Cut*, which he put out at Warners' request for the tenth anniversary in 2014.

They vary in their particulars, and in the tiptoeing gay focus. But one fundamental problem unites them. *Alexander*, in any form, is a film palpably unhappy with itself, itching at all times to go back to the drawing board. (A devastated, unusually humbled Stone all but confessed as much: messing up the story, he said, 'was my fault'.[8]) We either wait three hours for lift-off, or three and a half. The two main battle scenes – bewildering hack-and-slash marathons, gory, choppy and draining – have been praised by historians, not all of them Robin Lane Fox, as among cinema's most authentic attempts to show the way ancient warfare was actually waged. The trouble is, anyone without a master's in military history will have a hard time deducing who's even winning.

To figure that out, we're supposed to rely on the elder Ptolemy (Anthony Hopkins), a burbling authority whom the film's framing sections, set 40 years later, lean on in vapid desperation. While this surviving general potters around a rooftop in green-screened Alexandria, with a collection of exotic houseboys watering the plants, he dictates his memoirs to the waiting stylus of the film's single most thankless character, a half-naked secretary named Cadmos, who can barely disguise being bored out of his skull.

Ptolemy drones on about everything the film can't dramatise – pontificating about the nature of greatness, Alexander's mixing of the races, and the tragedy of his failure that 'towered over other men's successes'. This white-haired one-man PR team indulges in donnish fudging that would clear out whole lecture halls. 'Only now, when old, do I understand who this force of nature was. Or do I?' The film's bloated waffling matches this old duffer's pedantry – inflates it, even. Stone mainly succeeded in thumping the book shut hard on classical epics, leaving us to cough in a stale cloud of dust.

A SOUND OF THUNDER (2005)

Director: Peter Hyams
Studio: Warner Bros/Franchise Pictures
Budget: $80m (until more than halved)
Worldwide gross: $11.7m

'I don't have time for stupid idiots.'
'Well, why don't you make some time?'

Dr Sonia Rand (Catherine McCormack)
trades zingers with Travis Ryer (Ed Burns)

Ray Bradbury didn't coin the butterfly effect, except maybe – down one prong of a forking timeline – he did. In his 1952 short story 'A Sound of Thunder', a time-travel safari to the late Cretaceous goes awry, when a wealthy big-game hunter named Eckels panics at the approach of a T-Rex and breaks the rules by stepping off his prescribed path. When the expedition hops back to the present day (2055), everything has changed. English words are spelled differently. Colours, even smells, aren't quite the same. And the fascist candidate has just won an American election.*

Eckels, in a sweat, turns over the sole of his boot to find the culprit: a crushed butterfly.

---

* I know what you're thinking. Though Bradbury didn't live to see the rise of Trump, his affiliations switched wildly in that direction. Despite being raised as a staunch Democrat, he became an arch-Republican in later life, describing Bill Clinton as a 'shithead', George W. Bush as 'wonderful', and standing with the proto-Trumpian Tea Party in favour of small government. He was furious when Michael Moore modified the title of *Fahrenheit 451* for his Bush-bashing doc, *Fahrenheit 9/11*.

'It fell to the floor, more delicate and colorful than anything seen in this world. A small thing that could upset balances and cause small changes and then big changes and then huge changes, all down the years across Time.'

The story is taught in schools to introduce determinism in chaos theory, and I'd always assumed it was the origin of 'the butterfly effect'.* In fact, the meteorologist Edward Lorenz is the man credited for popularising that phrase, after a 1972 paper that speculated whether the flap of a butterfly's wings in Brazil might, weeks later, set off a tornado in Texas – an analogy suggested to Lorenz by a colleague, Philip Merilees. Lorenz speculated that Merilees might very well have been influenced by Bradbury's story, but it could just as easily be coincidence: the mark of a great science-fiction writer with a premonition for the perfect image.

The story is ten pages long. It might have lent itself beautifully to treatment on *The Twilight Zone* or *The Outer Limits*. As it happens, in 1989, Bradbury adapted it himself for a 23-minute episode of *The Ray Bradbury Theater* on USA Network, which has delightfully perfunctory, Sylvester-McCoy-as-Doctor-Who production values, but in retelling the tale beat by beat, with a steady pace and eerie score, comes off rather well.

Expanding this yarn, in a post-*Jurassic Park* era, into a feature-length effects blockbuster with an escalating three-act structure – and far steeper ramifications – was more of a challenge. Sadly, in almost every possible way that a film can go wrong, *A Sound of Thunder* managed to do so. There are reasons you may never have heard of this below-the-radar bellyflop, which almost no one I know has seen.

---

* In turn inspiring the trashy 2004 cult thriller of that name, in which Ashton Kutcher got himself in one heck of a tangle trying to fix all the psychological traumas of his childhood.

What the film does to Bradbury's tidy illustration of chaos theory is to embroider it on a grand scale, by going surreally out of control.

———

Plenty of films run out of money, or time, to be finished quite as smoothly as their makers first intended. *A Sound of Thunder* is far more tragic than your average example, because the budget it needed to be any good at all was slashed by about 60 per cent once they'd already shot it.

Time was not the pressing issue. Indeed, during the three years it took to get a release, the director, Peter Hyams, went through hell and back. This respected journeyman, a then 60-year-old SF veteran with a heap of entertaining potboilers on his résumé (*Capricorn One*, *Outland*, *Timecop*), could only try to salvage what he could, while outsourcing the effects shots to what he later called a 'mom-and-pop'[1] operation.

With baboon–lizard hybrids rampaging all over the place, futuristic Chicago at rush hour, a giant water serpent, humongous bats, sabre-toothed eagles, tidal-style 'time waves', shimmering jungle walkways, and an all-important Allosaurus on the safari (which has no business being in the late Cretaceous era, but that's the least of our worries), there was a vast amount of 'insert *xyz*' to achieve in post-production. It needed a pledged $50m that, suddenly, no one could find.

The reasons go way back, to well before *Thunder* was cast or Hyams put in charge. A flamboyant Lebanese producer named Elie Samaha – one of those 'colourful characters' around Los Angeles without whom an awful lot of dubious films would never have been made – was the man with the plan. Once a bouncer at Studio 54, Samaha established himself in Hollywood by running a dry-cleaning chain, then managing the VIP guest list at the Roxbury, a notorious celebrity hangout he co-owned on the Sunset Strip.

This schmoozer extraordinaire set up Franchise Pictures in 1997, an independent production company which 'rescued' star vehicles that had, usually for good reason, foundered elsewhere. He got them made on cheaper budgets than the major studios, tending to use salary deferments, presumably washed down with a lot of free champagne. Samaha scored a minor hit with the Bruce Willis–Matthew Perry mobster comedy *The Whole Nine Yards* (2000), but then put out a string of flops that made everyone look more closely at the company's accounting practices.

Franchise was already being sued by a producing partner, the German media company Intertainment, for inflating the budgets on 17 productions, so that Samaha's company could pocket the surplus funds. This case was dragging on. As *Variety* began its Samaha profile in 2003: 'There are several ways to finance a movie. There are split-rights pacts, equity deals, tax incentives and pre-sales. And then there's Elie Samaha's way, which nobody understands.'[2]

Meanwhile, the films themselves just kept crashing and burning. It was Samaha who picked up the phone to John Travolta and got *Battlefield Earth** off the ground after all the majors had been rejecting it for 15 years. Other bombs assembled by Franchise, all picked up for international distribution in a fluky deal with Warner Bros, included the infamously terrible *Matrix* rip-off *Ballistic: Ecks vs Sever* (2002),[†] the Kevin-Costner-and-Kurt-Russell-both-dressed-as-Elvis heist comedy *3000 Miles to Graceland* (2001) and a pair of duds

---

* See p. 197.

† Starring Antonio Banderas and Lucy Liu as opposing secret agents who throw their limbs around, this was the excruciatingly dull $70m Hollywood debut of Thai action maestro Kaos, whose fondness for slow-motion explosions (most of them inexplicable) even exceeds Renny Harlin's. Regularly turning up in worst-films-of-all-time lists, it's the recipient of a rare 0 per cent score on Rotten Tomatoes.

starring Samaha's close buddy Sylvester Stallone – his duff remake of *Get Carter* (2000), and the racing flick *Driven* (2001), which continued Renny Harlin's tumble from the big leagues.

It was under Harlin that *A Sound of Thunder* was supposed to be gearing up, with Pierce Brosnan attached to star, in a Montreal-based shoot scheduled for 2001. Then things got messy. Brosnan wasn't happy with the script, by *Sahara*'s Joshua Oppenheimer and Thomas Dean Donnelly, and demanded a rewrite, but that summer's threatened strike action in Hollywood would have left the film vulnerable to a shut-down, so it was put on ice.[3]

The film's Canadian producer, Nicolas Claremont, abruptly died in April 2001. A rumoured rift with Bradbury then caused Harlin to leave the project. When Hyams was brought in as a replacement, he had to recast the lead role with Edward Burns – he of *Saving Private Ryan* (1998), and a handful of chatterfests he'd written and directed about the love lives of Irish New Yorkers – after Brosnan, too, walked away.

If this already screams 'troubled production', it's not the half of it. The shoot in the summer of 2002, in the Czech Republic, was interrupted by a natural disaster, when an island in the Vltava had to be evacuated after Prague's worst floods in a century. Practically every makeshift stage in the city was being used for filming, including a Second World War-era sound stage, an ice rink and a swimming pool. The crew had to scramble to high ground, lugging equipment to safety and evacuating their waterlogged hotels. Even the Cretaceous jungle set, one-and-a-half storeys above ground, was very nearly inundated.[4]

Midway through production, one of the film's co-funding entities, the snappily named German company QiX Quality International Effects GmbH & Co. KG Jan Fantl Filmproduktion, financially collapsed. Meanwhile, the FBI started investigating Samaha for possible fraud, in tandem with the Intertainment lawsuit he was already defending.[5] There was nothing coming along to rescue Franchise Pictures – certainly not after *Ballistic* opened in September 2002, to the very opposite of a sound of thunder, and the uniquely unpleasant *FeardotCom** also tanked. A disconcerted Warner Bros, per a *Variety* story that autumn, was pressuring Samaha 'to increase quality control',[6] but everyone was really just waiting for the axe to fall.

Soon, it did. A federal court ruled in June 2004 that Franchise had, indeed, been scamming its investors. A company like Intertainment, which had agreed to part with 47 per cent of the budget on *Battlefield Earth*, had trusted the $73m budget figure Franchise had declared, but bank records revealed that film's true cost to be a mere $44m – meaning Intertainment had actually paid for 77 per cent of it. (There's a good reason, then, that Travolta's dreadlocked war against 'man-animals' does not have the reassuring look of a $73m production, to put it mildly. It's also less of a flop, dollar for dollar, than all the headlines reported.)

Totting up these distortions, the court ordered Franchise to pay back $77m to Intertainment. That was that: despite Samaha's vow to appeal, the company and all its subsidiaries filed Chapter 11 bankruptcy in August 2004.

Unsurprisingly, the post-production fund on *Thunder* had already been shrunk by a ray-gun – assuming, of course, that the pre-announced $80m budget was not just another shameless instance of inflation in the first place. Either way, instead of the high-end tech guys Hyams had expected to use, he and VFX supervisor Tim McGovern were forced to go around the houses cap in hand, subcontracting work from India, Hong Kong, Stuttgart and San Francisco. It took them over two years. In that time, a tie-in isometric

---

* See also p. 177.

shooter for the Game Boy Advance managed to come out in Europe, eighteen months before the film saw the light of day.

The fact that Hyams's picture got completed at all is some kind of miracle. But this B-movie-by-accident doesn't offer many other consolations. It's staggeringly ropey and forlorn, even for something scraped together with chump change.

———

We're in Ed Wood territory with *A Sound of Thunder* – especially armed with knowledge of its daunting production circumstances. That's to say, as an actual viewing experience, it's nowhere near odious so much as endearingly crummy with an eternal whiff of the bargain bin – an F (or Z) for execution that hovers around a C+ for pluck and ambition.

Perhaps the shiny monotony of computer effects in the Marvel era gives such palpably dire visuals a perverse kind of personality. When Burns's Travis Ryer (jaded expedition leader for the Time Safari company) and Catherine McCormack's Dr Sonia Rand (fuming software developer) are crossing a street in conversation, the green-screened backgrounds of slowly zooming commuter vehicles are so pathetically integrated into the frame you can't help but stare at them in awe. If the film achieves some actual semblance of time travel, it's back to the invention of full-motion video games in the early 1990s, such as *The 7th Guest*, the interactive haunted-mansion puzzler released on CD-ROM in 1993.

That was the same year as *Jurassic Park* – a standard-setting VFX Oscar-winner this film stares in the face, quite haplessly, from its very first sequence. The poor Allosaurus they've picked out to hunt, which is due to die any minute from a volcanic eruption, is dismally equipped by cinematic tech support to terrify anyone as an apex predator. *This* thing? It lumbers, looks flat and fake, repeats the same movements (which must have saved some dollar) and at no point looks in any danger of eating anybody.

In fact, such are the monumental ripples about to be caused by human error that it's not the most laughable creature in the movie: that's the final form of McCormack's Sonia when a climactic time wave rips its way into her, and she's hybridised into a quizzical-looking reptile–humanoid thing with catfish whiskers. You hope they used motion capture on it, just for laughs.

In the nick of time – a point emphasised by truly berserk editing, as every hatch in the Time Safari control room seems to blow at once – her last action is transporting Ryer back to the precise moment when it all went wrong, in the hope he can stop the butterfly being squished and save the world from this evolutionary meltdown.

It's the right idea for a climax – but the previous hour of screen time is inept padding, picking off the supporting cast like some desperate mash-up of *The Poseidon Adventure* and *The Last of Us*. David Oyelowo gets a very bizarre send-off at the mercy of the baboon lizards. Now there's a sentence I never thought I'd write. ('That was not a good movie,'[7] he has confessed.)

The other problem with the disaster-flick conceits of the middle act: we've forgotten entirely about Ben Kingsley. He's dismayingly underused as Charles Hatton, the glad-handing CEO of the corporation, who doesn't mind endangering the entire timeline of human civilisation if there are a few more silk-lined pockets to plunder.

He also sports a bouffant white wig and matching soul patch that look delightfully absurd, and match the film's daft personality. The thing is, you can throw almost any amount of cod-zingy dialogue at Kingsley and he'll spin it, lob it back, make it fly. Even this, to the rebellious Ryer: 'You work here so you can study your silly animals who don't exist any more.' What you probably can't do is drag Kingsley along for the logistically hellish brunt of a shoot in waterlogged Prague, so his appearance amounts to a smirking cameo in only one set at the beginning and end.

Pitted against the other recent test cases we've looked at, this comes closest to a *Pluto Nash* situation, in its slow-drip demolition of a director's morale. Lately, the reins of genre film-making in the Hyams family have been handed down to Peter's son John, who took over the *Universal Soldier* franchise with the brutal sequels *Regeneration* (2009) and *Day of Reckoning* (2012), the latter of which especially has accrued quite an intense cult following. Peter, having long tackled the cinematography on his own films, helped out with that role for his son's features, after all but giving up, sadly, on a directing career that spanned four decades and 20 movies.*

The experience of watching his father go through *A Sound of Thunder* turned Hyams *fils* off post-production effects for good – as it might have done anyone. 'I have to believe it was one of the hardest experiences of his career,' he said in 2012. 'It's got to be a real sinking feeling going into something shooting all of it against green screen, with all this trust that you're relying on this whole technology that ultimately you're not going to be able to afford, and you have to do it anyway. I took the lessons learned on that very seriously.'[8]

Down one fork in the *Sound of Thunder* timeline, this conceptually wild film drummed up the big-studio backing given to Roland Emmerich's next-ice-age disaster movie *The Day After Tomorrow* (2004) – which had $125m to work with – and was cooking with gas, stretching to several more drafts of its blatantly shonky script,

---

* He did make the Michael Douglas legal thriller *Beyond a Reasonable Doubt* (2009) and a cheapo Van Damme vehicle called *Enemies Closer* (2013), but the studio budgets of *Timecop* (1994) and *Sudden Death* (1995) were no longer within reach – or the enthusiasm was gone.

a more charismatic lead actor, and an effects budget that didn't dematerialise as it went along. In reality, every corner that was cut simply painted it into another. It's heroic that anyone persevered at all, even if it was just Peter Hyams jamming broken keys in some edit suite at the end of the world, while everybody else had long since thrown in the towel.

SPEED RACER (2008)

Director: The Wachowskis
Studio: Warner Bros/Village Roadshow
Budget: $120m
US gross: $43.9m

It was so different no one wanted to see it.

unnamed WB executive

We built a wall between the audience and the screen
and they ran into the wall at every scene.

Joel Silver

Speed Racer has many more fans these days – enraptured ones – than it did when Warner Bros brought it to market, only to watch it crushed by the gauntlets of *Iron Man* in the early summer of 2008.* This was a seminal moment for what blockbusters were going to look like for the next decade and beyond.

Though it became the springboard for Marvel's imminent world domination, *Iron Man* was by no means a sure-fire hit before it came out. Marvel, having declared bankruptcy in 1996, secured a $525m loan from Merrill Lynch in 2005, putting up the rights to the company's ten most famous characters as collateral, and gambling on major strides into film production. But *Iron Man* – not even one of those ten – was a funny choice to bet the house on.

---

* Crushed is the word: *Iron Man* had opened the week before to a fairly astounding $98.6m in the US alone, then topped its second weekend with $51.2m, while *Speed Racer* crawled in third with a tortoise-like $18.6m.

Some 30 screenwriters are said to have refused the gig because they thought the character too obscure. Jon Favreau's film also had to rehabilitate a faded star, Robert Downey Jr, whose career had been stalled by addiction and multiple arrests. Downey would later admit he was prepared for the worst: 'That thing was basically ready to be written off if it tanked,'[1] he said in 2022. Favreau confirms they were on shaky ground. 'I was constantly being reminded that if we screwed up and we couldn't pay back the loan, the bank was going to take all of the catalogue.'[2]

On paper, the Wachowskis must have been the favourites to win this fight, with a whizzy, family-friendly jamboree based on a cult anime series from the 1960s. Plucked as their follow-up to the *Matrix* trilogy (1999–2003), it was the next opportunity for them to push forward digital frontiers, while reaching out, as their producer Joel Silver was counting on, to a broader demographic in the process.

Speed Racer had been Silver's pet project since Warner Bros bought the option off Tatsunoko, the Tokyo-based anime pioneers, in the early 1990s. Various iterations of it came and went. There was a moment in 1994 when Johnny Depp was eyed up for the lead, with Henry Rollins as the masked, mysterious Racer X, a role Keanu Reeves was later offered by the Wachowskis but turned down. A couple of months before Depp's version was due to shoot in late 1995, he abruptly bailed, along with no less an *enfant terrible* than British director Julien Temple (*Absolute Beginners*). What a very different film *that* might have been. Vince Vaughn tried to revive it in 2004 – another false start, but enough to get the engine growling for the Wachowskis to hop in.

The duo had already given their own superhero – Neo – a messianic send-off, in the process doing a lot to amplify what 'state of the art' could mean in the blockbuster space, with the help of Oscar-winning VFX designer John Gaeta, the deviser of Bullet Time. *Matrix*ed-out, they were looking for another rollercoaster, and their visual experimentation was about to go into overdrive.

'We wanted to be expressive and fun and let our hair down a little,'[3] said Gaeta at the time, while Lana Wachowski went further: 'OK, we're going to assault every single modern aesthetic',[4] aiming to sculpt sequences 'like run-on sentences', which would abandon linear narrative, and citing James Joyce and Picasso, cubism and Lichtenstein as their models.

The technology was ready for their *Ulysses*-meets-*Guernica* washed down with soda pop, even if audiences were not, quite. A brave new world was dawning with the concept of the 'digital backlot' – essentially a warehouse-based production approach using wall-to-wall green screen and very few practical sets. Heavily utilised by George Lucas on his *Star Wars* prequels, this wraparound shooting style was James Cameron's big gamble on *Avatar* (2009), which started filming just before *Speed Racer*, in April 2007.

Sin City (2005)[5] and *300* (2007),[6] both grisly adaptations of Frank Miller comics, had proved the viability of digital backlots to make something broodingly stylised that could work at the multiplexes. But those were R-rated genre exercises, miles away from the goofy tone *Speed Racer* would aim for. A more ominous precedent was the commercial fate of *Sky Captain and the World of Tomorrow* (2004),[7] a vacant, PG slice of gee-whiz derring-do that proved a painfully hard sell, no matter how loudly the innovation of its making was trumpeted.

Speed Racer is nothing if not hyper-aware of the aesthetic boundaries it's playing with, not to mention the lineage in which it sits. Winks and sight gags abound towards the history of illustration and movie art. The WB logo blinks into view through a primary-coloured kaleidoscope that sets us up for a trip while recalling Looney Tunes. Zoetrope zebras flashing past at the Grand Prix will later tip the nod to the photography pioneer Eadweard Muybridge. Meanwhile, the film's J. J. Abrams-esque obsession with artificial lens flare makes every moment on the track feel mediated and on camera, even when we're watching a shot that's 100 per cent computer-rendered.

The first scene of young Speed (Nicholas Elia) in the classroom, fizzing with restlessness at the end of a test, is dazzlingly meta. In the corner of his schoolbook, he has pencilled a kineograph flicker-drawing of two cars colliding, and then his surroundings blur in a dolly-zoom shot, elongating all the colours into a stripy, one-point-perspective light show. The wacky theme tune bounds in, and we're off to the races in this kid's head. On his fantasy circuit, everything bar him and the vectors is a crudely hand-drawn prototype, from rival cars to the lumpy spectators, and 'Go Speed! Yay!' banners flutter at the finish line.

The film boldly weds the very idea of animation to the thrill of the race – equating them as feats of imaginative daring – and also letting the live action, CG and more traditionally animated elements tumble all over each other. (There are few films that deploy CGI less photorealistically.) In rhythmic terms, that classroom daydream sets us up for a signature move throughout, which is plunging us into the thick of the action at full pelt. The Wachowskis and their editors make the pretty bravura choice never once to show us the actual beginning of a race: they constantly cut to the chase.

Two hours later, the logical climax of this hyperactive assault is a dizzying abstract supernova that makes it hard to say who's just crashed into whom or what we're even looking at – the visuals simply explode. Speed (Emile Hirsch), whose surname is literally Racer, triumphs – and transcends – when the film's form achieves total, white-heat synthesis. His family (John Goodman as Pop, Susan Sarandon as Mom) whoop and holler in the spectator stands. In a dream world, we'd all be joining in, and the film would have been a word-of-mouth wow, and some kind of phenomenon.

Plainly, it wasn't just the marketing. *Speed Racer* didn't appeal to everyone, and there are built-in reasons. It still isn't fully my cup of tea: I like it in spurts but find there's a disjunct between the film we got and the one its giddiest enthusiasts tend to describe.

One problem – even if it was very much a conscious choice – is the prevailing flatness. Foregrounds and backgrounds crowd each composition on a single plane (save for the deep recesses of that dolly zoom). If the images could rightly be accused of being constantly up in your grill, it's because they have nowhere further back to retreat to. It's typical of the Wachowskis' rebellious streak that the 3D boom *Avatar* was about to initiate was preceded by this, perhaps the most belligerently 2D film of the modern era.

'Headachey' was a refrain in reviews, which were generally bad* and didn't all miss the point. Lacking depth on purpose for 135 minutes is bound to have its irritations: gorging on pop-art eye candy for that long is a down-the-line guarantee of a sugar crash.

With a couple of exceptions, the people on screen get flattened, and the actors are complicit. This is hardly a unique failing – it remains a serious problem of digital backlot film-making. Plonk yourself for 60 days in a giant, entirely green warehouse interior somewhere in Potsdam, strapped into a mocked-up car on a rig, being directed through monitors by technicians with a hundred other things to worry about, and no other actors nearby. The entire situation is not what you'd call a vibe. Is it any wonder that Natalie Portman's Princess Amidala seemed catatonic, or that none of the Spartans in *300* evinced much personality beyond the odd scowl?

I may be shot down for saying this, but human beings don't tend to be the Wachowskis' forte. We could make a counter-argument for

---

* 42 per cent on Rotten Tomatoes, buoyed by love from Wachowski loyalists in the blogosphere.

Bound (1996), their addictively pulpy chamber-movie debut, and parts of their next big flop, the sincere if strained *Cloud Atlas* (2012). But I'm not making one for any moment of *The Matrix*, which is driven by concepts and populated by cipherish avatars. *Speed Racer* at least knows John Goodman can handle fatherly advice and be gruffly touching, but you could try hunting all day for chemistry between Hirsch's Speed and his girlfriend Trixie (Christina Ricci at her most wide-eyed).

The standout character by a distance is Roger Allam's Arnold Royalton, smarmy CEO of the profit-hungry conglomerate hoping to ensnare Speed as an asset. Landing in front of the Racers' home in a helicopter that drowns out his greetings, he has the first dialogue in the film – inaudible as it is – that you actually *want* to hear. With his mauve cravat and hammy praise of pancakes in German, he's an irresistibly slimy patrician snob, with Allam seemingly channelling Christopher Hitchens up to the moment when Speed turns him down. The mask slips to reveal the rage below, and it's as if we're suddenly dealing with Peter Hitchens instead.

Speed Racer hangs on Royalton's every word, even when he walks us through how race fixing has allowed him to game the stock market, and then sues the Racer family for intellectual property infringement: subplots that can't have meant a great deal to tweens, unless they were Richie Rich types. He's capitalism incarnate, yet the film can't get enough of him, which foregrounds the weird paradox we're being sold in general. The Wachowskis are pitting corporate greed against the purity of following your dreams . . . in motor racing. And within the context of a wannabe franchise-starter released by one of the biggest multinational media conglomerates on Earth.

Just as Royalton (perfect name) is pushing his contract on Speed, younger brother Spritle Racer (Paulie Litt, a ringer for Sandi Toksvig) and his pet chimp Chim Chim go on a joyride through the factory and inhale a whole load of candy, in what amounts to a panicky admission of the film's split loyalties – quick, here's a manic bit to keep the kids on board, in case we're losing them in all the discourse about 'the unassailable might of money'.

Warners' marketing team had much the same impossible feat of juggling to attempt. The campaign cost $80m – the biggest in the studio's history at the time – and involved promotional support from McDonald's, Mattel, Target and Lego. They launched lines of toys and shoes, which actually flew off the shelves, but converting this enthusiasm into ticket sales was another matter.

This was no billion-and-a-half-grossing *Barbie* (2023), with its next-level market penetration, which became WB's biggest hit of all time, toppling even *Harry Potter*. Executives and press alike were especially shocked, according to a *Variety* report by Anne Thompson, at how young *Speed Racer* was actually skewing when they started screening it.[8]

Neither the Wachowskis nor Silver, who'd started to lose his touch commercially, seemed to know what they were doing in the arena of wholesome family entertainment, with all the merchandising that came along. (They might as well have had Arnold Royalton trying to strike all the deals.) The film's riskily bizarre form meant you couldn't really expect to sell it like a Pixar movie, but Warners tried anyway.

That strategy pushed the all-important *Matrix* demographic away, but the Wachowskis, who've never shown much discipline with their running times, were too convinced they'd made transcendent pop art to listen to the pleas of Warner chiefs Alan Horn and Jeff Robinov to get it down to a sensible duration. It would stay as 135 minutes, a film for everyone and no one, about remaining true to yourself no matter who was picking up the tab.

Perhaps they should have made a *Mario Kart* film instead. The Wii version of Nintendo's racing game was released exactly a month before *Speed Racer*, and became a global smash hit, the second highest-selling title ever in that franchise. It's a certainty that significant sections of the Wachowskis' target audience had no intention of leaving the sofa on opening weekend. Why watch Emile Hirsch try to outrace the ghost of his dead brother, with frankly indecipherable skills, when you could wrest a Wii controller off a sibling and do your own driving?

Speed Racer tried too hard in some areas, neglecting others, and left its viewers behind – doing stuff they simply preferred, one might add. It marked a rude dethroning of the Wachowskis as champs of the multiplex – a pattern that would continue with the successive failures of *Cloud Atlas*,[9] then *Jupiter Ascending* (2015)[10] and perhaps most brutally, *The Matrix Resurrections* (2021),[11] which couldn't only blame Covid for a wildly unprofitable release.*

In a rerun of what happened to the Wachowskis in *Speed Racer's* tussle with *Iron Man*, the sisters' attempt to defibrillate Neo was defeated right at the starting gate by the second weekend of *Spider-Man: No Way Home*[12] – the one that brought back all the previous Spider-Men for a gang's-all-here reunion. Officially, we had reached the dispiriting point where *nostalgia* for Marvel's product was a new way to reinvigorate it.

Headlines hailed this as cinema's salvation after the depredations of the pandemic. It saved *some* cinema. The Wachowskis could only look on from the sidelines – having already watched *Spider-Man: Into the Spider-Verse* (2018) come along and do zippy, abstract, pop-arty things with 3D animation that audiences and critics, on

---

* Its failure mired Village Roadshow in ultimately vain legal action against Warner Bros after the end of their four-decade co-production arrangement, with Roadshow alleging that WB had sabotaged the film's box office with a simultaneous streaming debut on HBO Max. WB convinced a judge to force arbitration of the dispute, and Village Roadshow withdrew their injunction.

that occasion, really went for. You can argue, as many do, that *Speed Racer* was ahead of its time, while also maintaining that it was the wrong film at the wrong time, and guilty of some major unforced errors. Perhaps it was just so busy hurtling past the competition that it disappeared into hyperspace.

SYNECDOCHE, NEW YORK (2008)

Director: Charlie Kaufman
Studio: Sony Pictures Classics/Sidney Kimmel Entertainment
Budget: $20m
Worldwide gross: $4.5m

Charlie Kaufman has never minced words about how *Synecdoche, New York* – the nonpareil achievement of his film career – came pretty close to ending it. Speaking in 2016 about why he found it impossible to get anything made after this, his monumental debut as a director, he simply replied, 'Because it lost a fortune. In a nutshell. And because it happened in 2008 when the economy tanked, and the movie business changed, completely, instantly, into superhero . . . garbage.'[1]

Pitching, funding and releasing stuff that wasn't made with the core aim of turning a profit: these were already uphill battles at the major studios, but they became assaults on Everest after the financial collapse. The days of, say, Sony wanting to jump into bed with Kaufman, the Oscar-winning screenwriter of *Being John Malkovich* (1999), *Adaptation* (2002) and *Eternal Sunshine of the Spotless Mind* (2004), were abruptly bygone. All the vital refuges for ruminative mid-budget film-making that had allowed such projects to be nurtured were swept away by this industrial sea change, leaving Kaufman bobbing without a raft.

The idea that an artist of this man's rebellious independence might take a call from Marvel to bat around concepts for (say) *Doctor Strange* was obviously laughable, not least to the man himself. (His fictitious twin Donald from *Adaptation*, a crass slave to all that sells, would have upended the sofa in his haste to answer, of course.) Kaufman turned, unsuccessfully, to TV, trying to tempt HBO with a fascinating idea for a show, in which his favourite actress, Catherine Keener, would have played a woman living the same day of her life in each episode, but with differences – some minor, some enormous – to the route her existence had taken. (Charlie Kaufman's *A Sound of Thunder*? Would watch.)

HBO passed. Then what? Kaufman got as far as filming a pilot for FX for an unaired series called *How & Why* (2014), which would have starred John Hawkes as the host of an educational kids' TV show, and Michael Cera as his new boss. Again, the response was: thanks but no thanks. To get his next film, the stop-motion fable *Anomalisa* (2015),* off the ground without submitting to all manner of grim studio compromises, Kaufman resorted to crowd-funding it through Kickstarter. That was only the beginning. 'While we were making the movie,' he explained on *Anomalisa*'s release, 'we didn't even know if we were going to finish it because the money situation was really dire.'[2]

These were hardly Wachowski budgets he was begging for. Even *Synecdoche, New York* itself – adjusting for inflation – is the cheapest flop in this book. Among 2008's rival attractions, it cost an eighth of David Fincher's *The Curious Case of Benjamin Button* – a film that inverts mortality like a party trick, to no valuable end – or less than a tenth of *The Chronicles of Narnia: Prince Caspian* (remember that, even slightly?) Because it stands to reason that you don't make something called *Synecdoche, New York*, or something *like* it, if the main agenda is ringing tills, those of us bowled over by Kaufman's taxing, one-of-a-kind magnum opus always have the option of simply not caring that it lost money.

---

* Co-directed with Duke Johnson, and featuring the voices of David Thewlis, Jennifer Jason Leigh and Kaufman favourite Tom Noonan.

Kaufman himself, though, could do no such thing. This is per-haps what makes him more like Caden Cotard (Philip Seymour Hoffman), his endlessly thwarted, increasingly decrepit protagonist, than he even knew at the time of its making.

Sketching this film for the uninitiated is no easy task, but here goes: Caden, a despondent playwright living in the New York suburb of Schenectady, is the unexpected recipient of a MacArthur 'genius' grant, which gives him the money to make something 'big and true and tough', which will also be all-encompassing: he'll mount a *Truman Show*-esque simulacrum of his whole life in a vast, disused Manhattan warehouse.

He's routinely doubtful, however, of his instincts as a theatre-maker, having just finished a regional production of Arthur Miller's *Death of a Salesman*, which he has cast young, with the instruction that the flailing actors exude a sense of their own mortality. The glimpses we get of this piece, without making it look exaggeratedly poor, give us an ample window on Caden's creative limitations. It goes without saying that he's a stand-in for Kaufman, whose main characters have always been painful introverts drowning in neuroses, suspicious of their own talents, and left to the mercy of a thousand physical and psychological frailties.

Meanwhile, Caden's constantly preoccupied wife, the perfectly named Adele Lack (Keener), specialises in exquisite portraits the size of postage stamps. She uses these as an excuse for missing his opening night, but when Caden comes home to their ramshackle digs, he finds Adele half stoned on the sofa with a lesbian pal played by Jennifer Jason Leigh.

Airily uneffusive about his art in general, this pair will soon emigrate to Berlin together in some ever-evolving polyamorous set-up, taking with them Caden's four-year-old daughter, Olive. Life, henceforth, rapidly slips away from Caden, who finds out in a magazine* that his wife has made it at last, and that his daughter, who's suddenly ten, has become the world's first child with a full-body tattoo. 'She's four!' he helplessly cries.

Caden has plenty of reasons to feel like a hack whose work no one gets, but it's hardly more reassuring when his *Salesman* actress and next wife, the (again) well-named Claire Keen (Michelle Williams), responds with knee-jerk gushing ('It's brilliant!') when he's trying to express complex thoughts about human attitudes to death. Plagued by pustules, dental trauma and an inability to salivate or cry, he's convinced, day to day, that he's dying, and it's not much consolation that we all are.

For his own artistic self-worth, Caden needs *someone* to understand profoundly what he's trying to put out there, but no one does. Most of these cash-strapped theatre types are just pathetically grateful for the work. 'When are we going to get an audience in here?' asks an actor called Tom (Daniel London) one day. 'It's been seventeen years?' Over the decades they devote to the project, a few colleagues *start* to get it, especially those played by Samantha Morton, Tom Noonan and Dianne Wiest. But Caden is forever changing his mind about how to go about it, and what purpose it all serves beyond a reason to get out of bed.

Synecdoche, New York was hatched as a horror film. It still is, vestigially, and certainly was for its financiers. After *Adaptation*, it was bandied around as such between Kaufman and Spike Jonze, when

---

* Only by hitting pause on this shot might you have time to absorb the hilariously brutal subhead: 'Six months ago, Adele Lack was an under-appreciated housewife in Eastern New York. Stuck in a dead-end marriage to a slovenly ugly-face loser, Adele Lack had big dreams for her and her then four-year-old daughter, Olive. That's when her paintings got small.'

Amy Pascal,* then head of Sony's film division, was curious to know how they'd approach a genre piece together – not about supernatural entities, but the everyday horrors of the real world.

Kaufman tried, but fitting a concept into that box just felt foreign to him. (His closest move in that direction came in 2020 with *i'm thinking of ending things* for Netflix, which, being derived from a novel, was an easier idea to pitch than his own stuff. Even that, adapted with wild liberty from Iain Reid's psychological thriller, was no one's idea of normal.) Jonze pivoted to make *Where the Wild Things Are* (2009), which left Kaufman with the option of directing his script or abandoning it.

Because Caden's project, which ends up consuming the rest of his life, is such a white elephant, and the ensemble cast for it is so enormous, Kaufman couldn't really get the film made for anything less than $18–20m. That's not much by Hollywood standards, and you feel it: you feel the grandiosity of the ideas chafing all the time against a ceiling of make-do-and-mend production values.

The subplot that has his friend/soulmate Hazel (Morton) renting a property that's permanently ablaze ('I'm concerned about the fire?' she confides to the estate agent) is almost a synecdoche in itself for the precarious process of getting the film made. When Caden contemplates sacking a minor cast member ('We have enormous budgetary concerns here!'), it's on one level a cosmic joke, because the cost of his boondoggle must easily have totted up to the GDPs of multiple countries by this point. But you can also read it as

* The powerful executive was made Sony's co-chair in 2006, having already made a huge success of the *Spider-Man* franchise. She then gave a home to such adult hits as *The Social Network* (2010), *Zero Dark Thirty* (2012) and *American Hustle* (2013). She resigned in 2015 after a cyberattack, thought to have emanated from North Korea, hacked Sony's servers, causing a huge scandal by leaking a slew of her personal emails.

an anxiously meta line about Kaufman himself trying to make the money stretch.

The company that footed the bill for *Synecdoche* (which Sony wound up only distributing, in the end) was Sidney Kimmel Entertainment, founded in 2004 by the financier of the same name, a philanthropist who'd already donated hundreds of millions to cancer charities and Jewish foundations. 'I wanted to make quality films,'[3] he told *Forbes* in 2010.

These included the likes of Bart Freundlich's New York romcom *Trust the Man* (2005),* Kasi Lemmons' period radio drama *Talk to Me* (2007)[†] and Ira Sachs's Sirkian four-hander *Married Life* (2007).[‡] None took off. What chance did *Synecdoche* have? Affording that budget was philanthropy by another name, even if it had practical consequences, emptying the company's coffers and making them inch forward into the next decade with far more commercial trepidation. 'It was the final straw for Kimmel,' Kaufman recalled in 2016.

The shoot, entailing 45 days inside an old armoury in New York's Bed-Stuy neighbourhood, thrust Kaufman's actors through the nightmarish ordeal of a summer heatwave inside fat suits, under thick ageing make-up, on top of the heavy emotional lifting they were already doing. 'It was very hard,' per Kaufman. 'It was very hot. There were times when the prosthetics guy had to come in and poke pin holes in Phil's costume because it was bubbling, because the sweat had nowhere to go. It was awful. Samantha [Morton] also had to contend with it.'[4]

---

* A fairly paltry business starring Freundlich's wife, Julianne Moore, alongside David Duchovny, Maggie Gyllenhaal and Billy Crudup.

† With Don Cheadle as Washington DJ Ralph 'Petey' Greene, Chiwetel Ejiofor and Taraji P. Henson.

‡ With Pierce Brosnan, Patricia Clarkson, Chris Cooper and Rachel McAdams.

There was also a near-disaster with a lift getting stuck, a harrowing enough thought without even considering the hellish functions lifts serve in Kaufman's scripts.* This phobia originates in a recurring anxiety dream he's had for decades, which he described once on NPR: 'The elevator is always old, and it's always ascending. And as it ascends, there's a sense that it's kind of not very well hanging, and that it's moving from side to side, and then it's going to fall. And it's rickety, and it's squeaking, and it's shaky, and it's claustrophobic.'[5]

In perhaps the most Charlie Kaufman-esque turn of events ever on a film set, then, he and 'like 10 crew people', mostly massive guys, found themselves stuffed into one lift at the end of a very long day. 'It got stuck between floors in the middle of the night in a building where nobody was. I thought it was going to plummet, and I think every-body else did, too. You couldn't breathe,'[6] he remembered. Somebody managed to prise open the doors and, one by one, they had to pluck up the courage to crawl out and jump half a floor down, in constant fear that the lift might spring back to life and decapitate someone.

Had Kaufman survived all this to reap the universal acclaim and cultural impact in which *Eternal Sunshine*† had already basked, it would have been one thing. But *Synecdoche* received nothing like unanimous praise. Many reviewers dithered about its merits or doubted them; some thought Kaufman had disappeared up his own self-admiring fundament; and even those besotted with the film led off, humbly enough, with Kaufman-esque professions of their own intellectual inadequacy in getting to grips with it.‡ Even the raves,

---

* There's that one you have to crowbar open to reach the 7½th floor in *Being John Malkovich*, and another that's the site of Nicolas Cage's first, mortifying encounter with Meryl Streep in *Adaptation*.

† Identically budgeted at $20m, that one managed to make $74m worldwide.

‡ For instance, Manohla Dargis, in her awestruck *New York Times* review.

in other words, were unintentional turn-offs. It failed to get a single Oscar nomination.*

Synecdoche's life in the cinemas would be much like Caden's – truncated and sad, and then over, because most people simply didn't fancy it. It never widened to more than 119 screens in the USA – compare 672 for *Adaptation*, which pulled off an equivalent slow roll-out – and dribbled its way to just over $3m domestically through the bleak midwinter of 2008. Since few foreign distributors thought it was a risk worth taking, the international grosses were less than half that. The UK premiere at that year's London Film Festival was met with boos and walkouts.

The film has gained many more fans in the streaming age, among them the comedian Jamie (*Stath Lets Flats*) Demetriou, who has talked about being totally obsessed with it. It exists to be rediscovered, argued about on Reddit threads, and periodically shown, one would hope, in 35mm screenings that will pack out cinemas far more comprehensively than they did in 2008.

There's no hiding that it's hard work – a fact practically broadcast in flashing neon lights with that title, even likelier to scare off casual ticket-buyers than *The Hudsucker Proxy* (or *Gigli*). Boy, though, does it repay the investment. It's unreal how much it packs into two hours; what loopy pathways it follows into Caden's senescence. His last scene with the ailing Olive (a German-accented Robin Weigert), whose flower tattoos have become lethally infected, is so bitter and woebegone you feel as if you've been flayed.

The section that has a jobbing actress called Millicent Weems (an astonishing Wiest) tackling the chores of a cleaning lady called Ellen Bascomb in Adele's mocked-up apartment, only for Caden suddenly

---

* *Being John Malkovich* got three, *Adaptation* four, and *Eternal Sunshine* two, winning for Kaufman's script.

to swap identities with her, has an ineffable yet strangely consoling logic. The last 15 minutes are quite extraordinary: Caden takes Millicent's direction through an earpiece while wandering through an apocalyptic wasteland strewn with the corpses of co-workers, and Jon Brion's generally amazing score sings him to his rest. I stumbled out of it sobbing on a first watch and could barely compose myself for hours.

You certainly won't find here the kind of structure Kaufman parodied in *Adaptation* – the one lifted from the precepts of screenwriting guru Robert McKee, with 'characters overcoming obstacles to *succeed* in the *end*' (those italics are for the contemptuous inflections of an all-time-classic Nicolas Cage line reading). Kaufman is 100 per cent committed in this thing to having everyone end and no one succeed. To throw 'self-admiring' at this gamble is exactly wrong: it's riven through with doubt, experiment, being powerfully unsure of itself. It's vulnerable art. That's its greatness.

Even the film's cheapjack stylings (comparatively) work to its advantage. Had it been slick, clever, more polished, could it possibly have *said* more? 'Being clever gets in the way of being raw,'[7] as Kaufman has declared. Would those qualities not have fumigated it, banishing the musty whiff of struggle and decay that comes off it so potently?

The photography, by Frederick Elmes (*Blue Velvet*), manages a mildewy, sickly feel that isn't far off the hues of Roy Andersson, the great Swedish director whose bleakly hilarious films observe our species in all its ridiculous dismay. Far from being something for actors to hide behind, and despite the indignities of working under them, the prosthetics become paradoxically exposing, too. Hoffman's stamina in this, his greatest part, is matched only by his supreme dedication to exploring it truthfully.

While the Writers Guild of America geared up in March 2023 for industrial action, Kaufman accepted the Laurel Award from them and gave a speech about resisting the power of box office numbers, as well as the studio executives employed to ringfence their importance. 'Our work is to reflect the world,' he protested, 'saying what is true in the face of so much lying.'

These are strong words, but he's absolutely right that films lie, and the ones that make the most money tend to lie the most: they fob us off with comforting fibs, unearned happy endings, Iron Man saving the day. They're the same bromides we've been sold a thousand times over. If you look at *Synecdoche, New York* in this light, of *course* it flopped. To comprehend failure this astutely, Kaufman had to follow it all the way down the plughole.

PAN (2015)

Director: Joe Wright
Studio: Warner Bros
Budget: $150m ($275m with marketing)
US gross: $35m

Warner Bros were going through a particularly rough patch in 2015, but it was about to get worse. The studio had waved goodbye to *Harry Potter* in 2011, with the eighth and final film in the original series, and still had a year to wait before launching the *Fantastic Beasts* spin-offs, with their hefty effects budgets and exponentially dwindling returns.* They'd also reached the end of the road with Middle-earth. Peter Jackson's *The Hobbit: The Battle of the Five Armies* (2014) had nearly cracked $1bn worldwide, even if it was basically a paragraph on steroids, with almost zero lingering impact in the culture.

All the other studios had whopping cash-cow franchises in rude health, from Disney's inescapable Marvel Cinematic Universe and about-to-return *Star Wars*, to Universal's *Jurassic World* and *Fast & Furious*, to Fox's *Planet of the Apes* and whatever more mileage they could scrape out of *X-Men*.

Warner Bros would keep clinging to DC Comics for dear life, but the post-Nolan era inaugurated by the successful-ish *Man of Steel*

---

* The first one (2016) placed 8th at that year's international box office, with $814m worldwide. The second (2018) slipped to 10th with $655m, and the third (2022) sagged down at 12th with $407m – these days, for any $200m production, that won't cut it. Original plans to make a fourth and fifth film have been scrapped indefinitely.

(2013) was about to go through years of teething pains. The summer of 2015 saw the studio trying to hatch a couple of fresh franchises of their own, with the Wachowskis' *Jupiter Ascending** and Guy Ritchie's *The Man from U.N.C.L.E.*,[1] but these splatted on impact.

It was during this rut that they decided to do something about *Peter Pan* – a piece of intellectual property that looked, on the face of it, ripe for *Harry Potter*-ising, with no tedious cut for the long-dead author. Though royalties for any direct adaptation have to be paid to Great Ormond Street Hospital, which owns the rights in perpetuity, this rather unique legal provision also carries a loophole, which is that sequels, prequels and spin-offs are exempted from paying the charity a penny. So Warners kept a tight fist, developing a *Pan* origin story instead.

We might long for the day when the very phrase 'origin story' is banned from pitch meetings, but the *Cruella*s and *Wonka*s that keep materialising suggest that fantasy is a way off. After the likes of *Batman Begins* (2005), *Oz: The Great and Powerful* (2013), and *Maleficent* (2014), the formula had become an absolute menace around this time. So why not tell Peter Pan's story from the top, then? And whatever we're not quite sure about, just make up?

No one had mounted a full-scale visit to Neverland since P. J. Hogan's underrated *Peter Pan* (2003),† which capsized at the box office, perhaps chiefly because it was so low on star power. *Pan* aimed, then, to be the first awfully *big* adventure since Spielberg's *Hook* (1991),‡ a film with a generational nostalgic pull that's been

---

* See p. 258 and note.
† See p. 209 and footnote.
‡ It snatched $300.9m from a $70m budget, but came in only sixth at that year's international box office, which would have been viewed as a mild disappointment for TriStar.

quite durable, even if Spielberg has often expressed a personal dislike for it, born of under-confidence.

Hook was conceived as a musical. 'I chickened out after the first week of shooting and took all the songs out,' Spielberg told the *Guardian* in 2021. 'It was the biggest paradigm shift I've ever had while directing a movie. It just didn't seem right.'[2] While he knew what he was doing with the film's outer sections, he never got comfortable with the body of it set in Neverland. As he told *Empire* in 2018, 'I tried to paint over my insecurity with production value. The more insecure I felt about it, the bigger and more colourful the sets became.'[3]

This lesson, as Joe Wright would learn on *Pan*, applies just as much in the digital era. The Englishman's film career, five pictures deep at this point, had majored in tried-and-tested literary adaptations (*Pride & Prejudice* in 2005, *Atonement* in 2007 and *Anna Karenina* in 2012). But the Wright intending to make *Pan* fly was really the mischievous innovator of the action romp *Hanna* (2011), starring Saoirse Ronan as a fifteen-year-old assassin. He'd been suggested by Ronan to *Hanna*'s producers after Danny Boyle and Alfonso Cuarón dropped out.

If the sheer glow of *Pride & Prejudice* makes it easily the pick of Wright's other films, *Hanna* is the exciting wild card that showed an antsy pop sensibility itching to get out. It blends a Lynchian, dark-fairytale aesthetic with *A Clockwork Orange* (1971), while Wright's choice of The Chemical Brothers to supply the pulsating soundtrack showed that the UK rave scene, where he'd learned his craft, was still very much in his bloodstream.*

* Wright started out as a roadie for a 1990s outfit called Vegetable Vision, who produced visuals for The Chemical Brothers, Underworld and others. 'I was definitely off my head on ecstasy for a few years,' he told the *Observer* in 2008.

The problem he faced was how to channel all this energy coherently into a film for kids, appropriate for his own sons to watch. 'It was a really interesting and super-expensive experiment,' he rued in 2018. 'I [wanted] to convey the anarchy of a child's imagination and so to make something totally and completely inconsistent.'[4] Wright's fondness for flashy, rather baroque editing might sporadically come to his rescue in *Pan*'s action scenes, but inconsistency was his self-inflicted downfall. He got hopelessly lost in trying to strike a gritty tone with the story – especially since it's not the story we all know, but a mélange of fill-in-the-gaps conceits.

The film's cod-Dickensian opening, with its *Oliver Twist* gruel, is remorselessly grimy: not for a good half-hour does any daylight dispel the studio-set gloom. It's set inside an orphanage in pre-war London, as if paving the way for Wright's *Darkest Hour* (2017) – which he'd foreshadowed already, with the look-at-me tracking shot around Dunkirk in *Atonement*. We learn that Peter (Levi Miller, the twelve-year-old Australian cast after an extensive talent search) was dumped on the doorstep of this low-fun establishment as a baby. He grows up battling a Trunchbull-esque foe in the shape of Mother Barnabas (Kathy Burke), whose mad glowering makes you wonder how much more OTT Burke could possibly have gone.

Once Peter's been whisked up from his dorm bed by a flying pirate ship, there are plenty more outsize theatrics to come from Hugh Jackman's baddie, a shouty, moustache-twirling buccaneer despot who is somehow *not* Captain Hook, a fact that would need to be explained to death by the marketing, still leaving everyone deeply confused.

Instead, he's Blackbeard, the real-life pirate, *né* Edward Teach, who rampaged around the West Indies in the early eighteenth century, and had just been played by Ian McShane in *Pirates of the Caribbean: On Stranger Tides* (2011). Blackbeard gets a tiny mention in J. M. Barrie, when Hook, who's equal parts Long John Silver, Captain

Cook, Ahab, and the hook-handed English sea captain Christopher Newport, is described as his former boatswain.

'I read that and thought, "Oh, that's our bad guy,"'[5] explained screenwriter Jason Fuchs (*Ice Age: Continental Drift*), whose script briefly made it onto Hollywood's Black List* in 2013. Aware that other studios were sniffing around *Peter Pan*, Warner Bros jumped on his pitch with possibly excessive haste, at the urging of production executive Sarah Schechter. Redrafted over the summer of 2013, it was assigned to Wright, cast with Jackman in January, and put into production at lightning speed by April 2014.

So we've met Blackbeard. To redouble the confusion, Captain Hook is then the next major character to be introduced. Pre-dismemberment, he's not even a boatswain, but a dashing young miner with an American accent, styled somewhere between Indiana Jones and Brendan Fraser in the *Mummy* films. Played by a pretty inexplicable Garrett Hedlund, this roguish adventurer, for whatever reason, seems to be doing a gratuitous impression of Daniel Plainview's baritone drawl from *There Will Be Blood* (2007) – you wouldn't trust him anywhere near a milkshake. But wait, he's one of the *good* guys? And he doesn't even meet the crocodile.

Scope was evidently being carved out for sequels: we barely meet Tinker Bell, who's a computer-generated spritz of light with no personality. As Fuchs put it mildly, 'There's a tremendous amount of narrative real estate between where our film ends and where Barrie's story begins.' You could build whole citadels on it.

Maybe Wright, charging headlong through pre-production, should have paid more attention to David Lean. 'I always resented

* Nothing to do with naming names under McCarthyism, but a survey of the best unproduced scripts, conducted and published every year since 2005 by development executive Franklin Leonard.

the quote when he said directing is 99 per cent casting,'[6] he has said, apropos of finding Saoirse Ronan for *Atonement*. 'I like to think that I have more control than that but, unfortunately, I think he was right, the old bugger.'

Pan proves Lean's point the other way, as an almost wholesale casting botch-up – we've barely scratched the surface. Jackman is bad, in a dastardly panto mode that doesn't come naturally to him at all. Hedlund is bad. Miller is fine, but not special, and has the film's toughest job: he seems like an obliging kid being directed to pull faces of awe and wonderment rather than drawing up those emotions from within. These are Wright's mistakes – unusually sloppy ones, from the man who got Keira Knightley to quit pouting and become a good actress.

The icing on the whole malformed cake, though, was Rooney Mara. Not just blankly wall-eyed as a tough-as-nails warrior maiden, she became the centre of undying controversy in her all-round troublesome role. The character of Tiger Lily, in Barrie, is a princess of Neverland's 'Piccaninny' tribe, described by the author as 'the most beautiful of dusky Dianas'. In 2015, you probably want to rethink the part, but not quite like the makers of *Pan* did.

She's usually depicted as Native American, most famously so in Disney's 1953 version, where she's stoically aloof, wearing a deerskin dress and eagle feather. Hogan's version cast her with the singer Carsen Gray, who's of Haida Indigenous and mixed descent. Way back in 1923, a silent effort from Paramount went a little off-piste by using then nineteen-year-old Anna May Wong, the Chinese-American star just on the cusp of major international fame.

One thing's for sure – Lily had certainly never been white before, let alone as terminally non-dusky as pale, interesting Rooney Mara. Wright would defend casting her as his prerogative, seeing as Neverland's a made-up place, and he wanted to create a world that was 'international and multiracial' – an argument that might have worked better if all three of his other leads weren't white, too. Doing their lone bit for Neverland's diversity were two supporting Brits, Adeel Akhtar as a cringing Smee and Nonzo Anozie as Blackbeard's hulking henchman, Bishop. But these were obvious sops.

Even Mara, within months of the film's release, admitted she shouldn't have done it. 'I really hate, hate, hate that I am on that side of the whitewashing conversation. I really do. I don't ever want to be on that side of it again,'[7] she told the *Telegraph*. She was redeemed by the near-simultaneous release of Todd Haynes's *Carol*, in which her career-best work scored an Oscar nomination.*

For *Pan* at large, the waves of negative publicity (casting announcement, trailer, then release) would be far harder to overcome. Whitewashing outcries had lately reached epidemic levels in the industry, doing hard-to-measure damage to the profitability of a slew of star vehicles. Cameron Crowe's lambasted romcom *Aloha* (2015) blundered into the debate by casting Emma Stone as a character stated to be one-quarter Chinese and one-quarter Hawaiian. Eyebrows were raised about the practically all-white cast of Ridley Scott's clomping biblical epic *Exodus: Gods and Kings* (2014).

Zoë Saldaña, the Afro-Latina *Avatar* star, had replaced Mary J. Blige as Nina Simone in the biopic *Nina*, with darkening make-up and prosthetics used to alter her appearance. The horror of Simone's estate, and from commentators such as Ta-Nehisi Coates, blighted the film almost to the point of making it unreleasable.† Further objections would follow about Matt Damon's white-saviour positioning as the hero of Zhang Yimou's period monster flick *The Great*

---

* Best Supporting Actress, which is absurd, as she's plainly the main character.
† Put out in a handful of cinemas in April 2016, more than three years after shooting wrapped, it sank without trace.

Wall (2016), and Scarlett Johansson as the cyborg supersoldier (conceived as a Japanese character) in the manga adaptation *Ghost in the Shell* (2017).

Pan scored a fairly catastrophic own goal in this department, and this was before people even knew about the songs. In an odd reverse of Spielberg's last-minute nerves, it was a snap decision by Wright, albeit a terrible one, to have the hundreds of pirates in Blackbeard's retinue enter to a mass singalong of Nirvana's 'Smells Like Teen Spirit', with the Ramones' 'Blitzkrieg Bop' held back till later. It certainly came as news to Jackman during rehearsals in pirate boot camp, when yo-ho-ho sea shanties weren't quite cutting it. As he confessed pre-release, 'I remember looking at the Warner Brothers executives who were like, "Uh, are we doing a *musical?*"'[8]

Wright was winging it, and they were letting him. 'I had a great time making it,' he shrugged to the *Independent* a few years later. By his own rationale, he was aiming the film at tweens, who certainly weren't *yet* Nirvana fans, and he'd cast pricey stars who can't have meant a lot to them, either. They had Lisbeth Salander from *The Girl with the Dragon Tattoo* (2011), the dude from *Tron: Legacy* (2010), and Jackman, whose pre-*Greatest Showman* (2017) filmography – all Wolverine, Jean Valjean and stuff like *Prisoners* (2012) – is almost relentlessly grim and vengeful.

Those very tweens, it turned out in the market research, didn't even fancy a film about Peter Pan, 'Because,' per Wright, 'they thought that was for little kids. So I had to recut [it] for *little* little kids, like, six, seven-year-olds, and therein lies one of the main problems with the movie.'[9]

Recalibrating *Pan* this way was an impossible endeavour, and everyone knew it was in deep trouble. Three months before the planned release in July 2015, Warners announced they were pushing it back to October, supposedly to refine the many, many effects, and to clear it out of the way of the summer scrummage. *Ant-Man* and *Mission Impossible: Rogue Nation* would certainly have done it some harm, but it was equally squelched in its new American berth by Ridley Scott's *The Martian* and the kiddie spookshow *Goosebumps*.

The only hope was an international marketing push, on which they continued to spend a fortune.[10] Leicester Square was transformed into Neverland before the world premiere on 20 September. Hong Kong built a whole installation in the Times Square Mall, featuring a Native village, the Jolly Roger, and Jackman, flying in for a meet and greet as part of an exhausting global tour. Cinema complexes in Tokyo and Mexico City got the full makeover, and Jacqueline Durran's kitschy costumes were exhibited everywhere.

But then the panning of *Pan* began. 'Headed for a low-altitude flight,' predicted Todd McCarthy in the *Hollywood Reporter*. Everyone yawned at how simultaneously over busy and rote it was; the garish clash of components; the Christmas-special performances.

Pan's so unwieldy that it's stressful to watch, in 2D *or* 3D. (I've tried both.) For all Wright's overconfidence, it has a hectic, why-don't-you-like-me desperation at its core, even in the parts where he summons some bright ideas to get it moving. There are flurries of Spielbergian business – a cable-car escape across the mountains – that almost come off, and then lethally dull character beats with our main quartet, bogging it down all over again. The climax, with two ships flying side by side in a crystalline Fairy Kingdom, is digitally backlotted to a degree that just seems deranged: you clock the expense and wild amounts of overtime it must have entailed, but there's no tangible peril to cling onto. It's state of the art, but how is it art?

Wright's film joined an ignoble list of 2010s flops with many of the same issues, and stands here for the lot of them. The running theme was a nervous unoriginality cloaked by an expensive facade of novelty – clutching at faded and/or obscure IPs they aimed to convert into the next *Pirates of the Caribbean*, the next *Star Wars*, or *Hunger Games*, or whatever.

Disney's wildly overpriced *John Carter* (2012)[11] is perhaps the most well trodden of these fiascos, even if the creepy, computer-animated *Mars Needs Moms* (2011)[12] got to the same planet first and sank without trace. Such failures as Gore Verbinski's admittedly ambitious *The Lone Ranger*[13] (which deserved better), Bryan Singer's *Jack the Giant Slayer*,[14] the Keanu Reeves samurai battle epic *47 Ronin*[15] and the unspeakable *R.I.P.D.*[16] made 2013 a banner year for bombing, just as *Pan* was being prepped.

A more unusual case was Brad Bird's *Tomorrowland* (2015),[17] if only because it was a missold original concept, nudged into existence by Walt Disney's obsession with futurism. Yet to come: Spielberg's glutinous misfire *The BFG* (2016),[18] Luc Besson's fun if reckless *Valerian and the City of a Thousand Planets* (2017),[19] Guy Ritchie's bloviating *King Arthur: Legend of the Sword* (2017)[20] and the Peter-Jackson-produced YA dud *Mortal Engines* (2018).[21]

Wright could take little solace from all these. He had his own wounds to lick after *Pan* failed everywhere – including China,* the film's last hope of recouping its investment,[22] where it opened two weeks after the US and grossed more pitiful sums than anywhere.

For Warner Bros, an already atrocious year was capped by a *Pan* write-off to the tune of at least $150m. But for Wright, the reviews stung hardest. 'They were rating me one star all over the place,'[23] he explained the next year, when his episode of *Black Mirror*, 'Nosedive',

---

* Fast headed towards overtaking the USA's gross annual box office, which it soon would (in 2020 and 2021). Several times already, popularity in China had redeemed Hollywood blockbusters that faltered in America, including Guillermo del Toro's *Pacific Rim* (2013) and *Terminator Genisys* (2015).

premiered at the London Film Festival. 'I'm a deeply insecure person . . . constantly looking for validation from other people.' To bounce back from his own nosedive, he needed to get his teeth into something fast, and what could be more apt: the theme of that teleplay was clinging onto your star ratings in a society where every interaction gets an Uber-style score.

Pan's imprint is not exactly massive. It comes down to fading memories of Mara in a bobbly multicoloured headdress, being dragged through one particular flashpoint at a tide-turning moment in the culture wars.

Come Disney's *Peter Pan & Wendy* (2023), it was the other side who saw red. Not because Tiger Lily was given to Alyssa Wapanatâhk, a member of Canada's Bigstone Cree First Nation, but in anti-woke fury at all the other changes: Peter was mixed race, Tinker Bell was Black, some of the Lost Boys were girls now, and Wendy had equal billing. (Wright's multicultural utopia was ironically achieved, at last.)

While more warmly received by critics than *Pan*, David Lowery's film still found itself relentlessly trolled by one-star ratings online, from the 'go woke, go broke' brigade, to give it the perception of being a flop – an impossible outcome to verify, seeing that it was ported straight to Disney+. In the heyday of the famous stage version, Tinker Bell needed vigorous applause to be resurrected from the brink of extinction. But now she gets booed. What a time to be alive.

CATS (2019)

Director: Tom Hooper
Studio: Universal Pictures
Budget: $95m (~$210m with marketing)
Worldwide gross: $75.5m

'You'll be playing a cat, in *Cats*!
We're using digital technology to make you a cat.'
'A relief, then, because I was about to ask a follow-up question
about whether I would be a befurred nude entity, smooth in weird places,
neither fully cat nor fully human.'

Alexandra Petri (@petridishes), Twitter, July 2019

Long before we knew about the buttholes, there were rumblings of *Cats* going astray. Shooting commenced at Hertfordshire's Leavesden Studios on 12 December 2018, almost exactly a year before the film was set to premiere. A year earlier, Andrew Lloyd Webber had written to the head of Universal Pictures, Donna Langley, warning her in no uncertain terms of the rough road ahead. 'I said, "This will be a car crash beyond belief if you don't listen to me,"'[1] the composer told the *Financial Times* in 2021. Langley never replied.

Lloyd Webber had sold the rights to Universal long before, keeping approval 'over some of the musical elements' as a courtesy, but found himself shut out of any deeper participation, especially when Tom Hooper came in to direct it.

'I've never known anything so ghastly,' the billionaire divulged. 'It was disgraceful, the whole process. They really rode roughshod over everything.' When he wound up seeing *Cats*, a day or two before walking the red carpet (and staying carefully on message) at the New York premiere, it left him reeling. 'I just thought, "Oh God, no." [It] was off-the-scale all wrong. There wasn't really any understanding of why the music ticked at all.'[2]

'I've never seen him so upset,' added his third wife, Madeleine Gurdon. Lloyd Webber was so traumatised by the whole experience, he went out and bought an emotional support dog – a Havanese puppy named Mojito. Faced with the issue of how to transport this pooch to New York in the middle of the pandemic, the composer tried writing to the airline for special dispensation. 'The airline wrote back and said, "Can you prove that you really need him?" "Just see what Hollywood did to my musical *Cats*." The approval came back with a note, "No doctor's report required."'[3]

———

Andrew Lloyd Webber does not get off quite so fast – nor does T. S. Eliot, the originator of the lyrics – as we sift through the wreckage of the good ship *Cats*, an inescapably weird stage musical with virtually no plot, which has grossed nearly $4bn worldwide since its West End premiere in 1981. That makes it second only in popularity to *The Phantom of the Opera* among Lloyd Webber's shows – the one that became an embarrassing Joel Schumacher film in 2004, which the composer admitted was horribly miscast.

There has never yet been a happy transfer of Lloyd Webber to cinema, and we probably shouldn't start holding our breaths for Christopher Nolan's *Starlight Express*. Resolutely stage-bound crowd-pleasers, these things have a hard time translating. This was obvious to anyone who saw *Cats* on the big screen, or read the uniquely savage reviews. But the long, tortured route it took to reach this benighted form had defeated many talented people before Tom Hooper got his paws on it.

Steven Spielberg wanted to do *Cats* as an animation in the early 1990s. Amblimation, the fledgling sub-division of his production company Amblin, struck a deal with Lloyd Webber and Universal to have a crack at it,[4] with Spielberg commissioning a tonne of concept art, pursuing an idea of setting it in London during the Blitz, and making it noirish and Brechtian. He hired Tom Stoppard, then some of *Toy Story*'s writers, to draft the script.

No amount of aggregated IQ power could fix the show's stubbornly obscure plot – however craftily they tried to explain what the heck a 'Jellicle' cat was, while workshopping ideas for Eliot's 'Jellicle Ball' – 'when the Jellicle Moon shines bright at night' – or unpicking Lloyd Webber's added conceit of ascending to 'the Heaviside Layer',* a trip to heaven in a hot-air balloon after some kind of feline singing contest. ('Jellicle', for the record, is a cutesy contraction of 'dear little', with no other legible meaning.)

Amblimation's *Balto* (1995), about the heroic dog rescuing kids from diphtheria, came out and tanked, causing the company to crumble, and Spielberg to shunt most of its employees to the newly formed DreamWorks Animation, just off its starting blocks with *Antz* and *The Prince of Egypt* (both 1998). That iteration of *Cats* might have run out of lives, then, but it haunts the one that got made. Production designer Hans Bacher, who'd moved to London to work on Spielberg's ideas, was surprised when catching the instantly infamous 2019 trailer, 'to spot a lot of visuals that apparently came from my designs'.[5] He could very well have saved face by pretending otherwise.

Universal's optimism in reviving *Cats* rested mainly on its success with Hooper's *Les Misérables* (2012), a medium-budget global smash,[6]

---

* Lloyd Webber borrowed this phrase, and notion, from an unpublished letter Eliot wrote to a friend, when he was figuring out how *Old Possum's Book of Practical Cats* could achieve closure. Eliot binned it; ALW fished it out of the bin.

despite being for the most part badly sung, hideously shot in its entirety, and directed with such ponderous, give-me-awards intensity you'd swear Hooper actually despised the musical form.

His much publicised method of recording the songs live on set, with live accompaniment, had snagged the Best Supporting Actress Oscar for Anne Hathaway singing 'I Dreamed a Dream'. It would be recapitulated wholesale on *Cats*, for Jennifer Hudson's would-be showstopping rendition of 'Memory' and all the other, less snotty-nosed solo numbers. New choreography by *Hamilton*'s Andy Blankenbuehler would be, in theory, another selling point, until everyone's first glimpses of James Corden pratting around as comedy glutton Bustopher Jones, Rebel Wilson trying to freestyle opposite a chorus line of cockroaches with human faces, and all the other moving parts, including imprisoned mice, played by children, forced to learn doo-wop.

Stars (Idris Elba! Ian McKellen!) were queuing up to work with Hooper. All three of his most recent films had won Oscars for act-ing,* and *The King's Speech* had caused a fair bit of film-nerd outrage by pipping *The Social Network* to Best Picture and Best Director, too. That accumulated prestige was about to come crashing down.

The date 18 July 2019, when the trailer landed and broke the Internet, was a very bad day to be the director of *Cats*.† It was hard to know where to start. Was that Judi Dench up there, wearing a massive coat that looked to be made out of tangerine cat fur? How

---

* Best Actor for Colin Firth in *The King's Speech* (2010), and Best Supporting Actress for Alicia Vikander in *The Danish Girl* (2015), with Hathaway in between them.

† An unexpected DM from an acquaintance, the director Graeme Arnfield: 'On the day the trailer for this came out, spotting Tom Hooper outside a Soho post-production house, with a lit cigarette in his mouth and another in his hand, is a defining image of what to avoid as a film-maker.'

had Jason Derulo, of all people, wound up in whatever this insanity was, yelling 'MILK!!!' and pulling lascivious faces? Why did all the female cats seem to be contoured with human breasts?

These and many other questions flooded social media, in what had to count as the most disastrous trailer launch of all time. 'The new *The Island of Doctor Moreau* trailer looks very creepy but I'm not sure about all the singing,'[7] deadpanned one tweet. 'I asked my eight-year-old to watch it to get her opinion,' said another, 'and she nope-ed out as soon as the first cat came on screen. Like, literally said "no" and walked away.'[8] Everyone agreed the cats were wrongly scaled – your brain would hazard a guess at 'too small', except it was hard to say what size they were at all. The sets towering over them looked terrifying, as if Alice in Wonderland had imbibed the wrong potion and/or tripped down a rabbit hole into the very living room of Lucifer.

As trailer backlashes go, this even exceeded the one that greeted *Sonic the Hedgehog*, Paramount's live-action transfer of the Sega game, whose release was pushed back into early 2020 after the teaser debuted in April that year. Everyone was perturbed by the appearance of the exceedingly toothy, CG-animated Sonic, which tumbled headlong into the uncanny valley. An all-out redesign was ordered to quell fans' conniptions, because no one, it turned out, wanted photorealistic CG hair on their favourite video-game character. But if they thought that looked wrong, they hadn't seen nothing yet.

The 'digital fur technology' Hooper had plumped for on *Cats*, after various failed tests with prosthetics and cat suits, was the source of most of his nightmares. 'I wanted to kind of create, I suppose, a covering of fur that was better than what a costume could do,' he explained in his DVD commentary, an impressively po-faced effort recorded soon after the premiere. 'But still be one-to-one with the real bodies, so that the way we captured the dance was utterly faithful to the way they did the dance.'

'Three years ago,' he told *Atlantic Monthly*, 'the best VFX guys in the business were like, "What you want to do cannot be done. The ability to track it in that detail is just not there." Two years ago, they were like, "You can do it, but it's crazily expensive." And then a year and a bit ago, they were like, "You can do it, and it's just about affordable."'[9]

To be fair to the fur in *Cats*, it does look remarkably like fur. It's not the 'how?' of that technology that threw everyone for a loop. (The actors all had to wear skin-tight leotards, and then an army of rotomators were set to work blending their faces in with the CG pelts.) It's the 'why?' that remains a hard one to answer.

Post-trailer, *Cats* had a whole lot of *Sonic*-style damage control to do, without the option of postponing the Christmas release date: any later than December and it wouldn't be eligible for the upcoming awards season. The effects staff at London's Mill Film were at their limit, having already worked around the clock for six months just to get the two-minute trailer ready. Left with only four months to finish the entire, 110-minute film, they found themselves working 80- and 90-hour weeks, often sleeping at their desks. Per one interview with an anonymous supervisor at Mill, they were also being collectively maltreated by the 'horrible' Hooper.

According to an interview the Daily Beast website published the following April, the situation was 'almost slavery'. Hooper's understanding of how rotomation worked was next to nil, but that didn't stop him sending denigratory emails to individual artists. He supposedly couldn't grasp the concept of work-in-progress animatics until they were fully rendered, and would also demand to see videos of real cats performing the stuff cats would do in the film. 'As you know,' the source said, 'cats don't dance.'[10]

Hooper certainly rubbed this unnamed collaborator up the wrong way. 'Disrespectful', 'demeaning' and 'condescending' were among the kinder descriptions of his managerial attitude. 'When you go into a conference room, you're not allowed to speak,' said the Beast's source. 'And he talks to you like you're garbage.'

It didn't help that Mill Film had underbid for the job. As a veteran insider told *GQ*, 'They crewed up a junior-heavy studio to do thousands of shots that would be incredibly hard even for an established studio with a proven pipeline. That apparent hubris was ultimately paid for by the artists.' As *Cats* reached crunch time, MPC in Vancouver was hired to take over a major chunk of the job, while simultaneously delivering the all-important rejig of none other than *Sonic the Hedgehog*.

The VFX industry has become a notoriously back-breaking profession in this century, because of situations just like this – working against the clock on impossible production schedules, with low pay, and then the grim likelihood of having everything blamed on you when the film looks awful. They were scrambling to fix the visuals until literally two hours before *Cats*' world premiere on 16 December – and even for days afterwards, because dozens of shots were still in such a poor state.

There was Judi Dench's wedding ring – clearly visible on her hand, which at one point seemed to be poking out of a fur sleeve. Jason Derulo's head wobbled all over the place. Tails became detached, while shadows were missing, or moved independently of dancers. People would lose whiskers, then gain them in the next shot. The atrocious closing number in Trafalgar Square had hands vanishing, cats standing off the ground, and Dench's Old Deuteronomy (amid her ultra-stern delivery of the soon-to-be infamous closing motto: 'A cat is not a dog') grabbing onto scenery that didn't exist. The list went on.*

---

* Catalogued (sorry) on a Reddit thread under r/vfx.

On Friday, 19 December, the film's opening day, thousands of cinemas were notified by Universal that they would be receiving updated versions of the DCPs* a few days later 'with some improved visual effects', according to a memo obtained by the *Hollywood Reporter*. For a finished title already on release, this was unheard-of – and the edict came straight from Hooper. It was the equivalent of handing in your homework, then trying to get mistakes scrubbed off during the marking process. Even so, the two chilling moments where Wilson's character unzips her own fur and steps out of it, to reveal a pink bodice beneath another layer of *sequined* fur, firmly stayed put.

If you'd paid for hideous tiles to be installed, would you blame the tilers for the end result? They tried to, all the same. When Corden and Wilson made an appearance at that year's Oscars, it was deemed lol-worthy for them to come dressed as their all-round charmless *Cats* characters, and even to present the award for Best VFX, a category in which *Cats* was, unsurprisingly, not nominated.

'As cast members of the motion picture *Cats*,' they announced, 'nobody more than us understands the importance of . . . good. Visual. Effects.' With that quip, a narrative salving the wounds of everyone else involved in the film was peddled, with only the department that had had the roughest time winding up as the whipping boys. Let's all forget the overarching design, shot choices, performances, colour palette, story concept, costumes, sets and most of the music – a pile-up of abominations – and just blame the whole thing on unfinished CGI.

One Canadian compositor at MPC, Yves McCrae, who'd been brought on to 'shit-fix' the film in October, clapped back at the actors on Twitter, writing: 'Hey guys, I haven't watched all of the Oscars, but I assume these two were really classy and thanked me for

* Digital cinema packages.

working 80-hour weeks right up until I was laid off and the studio closed, right?'

The buttholes were a whole other story. First reported in March, the existence of a fabled 'butthole cut' was confirmed online by various anonymous VFX staffers. Supposedly, the initial process of adding the fur created an unintentional byproduct, which was that the cats' skin looked 'groomed or just folded in a way that really, really looked like very furry lady genitals and buttholes by accident,'[11] per a crew member.

One particular producer, it transpired, had been given the months-long job of combing through the film and removing every one of the offending anuses. Upon these discoveries, #ReleaseTheButtholeCut* rapidly started trending, and kept a large swathe of the Internet pacified during the early days of Covid. *Cats* wasn't just the butt of jokes any more, but the butt of butt jokes.

———

Where do we all stand on *Cats*, then? I'll never quite forget the London press screening, on the same, gruelling night that *The Rise of Skywalker* was also unveiled. The anti-hype for *Cats* was at fever pitch by then, and it didn't disappoint: entire rows of critics, many beloved friends, were left agog, their eyes on stalks, jaws on the floor. Hooper's film was far from unwatchable, but practically the inverse: like Malcolm McDowell in *A Clockwork Orange*, we felt strapped in and helpless, eyelids peeled back, while the nightmarish imagery paraded itself.

* This was essentially a spoof of #ReleaseTheSnyderCut, the fan-fuelled movement to get Warner Bros to restore Zack Snyder's *Justice League* (2017) into the full, four-hour form Snyder originally envisaged.

This was viral failure, memed everywhere, and penetrating main-stream reporting beyond even a *Heaven's Gate*. It was noticed that Universal quietly pulled the film from Oscar consideration on its website in late December. Even the Golden Globes – the same taste-challenged body that had listed *The Phantom of the Opera* for Best Comedy/Musical – threw *Cats* the slimmest of bones, sucking up to Taylor Swift by nominating her for the film's one original song, 'Beautiful Ghosts', which she'd co-written with Lloyd Webber.

Swift's Bombalurina got off comparatively unscathed in reviews, because she summons a cat-like aura, doesn't hang around, and vamps through 'Macavity' in the rare sequence that actually clicks – at least until naked, neutered Idris Elba shows up to do a lewd shimmy. But 'Beautiful Ghosts' sucks, especially lyrically – it's roughly what you'd get if you asked ChatGPT to rearrange all the words from 'Memory' into something you wanted nominated for a Golden Globe.

Cats lore only continued to grow. Jason Derulo felt moved to clarify that his crotch bulge had been CGI-ed out of the film.[12] Everyone knew someone who knew someone who worked on it, and had stories. My favourite, which I heard in person, concerns the ballet-trained dancers hired to play the troupe of cockroaches in Wilson's unforget-tably gruesome number, 'The Old Gumbie Cat'. On good authority, they had a dance-off after the casting process, and the winners of this were the lucky ones whose heads got bitten off.

Was zero stars, a once-per-decade call, overly harsh? Almost cer-tainly – an editor's snappy suggestion after my review was emailed in. And yet, what's the correct star rating for *Cats*? It fits into no known niche of quality. I can't think of any *one*-star films I've now seen four times, and not many twos or threes, either. It's simply beyond stars – or above them, as we should all be.

On release, I can't shake the image of a few straggling Andrew Lloyd Webber fans keeping faith, maybe even indignantly, amid rude sensation hunters who had come in to get drunk and see how bad it could possibly be. A film marketed to families wound up being a site of experimentation for hundreds of millennials high on mushrooms. Who'd have guessed that it would be this generation's ironic answer to *2001: A Space Odyssey*?

London's beloved Prince Charles Cinema was quick off the mark in identifying this growing cult, just as it had done for *The Room* (2003),* Tommy Wiseau's legendarily abysmal indie vanity project. Soon after the first run of *Cats* had petered out, the PCC catered to everyone's ironic curiosity by arranging several singalong 'Jellicle Ball' screenings. I couldn't resist booking a ticket for one, but the pandemic put paid to it that March. Any immediate hope for a *Cats* afterlife – the film's ascent to its very own Heaviside Layer – was whipped away.

Hooper hasn't made a film since *Cats*, though he did direct a 2022 Christmas advert for McDonald's. And he did go about explaining, in the aforementioned commentary track, what the dancing before Dench's 'Jellicle Choice' was all about. 'It becomes about a different way of accessing the spiritual high or a spiritual place. You're arriving at a spiritual state through the kinesis and the catharsis of a sort of tribalistic, atavistic dance. So it kind of taps into the deepest traditions of how dance has existed in our culture, where the movement and the intensity transports you and takes you to a different space.'

On planet *Cats*, we're all just visitors.

---

* *The Room* barely counts as a flop by this book's metric: though it cost $6m, an insane amount given the shoddiness of its craft, it has by now recouped almost all of that (at least $5m) on the cult repertory circuit. So there's hope for *Cats*, one day.

AFTERWORD

It's hard to imagine another *Cats* coming along now – or, certainly, making it into cinemas to flop in such a blatant, measurable way. The pandemic, which followed almost suspiciously fast upon it, has transformed the economics of the industry, and there may be no going back. Hits are measured very differently from how they were in 2019, and flops don't flop the same way, either – not since the likes of Pixar's *Onward* and Christopher Nolan's *Tenet* (both 2020) were inevitably caused to underperform by the effect of global lockdowns.

Covid certainly accelerated the rise of streaming, but then saw the rapid effects of viewing fatigue, as subscriptions to the likes of Netflix and Disney+ peaked, then atrophied. You'd think this might be good news for old habits of cinema-going. Instead, it has created an ecosystem of megahits – 'special occasion' outings, such as the *Barbie*/*Oppenheimer* twofer, or *Top Gun: Maverick*. But the middle has dropped right out of the business, making studios more risk-averse than ever.

Even the safety of the past decade's most sure-fire blockbuster franchises, which used to be relied on to offset genuine commercial risks, is no longer guaranteed. *Fast X* (2023) topped out at $704m globally, less than half the $1.5bn *Fast 7* made back in 2015. *Mission: Impossible – Dead Reckoning Part One* (2023), that franchise's most expensive entry, cost $291m to make, and landed only fourth among the series to date, grossing $567.5m. With the ever heftier tolls of distribution and advertising, that's a marginal loss on its theatrical run. Yes – even *Mission: Impossible* flops, these days.

Disney's policy of rinsing its back catalogue for live-action remakes is starting to backfire, at the worst possible time. The poor figures for *The Little Mermaid* (2023) – $569.4m, versus $1.26bn for *Beauty and the Beast* (2017) and $1.66bn for *The Lion King* (2019) – can partly be explained by a shockingly bad performance in China, where audiences roundly rejected the recasting of Ariel with an African-American actress, Halle Bailey.* (Plus, the film is really woeful.) Massive restructuring and layoffs in 2023, and the legal tug-of-war between Disney and Ron DeSantis in Florida, furthered the impression of a major corporate crisis, and Disney's next remake, *Snow White*, was ominously pushed back a whole year (to spring 2025).

Even once trusty superheroes are suddenly on borrowed time, with Spider-Man one of few runaway exceptions. Marvel and Disney could blame the pandemic for losing hundreds of millions on *Black Widow*, *Eternals*, and *Shang-Chi and the Legend of the Ten Rings* (all 2021), but they had no such excuse for the badly reviewed *Ant-Man and the Wasp: Quantumania* (2023), which barely out-grossed all those with $476m, or the megaflop that was *The Marvels* (also 2023), which cratered instantly with Marvel's worst opening weekend to date.† Had I been able to face chapters on DC's *The Flash* or *Blue Beetle* (both 2023)[1], or Sony's instant laughingstock *Madame Web* (2024), we could have delved into the thuddingly obvious phenomenon of comic-book fatigue. But I think we all saw this coming.

---

* *Mermaid's* Chinese gross was an astonishingly low $3.7m, compared with $120.4m for *The Lion King*.

† First weekend gross: $47m. Worldwide total: $206m. Bearing inflation in mind, this is well behind Marvel's second worst, *The Incredible Hulk*, which opened with $55.4m in 2008 en route to a global total of $264.8m.

There's a postscript to *Catwoman*, which is that it probably wouldn't even be released these days. Consider the fate of *Batgirl*, an offshoot in the DC Extended Universe on which $90m was spent, with a destined berth on HBO Max. It was shot, then scrapped deep into post-production in August 2022, supposedly the victim of a suspiciously Machiavellian corporate rethink. It's unlikely ever to see the light of day.

According to co-chair of DC Studios Peter Safran, the film was 'not releasable', would have hurt the brand, and damaged the careers of all involved. But there's a difference. That film's Afro-Latina star, Leslie Grace, was relying on it to gain a foothold; unlike Halle Berry, she was hardly an Oscar-winning megastar when she got cast. To stop a flop, the option of a tax write-off for Warner Bros was a cold, hard fix no one saw coming. It was conscience-free. Maybe they just thought back to the furball they'd coughed up in 2004, read the room, and shuddered.

The post-*Cats* film that got closest to earning a chapter was Damien Chazelle's *Babylon* (2022),[2] an ambitious, critically divisive, chaotic and debauched valentine to the early days of populist film-making. Reflecting on it does bring us back full circle, not only to Kenneth Anger's famous book on early Hollywood and the vast sets Griffith had built, but to the dawn of sound (which caused Stroheim and Swanson so many of their problems on *Queen Kelly*).

Babylon was a hard sell – sprawling over the three-hour mark – and the marketing campaign screwed up by giving no real sense of the story. It relied completely on Brad Pitt's and Margot Robbie's star power, and possibly excessive confidence that viewers who'd loved Chazelle's *La La Land* would be content to follow his every whim.

Paramount's biggest mistake was pitting it against the also-three-hours-plus *Avatar: The Way of Water*. Like two other auteur flops that year, David O. Russell's *Amsterdam*[3] and George Miller's *Three*

Thousand Years of Longing,* it lacked the ringing critical support needed to make a prestige film break through: there were too many carping voices, accusations of coddling and indulgence. *Avatar* is review-proof; they're not.

Babylon does bottle *some* of the essence of a classic flop, maybe without quite enough of the madness behind the scenes. The circumstances of it failing sum up where we're at, but the story of its undoing is simply too routine. It's no *Cats*. For if that wasn't technically the flop to end all flops, it's still the one to tie the ribbon on. They already don't make 'em like *Cats* any more.

* See page 172, and footnote.

ACKNOWLEDGEMENTS

Except Max Bialystock and Leo Bloom in *The Producers*, no one sets out to make a flop. My sincere thanks go out, then, to every single person involved on these films. The individual efforts of these many talented folks vastly exceed my own in trying to chronicle what went wrong. Several of the productions chosen here aren't just my favourite flops but among my favourite films ever made, and I have an ever-growing affection even for the runts of the litter.

This book wouldn't exist without the encouragement of Jon Wood, my agent at RCW, and the stewardship of Angus Cargill, my editor at Faber, who received the idea with immediate enthusiasm and has improved it every step of the way with his cheery guidance. Andy Miller gave moral support at an embryonic stage. I also owe a debt to Veronica Goldstein at United Talent Agency and Peter Joseph at Hanover Square Press for masterminding the American edition with perfect timing.

Jill Burrows took on the copyedit with exacting grace, fixing many things and making me smile. I'm grateful also to James Degnan for the author photo, to Eden Railsback, to Joanna Harwood, Barbara Mignocchi, Hannah Turner and Hannah Marshall at Faber, to Safae El-Ouahabi at RCW, to Rico Gagliano at MUBI, to Paul Vickery at the Prince Charles Cinema, and to the good folk at the BFI: Justin Johnson, Katie Reddington, Stuart Brown and especially Jason Wood. Input on the release of *The Hudsucker Proxy* was provided by Julia Short, David Livingstone and Stewart Till, while the disability issues raised within (and by) the chapter on *Freaks* were very helpfully critiqued by Cathy James and Bill Chambers. Kim Newman, Mark

Kermode and Tom Teodorczuk collectively dredged up memories of *Nothing But Trouble* reaching the UK.

Meanwhile, many friends looked through individual chapters and/or watched the films with me and gave their feedback along the way. Thank you to Jacob Stolworthy, Jon Robertson, Catherine Bray, Ryan Miles, Charles Gant, Simon Renshaw, Harry Macqueen, Myles Robey, and my three most industrious early readers: Nick Davis, Thomas Small, and (the best of the best) Ryan Gilbey, who were supportive beyond the call of duty, offering hundreds of notes I took on board. Finally, gratitude goes out to my whole family, to Stephen Turnock, and to Nina, our Beagle puppy, who curled up on my lap through long afternoons of writing this, yelped at cats in the garden, and put up with being walked at weird times.

BIBLIOGRAPHY

Anger, Kenneth, *Hollywood Babylon* (first published in French by J. J. Pauvert, 1959)

Arnaud, Georges, *Le salaire de la peur* (Juilliard, 1950)

Bach, Steven, *Final Cut: Dreams and Disaster in the Making of Heaven's Gate* (William Morrow & Co., 1985; revd edn, 1999)

Berg, Scott A., *Kate Remembered: Katharine Hepburn, a Personal Biography* (Putnam Publishing Group, 2003)

Biskind, Peter, *Easy Riders, Raging Bulls: How the Sex 'n' Drugs 'n' Rock 'n' Roll Generation Saved Hollywood* (Simon & Schuster, 1998)

—, 'Madness in Morocco: The Road to *Ishtar*' (*Vanity Fair*, February 2010)

Bogdanovich, Peter, *Who The Devil Made It: Conversations with Legendary Film Directors* (Ballantine Books, 1998)

Bradbury, Ray, 'A Sound of Thunder', *Collier's*, 1952

Britton, Andrew, *Katharine Hepburn: Star as Feminist* (Studio Vista, 1995)

Brown, Karl (Kevin Brownlow, ed.), *Adventures with D. W. Griffith* (Farrar, Straus & Giroux, 1973)

Callow, Simon, *Orson Welles*, Volume 2: *Hello Americans* (Penguin, 1999)

Carringer, Robert, *The Magnificent Ambersons: A Reconstruction* (University of California Press, 1993)

de Semlyen, Nick, *The Last Action Heroes: The Triumphs, Flops, and Feuds of Hollywood's Kings of Carnage* (Pan MacMillan, 2023)

Dunne, John Gregory, *The Studio* (Farrar, Straus & Giroux, 1969)

Evry, Max, *A Masterpiece in Disarray: David Lynch's Dune – An Oral History* (1984 Publishing, 2023).

Fleischer, Richard, *Just Tell Me Where to Cry* (Carroll & Graf, 1993)

Fox, Robin Lane, *Alexander the Great* (Penguin, 1973)

Friedkin, William, *The Friedkin Connection: A Memoir* (Harper, 2013)

Fruchter, Rena, *I'm Chevy Chase . . . and You're Not* (Virgin Books, 2008)

Griffin, Nancy, and Kim Masters, *Hit & Run: How Jon Peters and Peter Guber Took Sony for a Ride in Hollywood* (Simon & Schuster, 1996)

Harris, Mark, *Scenes from a Revolution: The Birth of the New Hollywood* (Canongate, 2008)

Herbert, Frank, *Dune* (Chilton Books, 1965)

Fitzgerald, F. Scott, 'Crazy Sunday', *American Mercury*, 1932

Gish, Lillian, and Ann Pinchot, *The Movies, Mr Griffith, and Me* (Prentice-Hall, 1969)

Hepburn, Katharine, *Me: Stories of My Life* (Alfred P. Knopf, 1991)

Howard, Noël, *Hollywood sur Nil* (Fayard, 1977)

Kamp, David, 'Magnificent Obsession', *Vanity Fair*, April 2010.

Kennedy, Matthew, *Roadshow! The Fall of Film Musicals in the 1960s* (Oxford University Press, 2014)

King, Lynnea Chapman, *The Coen Brothers Encyclopedia* (Roman & Littlefield, 2014)

Koszarski, Richard, *The Man You Loved to Hate: Erich von Stroheim and Hollywood* (Oxford University Press, 1983)

Lambert, Gavin, *On Cukor* (G. P. Putnam's Sons, 1972)

Lennig, Arthur, *Stroheim* (The University Press of Kentucky, 2000)

Lofting, Hugh, *The Story of Doctor Dolittle, Being the History of His Peculiar Life at Home and Astonishing Adventures in Foreign Parts* (Frederick A. Stokes, 1920)

Long, Robert Emmet, *George Cukor: Interviews* (University Press of Mississippi, 2001)

Loos, Anita, *A Girl Like I* (Viking Press, 1966)

Matthews, Jack, *The Battle of Brazil* (Crown Publishers, 1987)

Mackenzie, Compton, *Sylvia Scarlett* (Martin Secker, 1918)

McCarthy, Todd, *Howard Hawks: The Grey Fox of Hollywood* (Grove Press, 1997)

McGilligan, Patrick, *George Cukor: A Double Life* (St Martin's Press, 1991)

Naha, Ed, *The Making of Dune* (Berkley Books, 1984)

Nayman, Adam, *It Doesn't Suck: Showgirls* (ECW Press, 2014)

Noble, Peter, *Hollywood Scapegoat: The Biography of Erich von Stroheim* (Fortune Press, 1950)

Parish, James Robert, *Fiasco: A History of Hollywood's Iconic Flops* (Turner Publishing, 2006)

Peary, Danny, *Cult Movies* (Delta Books, 1981)

Phillips, Gene D., *George Cukor* (Twayne Publishers, 1982)

Polley, Sarah, *Run Towards the Danger: Confrontations with a Body of Memory* (September Publishing, 2022)

Rabin, Nathan, *My Year of Flops* (Scribner, 2010)

Raspe, Rudolf Erich, *Baron Munchausen's Narrative of his Marvellous Travels and Campaigns in Russia* (Smith, 1785)

Robbins, Tod, 'Spurs', *Munsey's Magazine*, 1923

Ross, Lillian, *Picture* (Rinehart & Co., 1952)

Salamon, Julie, *The Devil's Candy: The Bonfire of the Vanities Goes to Hollywood* (Houghton Mifflin, 1991)

BIBLIOGRAPHY

Schickel, Richard, *D.W. Griffith: An American Life* (Simon & Schuster, 1984)

Segaloff, Nat, *Hurricane Billy: The Stormy Life and Films of William Friedkin* (William Morrow & Co., 1990)

Skal, David J., and Elias Savada, *Dark Carnival: The Secret World of Tod Browning* (Anchor Books/Doubleday, 1995)

Stewart, Patrick, *Making It So: A Memoir* (Simon & Schuster, 2023)

Streisand, Barbra, *My Name is Barbra* (Viking Press, 2023)

Swanson, Gloria, *Swanson on Swanson* (Random House, 1980)

Tarkington, Booth, *The Magnificent Ambersons* (Doubleday, Page and Co., 1918)

Taylor, Dwight, 'This Side of Malibu', in *Joy Ride* (G. P. Putnam's Sons, 1959)

Towlson, Jon, *Subversive Horror Cinema: Countercultural Messages of Films from Frankenstein to the Present* (McFarland & Company, 2014)

Walters, Ben, *Orson Welles* (Haus Publishing, 2005)

Welles, Orson, and Peter Bogdanovich, *This is Orson Welles* (HarperCollins, 1992)

Welsch, Tricia, *Gloria Swanson: Ready for Her Close-Up* (University Press of Mississippi, 2013)

Wolfe, Tom, *The Bonfire of the Vanities* (Farrar, Straus & Giroux, 1987)

Yule, Andrew, *Losing the Light: Terry Gilliam and the Munchausen Saga* (Applause Books, 1991)

NOTES

PREFACE

1   https://www.washingtonpost.com/archive/lifestyle/1979/09/02/shoot-out-at-heavens-gate/c9785a69-2f68-437b-852f-bec237f0afc8/

INTOLERANCE (1916)

1   Richard Schickel, *D. W. Griffith: An American Life*, p. 304.
2   Lillian Gish and Ann Pinchot, *The Movies, Mr Griffith and Me*, p. 166.
3   Schickel, p. 306.
4   Ibid, p. 309.
5   Karl Brown, Adventures with D.W. Griffith, p. 161.
6   Schickel, p. 320.
7   Anita Loos, *A Girl Like I*, p. 102.
8   Gish and Pinchot, p. 180.
9   Ibid., p. 185.

QUEEN KELLY (1929)

1   Richard Koszarski, *The Man You Loved to Hate: Erich von Stroheim and Hollywood*, p. 221.
2   Arthur Lennig, *Stroheim*, p. 275.
3   Koszarski, p. 216.
4   Gloria Swanson, *Swanson on Swanson*, p. 369.
5   Koszarski, p. 206.
6   Swanson, p. 373.
7   Ibid., p. 372.
8   Ibid., p. 373.
9   Tricia Welsch, *Gloria Swanson: Ready for Her Close-Up*, p. 227.
10 Lennig, p. 288.
11 Swanson, p. 373.
12 Peter Noble, *Hollywood Scapegoat: The Biography of Erich von Stroheim*, p. 79.

FREAKS (1932)

1 Quoted in David Skal's commentary on the 2004 Warner Bros DVD.
2 David J. Skal and Elias Savada, *Dark Carnival: The Secret World of Tod Browning*, p. 166.
3 Dwight Taylor, 'This Side of Malibu'.
4 Quoted in Skal and Savada, p. 169.
5 Quoted in *Tod Browning's Freaks – The Sideshow Cinema* (Warner Home Video, 2004).
6 Skal and Savada, p. 170.
7 Ibid., p. 172.
8 Quoted in ibid., p. 174.
9 Ibid., p. 177.
10 Mrs Ambrose Nevin Diehl, letter to Will Hays, 26 February 1932.
11 Personal email to author.
12 For example, Jon Towlson, *Subversive Horror Cinema: Countercultural Messages of Films from Frankenstein to the Present*.

SYLVIA SCARLETT (1935)

1 Scott A. Berg, *Kate Remembered: Katharine Hepburn, a Personal Biography*, p. 59.
2 Patrick McGilligan, *George Cukor: A Double Life*, p. 127.
3 Katharine Hepburn, *Me: Stories of My Life*, p. 193.
4 McGilligan, p. 127.
5 Gavin Lambert, *On Cukor*, p. 92.
6 Ibid.
7 Gene D. Phillips, *George Cukor*, p. 69.
8 Pulled direct from the RKO archives by Ed Asner, in the 1987 documentary *A Woman's Lot – The RKO Story*.
9 Ibid.
10 Hepburn, p. 233.
11 Robert Emmet Long, *George Cukor: Interviews*, p. 106.
12 Ibid.
13 Lambert, p. 96.
14 Hepburn, p. 201.
15 McGilligan, p. 127.

THE MAGNIFICENT AMBERSONS (1942)

1   Simon Callow, *Orson Welles*, Volume 2: *Hello Americans*, p. 25.
2   Orson Welles and Peter Bogdanovich, *This Is Orson Welles*, p. 130.
3   Robert Wise, final interview with Mike Thomas, in Joel Eisenberg (ed.), *Aunt Bessie's How to Survive a Day Job While Pursuing the Creative Life* (2005); available at https://joeleisenberg.medium.com/the-lost-and-the-last-robert-wise-interview-a-medium-com-exclusive-d88651fba865.
4   Quoted in David Kamp, 'Magnificent Obsession', *Vanity Fair*, April 2010.
5   Wise.
6   Quoted in Kamp.
7   Wise.

LAND OF THE PHARAOHS (1955)

1   Noël Howard, *Hollywood sur Nil*, pp. 157–8.
2   Ibid., p.19.
3   Quoted in Todd McCarthy, *Howard Hawks: The Grey Fox of Hollywood*, p. 518.
4   Peter Bogdanovich, *Who the Devil Made It: Conversations with Legendary Film Directors*, p. 355.
5   Howard, p. 95.
6   McCarthy, p. 530.
7   Ibid., p. 522.
8   Ibid., p. 526.
9   Ibid., p. 530.
10 Ibid., p. 525.
11 Ibid., p. 526.
12 Howard, p. 236.
13 McCarthy, p. 531.
14 Ibid., p. 533.
15 Bogdanovich, p. 283.

DOCTOR DOLITTLE (1967)

1   All quotes from 'Miss Taylor and Burton Sued For $50 Million on *Cleopatra*', *New York Times*, 23 April 1964.
2   Matthew Kennedy, *Roadshow!*, p. 37.
3   Mark Harris, *Scenes from a Revolution*, p. 43.
4   Richard Fleischer, *Just Tell Me Where to Cry*, p. 247.
5   John Gregory Dunne, *The Studio*, p. 35.

6 Harris, p. 200.
7 Ibid., p. 201.
8 Ibid., p. 240.

SORCERER (1977)

1 Peter Biskind, *Easy Riders, Raging Bulls*, p. 337.
2 William Friedkin, *The Friedkin Connection*, p. 320.
3 Ibid.
4 Ibid., p. 329.
5 Friedkin, in *Sorcerers: A Conversation* (see fn p. 84).
6 Friedkin, p. 325.
7 Ibid., p. 326.
8 *Sorcerer* press book, 1977.
9 Nat Segaloff, *Hurricane Billy: The Stormy Life and Times of William Friedkin* (1990), p. 164.
10 Friedkin, p. 333.
11 Friedkin interviewed by Alex Simon for the *Hollywood Interview*, 1 April 2014.
12 Friedkin, p. 335.
13 Ibid., p. 337.
14 Ibid., p. 338.
15 Ibid., p. 346.

DUNE (1984)

1 In the 2001 BBC2 documentary *The Last Movie Mogul*.
2 Michael Cimino interviewed by Steve Garbarino, *Vanity Fair*, March 2002.
3 Quoted in *Jodorowsky's Dune*, 2013 documentary directed by Frank Pavich.
4 Ridley Scott interviewed by Jack Shepherd in *Total Film*, November 2021.
5 Lynch interview by David Breskin for *Inner Views: Filmmakers in Conversation* (1992), p. 63.
6 'Is there life after Dune?' *Cinefantastique*, October 1986.
7 Universal-approved, written by SF author Ed Naha, and published in 1984.
8 Ed Naha, *The Making of Dune*, p. 52.
9 Francesca Annis, interview with *Deadline*, September 2021.
10 Naha, p. 84.
11 ComicCon interview with Patrick Stewart, 2013, and repeated in Stewart's 2023 memoir *Making It So*.
12 Quoted in Max Evry's meaty tell-all *A Masterpiece in Disarray: David Lynch's Dune – An Oral History* (1984 Publishing, 2023).

13 Ibid.
14 Naha, p. 110.
15 Ibid. p. 181.
16 Ibid., pp. 283–4.
17 Quote from the 2009 documentary *Great Directors*, directed by Angela Ismailos.
18 Both quoted in Evry, p. 316.
19 Ibid., p. 236.
20 Ibid., p. 364.
21 Ibid., p. 361.
22 Ibid., p. 283.
23 Ibid., p. 344.

THE ADVENTURES OF BARON MUNCHAUSEN (1988)

1 See, for example, *The Battle of Brazil* (Jack Matthews, 1987).
2 *Time Bandits* took $42.5m from a $5m budget for Handmade Films/Avco Embassy Pictures; *The Fisher King* managed $72.4m worldwide for TriStar off $24m, and *12 Monkeys* a whopping $168.8m worldwide for Universal off $29.5m. *Brazil*, by comparison, managed only $9.9m in the US from its $15m budget.
3 Directed by Matthew Robbins. Budget: $18m, worldwide gross: $14.1m for Paramount/Disney.
4 Directed by Peter Yates. Budget: $27m ($50m with marketing), worldwide gross: $16.9m for Columbia.
5 Directed by Richard Donner. Budget: $20m, worldwide gross: $18.4m for WB/Fox.
6 Budget: $25m, worldwide gross: $23.5m for Universal and Fox.
7 Directed by Jim Henson. Budget: $25m, worldwide gross: $34m for Columbia/TriStar.
8 Directed by Wolfgang Petersen. Budget: ~$27m, worldwide gross: ~$100m for Warner Bros.
9 Directed by Ron Howard. Budget: $35m, worldwide gross: $137.6m for MGM/UA.
10 Budget: $28m, worldwide gross: a brutal $11.1m for Disney.
11 In *The Madness and Misadventures of Munchausen* (hereafter *TMAMOM*), a feature-length 2008 documentary on the DVD extras.
12 Andrew Yule, *Losing the Light: Terry Gilliam and the Munchausen Saga* (1991), p. 4.
13 Ibid., p. 68.
14 *TMAMOM*.

15 Ibid.
16 Ibid.
17 Yule, p. 85.
18 *TMAMOM.*
19 Yule, p. 56.
20 Ibid., p. 78.
21 Ibid., p. 99.
22 *TMAMOM.*
23 Ibid.
24 Sarah Polley, *Run Towards the Danger: Confrontations with a Body of Memory* (2022), p. 152.
25 Ibid., p. 151.
26 Ibid., p. 153.
27 Yule, pp. 44 and 115.
28 Ibid., p. 160.
29 Ibid., p. 189.

NOTHING BUT TROUBLE (1991)

1 Rena Fruchter, *I'm Chevy Chase, and You're Not* (2008), p. 135.
2 Hal Hinson, 16 February 1991.
3 Julie Salamon, *The Devil's Candy* (Picador paperback edition), p. 418.

THE HUDSUCKER PROXY (1994)

1 Quoted in *The Coen Brothers Encyclopedia*, p. 90.
2 Michel Ciment and Hubert Niogret, 'Closer to Life Than the Conventions of Cinema', *Positif*, September 1996.

CUTTHROAT ISLAND (1995)

1 $240m worldwide from a budget somewhere between $62m and $70m.
2 $255m from a $70m budget.
3 'Hollywood's Billion-Dollar Man', *Los Angeles Times*, 23 September 1990.
4 Without adjusting for inflation.
5 Daniel Jeffreys, 'The Vanity That Led to a $100m Bonfire', *Independent*, 10 April 1996.
6 James Sterngold, 'Debacle on the High Seas', *New York Times*, 31 March 1996.
7 KCRW, *The Business with Kim Masters*, 12 September 2011.
8 *Spy* magazine, March–April 1995.

9   Quoted in James Robert Parish, *Fiasco* (2006), p. 211.
10 Matthew Modine interview, *Entertainment Weekly*, 3 June 2013.
11 Jeffreys.

SPEED 2: CRUISE CONTROL (1997)

1   Interview with Bilge Ebiri for *Vulture*, July 2020.
2   Interview with *Yahoo! News*, September 2022.
3   Interviews with *Entertainment Weekly*, 10 May 1996.
4   Keanu Reeves, interview with the *Calgary Sun*, October 1997, while on the promo tour for *The Devil's Advocate*.
5   Speaking to Kristopher Tapley for *Uproxx*, June 2014.
6   Ibid.
7   *The Nation*, 13 June 1997.
8   Ibid.

BABE: PIG IN THE CITY (1998)

1   George Miller, interview with *The Australian Financial Review Magazine*, May 2007.
2   James Cromwell, interviewed by Seth Abramovitch in the *Hollywood Reporter*, 8 August 2020.
3   Now Disney Studios Australia.
4   'The Set Was a Zoo, the Actors Were Animals', *Los Angeles Times*, 27 November 1998.
5   Cromwell.

SUPERNOVA (2000)

1   Bill Chambers, Film Freak Central website, DVD review of *Supernova* (August 2000).
2   Walter Hill, interviewed by Paul Fischer for *Dark Horizons*, August 2002.
3   Jack Sholder, interviewed by Dan Epstein for www.UGO.com, February 2003.

ROLLERBALL (2002)

1   See 'How They Built the Bomb', the chapter devoted to *Last Action Hero* in the 1996 book *Hit & Run: How Jon Peters and Peter Guber Took Sony for a Ride in Hollywood*, by Nancy Griffin and Kim Masters.

2 *Movieline*, August 2001.
3 McTiernan interview with *Radio Times*, 28 July 2022.
4 Ibid.
5 '*Rollerball* Test Print Review', Ain't It Cool News website, 7 June 2001.
6 *Los Angeles Times*, 31 March 2008.
7 *HuffPost*, 3 April 2008.
8 For example by Nikki Finke, *Deadline*, 3 April 2006.

THE ADVENTURES OF PLUTO NASH (2002)

1 Directed by Roger Christian. Budget: reported as $73m, but actually $44m – see p. 246. Worldwide gross: $29.7m for Warner Bros.
2 Directed by Peter Chelsom, starring Warren Beatty, Diane Keaton, Goldie Hawn, Garry Shandling. Budget: $90m. Worldwide gross: $10.4m for New Line Cinema.
3 Ron Underwood interviewed by Blake Harris, *Slash*, 24 July 2020.
4 Ibid.
5 'The Freshmaker says PLUTO NASH should be blown out an airlock!!!' *Ain't It Cool News*, 27 January 2001.
6 Underwood interview.

GIGLI (2003)

1 *Gigli* production notes.
2 Ibid.
3 Ben Affleck, interviewed by Army Archerd for *Variety*, 4 August 2003.
4 Affleck, interviewed by Matt Damon in *Entertainment Weekly*, January 2022.

CATWOMAN (2004)

1 Halle Berry, interview for *Variety*, September 2020.
2 John Rogers, Twitter, in February 2018.
3 Berry, interview for *Blackfilm*, July 2004.

ALEXANDER (2004)

1 *New York Times*, 1 September 2004.
2 'Kings of Hollywood in epic battle to film *Alexander*', Fiachra Gibbons, *Guardian*, 30 December 2002.
3 'An Oxford professor is leading the charge!' *Guardian*, 19 November 2004.

4   Wesley Morris in the *Boston Globe*, 24 November 2004.
5   Lou Lumenick, *New York Post*, 18 November 2004.
6   Stone interview in the *Sunday Telegraph*, 3 January 2005.
7   Ibid.
8   Ibid.

A SOUND OF THUNDER (2005)

1   Interviewed by Phil Florence in *Starlog* magazine, October 2005.
2   Jonathan Bing, 'The Samaha Syndrome', *Variety*, 8 June 2003.
3   'Brosnan film falls victim to Hollywood strike action', *Guardian*, 8 March 2001.
4   '*A Sound of Thunder*: Combining the Futuristic with the Prehistoric', *VFX World*, 2 September 2005.
5   *Los Angeles Times*, 6 June 2002.
6   'Franchise scales back sked', *Variety*, 6 October 2002.
7   'David Oyelowo Fills in the Blanks', video interview for Internet Movie Database, 31 August 2019.
8   John Hyams interview with *Collider* (website), 7 December 2012.

SPEED RACER (2008)

1   *Digital Spy* (website), December 2022.
2   *Variety*, 16 April 2019.
3   John Gaeta, interviewed in *Variety*, 1 May 2008.
4   The Wachowskis interviewed in *HitFix*, 10 October 2012.
5   Directed by Robert Rodriguez, starring Bruce Willis, Clive Owen, Jessica Alba, Mickey Rourke. Budget: $40m; global box office: $158.7m for Miramax.
6   Directed by Zack Snyder, starring Gerard Butler, Lena Headey, Rodrigo Santoro. Budget: $65m; global box office: a whopping $456m for Warner Bros.
7   Directed by Kerry Conran, starring Jude Law, Gwyneth Paltrow, Angelina Jolie. Budgeted at $70m, it scraped $58m back worldwide for Paramount.
8   'Why *Speed Racer* sputtered', *Variety*, 13 June 2008.
9   Budget: ~$128m; global box office: $130.5m.
10 Budget: ~$200m; global box office: $183.9m.
11 Budget: $190m; global box office: $159.2m.
12 Budget: $200m; global box office: $1.9bn.

SYNECDOCHE, NEW YORK (2008)

1 Charlie Kaufman interviewed at the 2016 edition of the Karlovy Vary Film Festival.
2 Kaufman interview with *Vulture*, December 2015.
3 Sidney Kimmel interview, *Forbes*, 11 October 2010.
4 Kaufman interview with *IndieWire*, 24 October 2008.
5 Kaufman interview with NPR, 23 October 2008.
6 Ibid.
7 Kaufman interview at the Karlovy Vary Film Festival.

PAN (2015)

1 Budget: $75m; worldwide gross: $107m.
2 Spielberg interviewed by Ryan Gilbey in the *Guardian*, 8 December 2021.
3 *Empire*, April 2018.
4 Wright interviewed by Jacob Stolworthy, *Independent*, May 2018.
5 Jason Fuchs interview with ScreenCraft (website), October 2015.
6 Wright, *Independent* interview.
7 Mara interviewed in the *Telegraph*, February 2016.
8 Jackman interviewed by King5 News (YouTube), 6 October 2015.
9 Wright, *Independent* interview.
10 '*Pan* To Get Worldwide Welcome in Warner Bros. Marketing Blitz', *Deadline*, 17 September 2015.
11 Directed by Andrew Stanton. Budget: $306m, worldwide gross: $284m for Disney.
12 Directed by Simon Wells. Budget: $150m, worldwide gross: $39.2m for Disney.
13 Budget: $250m, worldwide gross: $260.5m for Disney.
14 Budget: $200m, worldwide gross: $197m for Warner Bros.
15 Directed by Carl Rinsch. Budget: $225m, worldwide gross: $151.8m for Universal.
16 Directed by Robert Schwentke. Budget: $154m, worldwide gross: $78.3m for Universal.
17 Budget: $190m, worldwide gross: $209m for Disney.
18 Budget: $140m, worldwide gross: $195.2m for Disney.
19 Budget: $205m, worldwide gross: $226m for a hodgepodge of international distributors.
20 Budget: $175m, worldwide gross: $148.7m for Warner Bros.
21 Budget: $150m (with marketing), worldwide gross: $83.7m for Universal.

22 'Pan Looks for China Life Raft as it Faces $100 Million Writedown', *Variety*, 13 October 2015.

23 Wright interviewed by the author at the 'Nosedive' premiere in London, October 2016.

CATS (2019)

1 Andrew Lloyd Webber interviewed by Henry Mance in the *Financial Times*, 16 July 2021.

2 Lloyd Webber interviewed in *Variety*, October 2021.

3 Ibid.

4 Reported in the *Los Angeles Times*, 25 June 1990.

5 'How a Dog Film Killed an Animated Version of *Cats*', *Forbes*, 20 December 2019.

6 $442.3m, costing a mere $61m.

7 @CethanLeahy, 18 July 2019.

8 @JessicaValenti, 18 July 2019.

9 Tom Hooper interviewed in *Atlantic Monthly*, 26 December 2019.

10 *Daily Beast* website, 7 April 2020.

11 Shared with Twitter prankster Ben Mekler.

12 Jason Derulo interviewed on SiriusXM (online), 19 December 2019.

AFTERWORD

1 *The Flash*: budget $200–220m, worldwide gross $271.3m; *Blue Beetle*: budget $104–125m, worldwide gross $130.7m; *Madame Web*: budget $80m, worldwide gross $100.3m.

2 Budget: $110m; worldwide gross: $63.4m. It would have needed $250m to break even.

3 Budget $80m, worldwide gross $31.2m (calculated to have lost over $100m with all other costs factored in).

IMAGE CREDITS

PAGE ONE

A set photo of the thirty-foot 'white elephants' D. W. Griffith had made for *Intolerance*. There was no evidence they'd ever featured in Babylonian iconography, but Griffith couldn't care less. *Public domain.*

Fuming Ruritanian queen Regina V (Seena Owen) whips Gloria Swanson's convent lass, dubbed *Queen Kelly* in her African exile. This saucy epic was overtaken in the rush to make talkies. *Public domain.*

PAGE TWO

The circus troupe in *Freaks* welcome the so-called 'normal' bride, Cleopatra (off-screen), for the famed banquet. When she responds with cackling disgust, they close ranks to get even. *Photo 12 / Alamy Stock Photo*

Katharine Hepburn in her fizzy element was no draw; instead, her cross-dressing romcom became notorious. Her next few vehicles would bomb, but none as badly as *Sylvia Scarlett*. *Everett Collection Inc / Alamy Stock Photo*

PAGE THREE

An army of Egyptian extras herald Pharaoh Khufu (Jack Hawkins) in *Land of the Pharaohs*. Warner Bros put the local workforce through hell, with minimal pay for back-breaking labour. *Entertainment Pictures / Alamy Stock Photo*

317

Taming Rex Harrison on *Doctor Dolittle* was hard enough, let alone his four-legged co-stars. This accident-prone giraffe scarcely made the cut – an emblem of the elusive fun being missold. *Allstar Picture Library Ltd / Alamy Stock Photo*

PAGE FOUR

Sumptuous craft in *Dune*: Tony Masters' jade-floored throne room; a few of Bob Ringwood's 8,000+ costumes; and Carlo Rambaldi's Guild Navigator, which so blindsided customs officials. *Allstar Picture Library Ltd / Alamy Stock Photo*

Eschewing the likes of Sean Connery, Terry Gilliam's casting idea for *The Adventures of Baron Munchausen* was to pick 'a great actor who'd been forgotten': sixty-two-year-old John Neville. *Cinematic / Alamy Stock Photo*

PAGE FIVE

Chevy Chase and Demi Moore take a plunge into the booby-trapped Gothic funhouse that was *Nothing But Trouble*. Behind Moore's back, Chase griped that her costume was 'too revealing'. *Moviestore Collection Ltd / Alamy Stock Photo*

Geena Davis and Matthew Modine brave *Cutthroat Island*'s carriage chase – cue exploding cannonballs. 'He likes to blow things up,' Modine remarked of her husband, Renny Harlin. *Universal Images Group North America LLC / Alamy Stock Photo*

PAGE SIX

Same pig, new friends: the waifs and strays who look to him as the moral centre of *Babe: Pig in the City*. More than half the

120-strong canine cast came from dog shelters around Sydney. *Universal Images Group North America LLC / Alamy Stock Photo*

If it worked at Agincourt? *Alexander* (Colin Farrell) peps up his band of brothers before the battle of Gaugamela in 331 BC. The speech-writing, not by Shakespeare, visibly lets the side down. *AJ Pics / Alamy Stock Photo*

PAGE SEVEN

Prepare for *Catwoman*'s boss battle between black widow Laurel Hedare (Sharon Stone) and once-meek Patience Phillips (Halle Berry), who's seen into the wicked heart of Big Make-Up. *AJ Pics / Alamy Stock Photo*

Ben Kingsley's Time Safari CEO gives marching orders to peeved Edward Burns in *A Sound of Thunder*: a scene shot roughly three years before the film hobbled broken into cinemas. *Cinematic / Alamy Stock Photo*

PAGE EIGHT

'Genius' playwright Caden Cotard takes five in *Synedoche, New York* – letting Philip Seymour Hoffman catch his breath, too. It was a punishingly hot shoot under heavy latex in Bed-Stuy. *Album / Alamy Stock Photo*

Taylor Swift's one scene in *Cats* before she prudently scrammed. Belting out 'Macavity' as flirtatious cabaret puss Bombalurina, she got away with the only kind mentions in reviews. *Pictorial Press Ltd / Alamy Stock Photo*

INDEX

Film titles in **bold** are chapter topics. Page numbers followed by n indicate footnotes on the same page.

12 Monkeys, 107
The 13th Warrior, 187, 188
20th Century Fox, 20, 24, 60, 69–71, 82, 155, 157, 158, 221, 227, 271; *see also Doctor Dolittle*; *Speed 2: Cruise Control*
47 Ronin, 280
300, 253
3000 Miles to Graceland, 244

Academy Awards *see* Oscars and nominations
accents, dubious, 234, 235–6
Adams, Joey Lauren, 213
Adaptation, 261–2, 267n, 268, 269
The Adventures of Baron Munchausen, 107, 108–17, 231
The Adventures of Pluto Nash, 197–205
Affleck, Ben, 207, 210–11, 212–17
Aherne, Brian, 41
Akhtar, Adeel, 277
An Alan Smithee Film: Burn Hollywood Burn, 177
Alexander, 229–39
Alice Adams, 42
Alien series, 96, 179, 224
Allam, Roger, 256
Allosaurus, anachronistic and unthreatening, 243, 247–8
Aloha, 277
Ambler, Eric, 51
America's Sweethearts, 208–9
Amidou (Hamidou Benmessaoud), 84, 85, 91
Amsterdam, 297–8
Anderson, Paul W. S., 183
Anderson, Wes, 52
Andersson, Roy, 269
Andress, Ursula, 63
Andrews, Julie, 71, 72, 73, 78
Andrews, Naveen, 191
Anger, Kenneth, 7, 8, 297
animals, live: *Babe: Pig in the City*, 165–7, 168–9; *Doctor Dolittle*, 74–6, 78; *Heaven's Gate*, 75n; *Intolerance*, 10–11; *Land of the Pharaohs*, 62; *Queen Kelly*, 20–1; *Roar*, 156; *see also specific animals*
Annaud, Jean-Jacques, 109n
Annis, Francesca, 99
Anomalisa, 262
Anozie, Nonzo, 277
Ant-Man and the Wasp: Quantumania, 296
Apocalypse Now, 4, 89n
Argo, 217
Arnfield, Graeme, 286n
Arzner, Dorothy, 42
Atonement, 273, 274, 276
audience exits, 33, 37, 43, 54, 164, 181–2
Avatar, 253, 255, 277
Avatar: The Way of Water, 297–8
The Aviator, 43, 232
awards *see* Golden Globe Awards; Golden Raspberry Awards; Laurel Awards; Oscars and nominations; Palme d'Or awards
Aykroyd, Dan, 119–24, 125n, 126–30

Babe, 163, 164, 171
Babe: Pig in the City, 163–72, 173
babies, giant mutant, 120, 122, 124
baboon–lizards, 243, 248
Babylon, 297, 298
Bach, Steven, 93–4
Bacher, Hans, 285
Baclanova, Olga, 30
Bailey, Halle, 296
Ballard, Carroll, 146n
Ballistic: Ecks vs Sever, 244, 246
Balto, 285
Banderas, Antonio, 191, 237, 244n
bankruptcy: Carolco Pictures, 142, 147, 150; Dan O'Bannon, 96; Franchise Pictures, 246; Francis Ford Coppola, 182; Gloria Swanson, 24; Marvel, 251; MGM studios, 178n
Barker, Clive, 121
Barrymore, John, 42
Bartha, Justin, 212

Barton Fink, 132
Basic, 193
Basic Instinct, 143, 145
Bassett, Angela, 176, 178, 181, 220n
Batgirl (unfinished), 297
The Batman, 228
Batman and Robin, 221
Batman Begins, 272
Batman Forever, 136, 222
Batman Returns, 222
Batman trilogy (*Dark Knight* trilogy), 221, 227
Batman vs Superman (unmade), 221–2
batshit, actual, 120
Battlefield Earth, 197, 244, 246
Baxter, Anne, 52
beard, marcelled, 31
Beatty, Warren, 5, 197
Beauty and the Beast (2017), 296
Beetlejuice, 119, 124
Being John Malkovich, 261, 267n
Bellucci, Monica, 209n
Bergman, Ingrid, 41
Berman, Pandro S., 43, 44
Berry, Halle, 207, 219–21, 222, 224–7, 228
Besson, Luc, 280
Beverly Hills Cop, 105, 198, 199n, 211
Bewitched, 136
The BFG, 280
Bhowani Junction, 44
The Big Sleep, 61
A Bill of Divorcement, 42
Biondi, Frank, Jr, 169, 170
Bird, Brad, 280
Birds of Prey, 228
The Birth of a Nation, 7–8, 12, 13–14, 17
Bitzer, Billy, 11
Black, Shane, 152
blackface, 8, 28
Blade and *Blade II*, 221
Blade Runner, 97, 108, 201
Blades of Glory, 230
Blank, Les, 89n
Blankenbuehler, Andy, 286
Blattner, Gerry, 65
Blind Husbands, 18
Blood Simple, 134
Bloom, Harold Jack, 61, 62
Bloom, Orlando, 232

Blue Velvet, 106
The Blues Brothers, 121, 123n, 129
Bluhdorn, Charles, 86, 87
Bogdanovich, Peter, 53, 84
Boleslavsky, Richard, 23
The Bonfire of the Vanities, 125–6, 128–9
Booth, Elmer, 28
Borman, Moritz, 232
Bosch, Francisco, 236–7
Bound, 256
Bowie, David, 108
Box, John, 88
Bradbury, Ray, 241–2, 245
Brancato, John, 223
Brando, Marlon, 111
Brandt, Harry, 39–40
Bratt, Benjamin, 225
Bravo, Ricky, 88
Brazil, 107, 108, 109, 137
Bregman, Martin, 198, 199–200
Brest, Martin, 211–16, 217
Bricusse, Leslie, 74
Bringing Up Baby, 40
Brosnan, Pierce, 188, 220, 245, 266n
brothels, on screen, 19, 21, 22
Brown, Karl, 10–11
Browning, Tod, 27–37
Bruckheimer, Jerry, 232
Bullock, Sandra, 154, 155, 157, 158, 160, 162, 208n
Burden of Dreams, 89n
Burke, Kathy, 274
Burns, Edward, 245, 247
Burton, Richard, 60n, 70, 72
Burton, Tim, 124, 222
Burwell, Carter, 137
Bush, Dick, 88
butterfly effect, 241–2
'butthole cut,' 291
Byron, Walter, 19

Caan, James, 189
Cabiria, 9
Cage, Nicolas, 134, 267n
Callow, Simon, 52
Camelot, 72, 78
camels, 62
Cameron, James, 1, 4, 161, 253
Candy, John, 120, 123, 126, 129

Cannes Film Festival, 132, 138, 144
Capra, Frank, III, 204–5
Captain Marvel, 228
Carol, 277
Carolco Pictures, 142–50
Carradine, David, 96
Casino, 67
Castle Rock, 197–205
cats: covering modesty with, 20–1; lethargic, 21
Cats, 283–93, 295, 298
Catwoman, 219, 222–7, 228, 297
The Cell, 200
censorship: *The Birth of a Nation*, 8; *Freaks*, 34, 35–6; Hays Code, 27, 40, 46; Mae West, 40; *Tarzan and His Mate*, 40
Chain Reaction, 158
Chambers, Bill, 36
Champlin, Charles, 90
Chandler, Fred, 50
Chaney, Lon, 28, 29
Chaplin, Geraldine, 96
Chaplin, Sydney, 64, 65
Charlie's Angels, 223n
Chase, Chevy, 120, 123, 125, 126–7, 129, 130
Chasing Amy, 213
Chazelle, Damien, 297
The Chemical Brothers, 273
chimpanzees: cooking skills, 74; gum-chewing, 167
Chinatown Nights, 23
Chinese audiences, saving films, 152, 280n
Christopher Strong, 42
Chuba, Daniel, 177
Cimino, Michael, 4, 75n, 93n, 94
Citizen Kane, 51
Claremont, Nicolas, 245
Cleopatra, 67, 70–1
Cliffhanger, 143, 144, 148
Cloud Atlas, 256, 258
Clouzot, Henri-Georges, 83
cockfights, 75n
cockroaches, dancing, 286, 292
Coen, Joel and Ethan, 131–40
Collier, John, 41
Collins, Joan, 63–4, 67
Collins, Ray, 52
Columbia Pictures, 63n, 105, 112, 143, 209; see also *The Adventures of Baron Munchausen*

Comar, Jean-Christophe (Pitof), 223–4, 226, 228
comic-book fatigue, 296
condoms, innovative use of, 100
Coneheads, 129
Connery, Sean, 109n, 110–11, 186
Contact, 182
Coppola, Eleanor, 89n
Coppola, Francis Ford, 4, 84, 176, 182, 232
Corden, James, 286, 290
Cosmo, James, 167
Costello, Dolores, 52
Costner, Kevin, 4, 5, 141, 244
Cotten, Joseph, 52, 53, 56
The Cotton Club, 4
Covid-19 pandemic: delays due to, 5; impact on box office figures, 5, 258n, 295; prevents 'Jellicle Ball' singalong screening, 293
cows, disembowelled, 75n
Craven, Wes, 120n
Crawford, Joan, 40, 46
Cremer, Bruno, 84
crew walk-outs, 88, 148; see also directors quitting/being fired
Crichton, Michael, 187
Crimewave, 134
Cromwell, James, 163, 164–5, 169
cross-dressing and drag, 39, 40–1, 46, 47, 120, 126
Crowe, Cameron, 277
Cruise, Tom, 108, 135, 146, 159, 214, 232
Crusade (unfinished), 145
Cruz, Wilson, 184
Cukor, George, 39–44, 45, 47
The Curious Case of Benjamin Button, 262
Curry, Tim, 108
Cuthbert, Neil, 198
Cutthroat Island, 141–2, 145–52, 158

Daddy Day Care, 205
Dafoe, Willem, 153, 162
Daily, E. G., 166
Dalí, Salvador, 96
Damas, Bertila, 129
Damon, Matt, 277–8
Dances with Wolves, 5
Dangerous, 42
dangerous sets, 10–11, 32
The Danish Girl, 286n

Dargis, Manohla, 267n
Darin, Bobby, 76
Dark Knight trilogy, 221, 227
Darkest Hour, 274
Darkman, 134
Darling Lili, 73
Daveikis, John, 124
Daves, Delmer, 23
Davis, Bette, 42, 46
Davis, Geena, 142–3, 145, 146, 147, 148, 149–52
Davis, Sammy, Jr, 74, 76
Dawson, Rosario, 200, 203, 204, 229
The Day After Tomorrow, 249–50
DC Studios, 296, 297
de Bont, Jan, 153, 155–61, 162, 185
De Laurentiis, Dino, 93, 96–7, 99, 100–1, 103, 105, 233–4
De Laurentiis, Raffaella, 97, 103
De Niro, Robert, 67, 203
De Palma, Brian, 125
Dead Calm, 176, 179, 184
Deakins, Roger, 137
death of extra, 64; *see also* injuries, sickness and fatalities
Debney, John, 151
Deep Blue Sea, 152
Delon, Alain, 96
Demetriou, Jamie, 268
Demme, Jonathan, 237
Dench, Judi, 286, 289
Depp, Johnny, 151, 152, 252
Dequina, Michael, 216n
Derulo, Jason, 287, 292
DeSantis, Ron, 296
The Devil-Doll, 35
The Devils, 188n
Devis, Jimmy, 101
Di Novi, Denise, 222
Diaz, Cameron, 208n
DiCaprio, Leonardo, 160, 233, 234
Die Another Day, 220
Die Hard series, 134, 143, 155, 185, 187, 193
Diehl, Mrs Ambrose Nevin, 34–5
Dietrich, Marlene, 40, 46
'digital backlot' film-making, 253, 255, 279
Digital Underground, 122, 126n
directors quitting/being fired: *The Adventures of Baron Munchausen*, 112–13; and 'Alan

Smithee' pseudonym, 177; *Cutthroat Island*, 148; *Merry-Go-Round*, 18–19; *Queen Kelly*, 22–3; *A Sound of Thunder*, 245; *Speed Racer*, 252; *Supernova* (2000), 175, 176, 177, 178–9, 181; *Waterworld*, 141; *see also* crew walk-outs
disabilities and differences, portrayal on screen, 27–37, 166, 169
Disney, 5, 60n, 71, 78, 151, 276, 280, 281, 296; *see also* Marvel Cinematic Universe (MCU)
Doctor Dolittle, 72–8; *see also* Dr Dolittle
dogs: for coping with *Cats*, 284; rehoused, 165; on witness stand, 78; yelping at cats, 300
Donnelly, Thomas Dean, 245
The Doors, 143, 231
Douglas, Illeana, 204
Douglas, Michael, 145–6, 147, 149, 249n
Downey, Robert, Jr, 252
Dr Dolittle, 198; *see also Doctor Dolittle*
Dr Jekyll and Mr Hyde, 36
Dracula, 29
drag *see* cross-dressing and drag
Dragonslayer, 108
dream-derived plots, 155, 157
Dreamgirls, 205
Driven, 245
ducks, sinking, 75
Dune (1984), 94–5, 97–105
Dune (other aborted attempts), 95–7
Dune: Parts One and Two (2021, 2024), 104
Dunne, John Gregory, 72
Durning, Charles, 136
Dykstra, John, 103

Earles, Daisy, 30
Earles, Harry, 29
Ebert, Roger, 127–8, 166, 188, 213n, 228
Eck, Johnny, 32
Ekins, Bud, 86n
Elba, Idris, 172n, 286, 292
electric shocks, from lighting rigs, 32
Elektra, 227
elephants, white and otherwise, 7, 9, 11, 12
Elia, Nicholas, 254
Eliot, T. S., 284, 285
Elmes, Frederick, 102, 269

Emmerich, Roland, 249–50
Eno, Brian, 102
Eternal Sunshine of the Spotless Mind, 261,
    267, 268n
Event Horizon, 183
The Evil Dead, 134
Exodus: Gods and Kings, 277
The Exorcist, 83
explosions: *The Adventures of Baron
    Munchausen*, 114–15, 116; *Cutthroat
    Island*, 148, 149, 151, 152; *Dune*, 101;
    Ranulph Fiennes's heroics, 82; *Sorcerer*,
    85, 87
extras: paid in shoes, 100; problems with,
    59–60, 64–5
extravagant sets *see* sets and props,
    extravagant

The Fabelmans, 69
Facinelli, Peter, 176, 179, 180, 184
Faiman, Peter, 198
Fairbanks, Douglas, 12, 18, 210n
Fantastic Beasts series, 271
Fargo, 139–40
Farrell, Colin, 229, 234, 235–7
Fassbinder, Rainer Werner, 109
Fast & Furious franchise, 271, 295
Faulkner, William, 61–2, 63
Favreau, Jon, 252
fawn, eats paint, 76
FeardotCom, 177, 246
Fehr, Rudi, 65–6
Feldman, Charles, 65
Ferretti, Dante, 110
Ferris, Michael, 223
Fiennes, Ranulph, 75
film reel destruction (deliberate), 49
Finney, Albert, 132
Fire and Ice: The Dragon Chronicles, 228
fires on set, 103, 194
First World War, 14, 18
Firth, Colin, 175n, 286n
The Fisher King, 107
Fitzcarraldo, 89n
Fitzgerald, F. Scott, 30
Five Graves to Cairo, 25
Fleck, Freddie, 56
Fleischer, Richard, 73–5
floods, rescuing equipment from, 245

flops: criteria for, 3; Golden Raspberry
    Awards, 5, 125n, 215, 228; media
    prediction, 4
Foolish Wives, 18
Ford, Harrison, 82, 143, 198, 209n
Ford, Roger, 165, 166
Forster, Robert, 180
Foster, Norman, 51
Four Weddings and a Funeral, 139
Fox *see* 20th Century Fox
Fox, Robin Lane, 231, 234–5
Franchise Pictures, 244–6
Francis, Freddie, 100
Frankenstein, 29, 36
fraud, 12, 113, 246
Freaks, 27
French, Don, 112–13
Freundlich, Bart, 266
Friedkin, William, 81, 82–92
Fuchs, Jason, 275
Fuqua, Antoine, 209n
fur, digital, 287–91
Furiosa, 172

Gaeta, John, 252
Garbo, Greta, 40, 41, 46
Garland, Judy, 41
Garner, Jennifer, 227
Gaslight, 41
Gassner, Dennis, 135–6
gay icons, 46; *see also* homosexuality and
    bisexuality
gender fluidity, 41, 47, 151; *see also* cross-
    dressing and drag; homosexuality and
    bisexuality
gender pay gap, 143n, 145, 207–8
Get Carter (2000), 245
Ghost, 123, 129
Ghost in the Shell, 278
Ghostbusters, 121
Gibson, Mel, 172, 232–3
Giger, H. R., 96
Gigli, 207–8, 209–17
Giler, David, 179
Gilliam, Terry, 107, 108–17
giraffe, self-injury, 75, 77
Gish, Lillian, 9, 14–15
Gladiator, 232
goat, mutinous, 75

Godzilla, 136, 156
Goldberg, Adam, 166
Golden Globe Awards, 292
Golden Raspberry Awards, 5, 125n, 215, 228
Goodman, John, 254, 256
Gothika, 221
Goulding, Edmund, 22, 23, 24
Goyer, David S., 221
Grace, Leslie, 297
La Grande Illusion, 18
Grant, Cary, 40–1, 45–6
Gray, Carsen, 276
The Great Wall, 277–8
Greed, 18
Green, Walon, 84, 145
Griffith, D. W., 7–15, 17, 28
Griffith, Melanie, 125n

hair and wigs, comical, 230, 236, 248
Hanks, Tom, 125, 125n, 237
Hanna, 273
Happy Feet and *Happy Feet Two*, 172
Harlan, Russ, 64
Harlin, Renny, 142, 143, 145, 146–9, 151–2, 245
Harlow, Jean, 30
Harris, Mark, 72
Harris, Richard, 72
Harrison, Rex, 73, 75, 76, 77, 78
Harron, Bobby, 8
Hartnett, Josh, 209n
Hatari! 65
Hathaway, Anne, 286
The Haunting, 156, 162
Hawkins, Jack, 59, 63
Hawks, Howard, 59–62, 64–7
Haynes, Todd, 277
Hays Code, 27, 40, 46; *see also* censorship
Headly, Glenne, 167
The Heart of Humanity, 18
Hearts of Darkness: A Filmmaker's Apocalypse, 89n
Heaven's Gate, 4, 75n, 93–4
Heder, Jon, 230
Hedlund, Garrett, 275, 276
Hello, Dolly! 78–9
Hello, Sister! 24
Hellraiser, 121, 177, 184
Henabery, Joseph, 9–10

Hepburn, Katharine, 39–41, 42–4, 45, 46–7, 137
Hepburn, Katharine Martha Houghton, 45
Herbert, Frank, 94, 95, 96, 97–8, 104
Heyman, Paul, 192
Hill, Walter, 176, 181–2
Hiller, Arthur, 177
Hirsch, Emile, 254, 256
His Girl Friday, 137
The Hobbit series, 271
Hoffman, Dustin, 5, 212
Hoffman, Philip Seymour, 263, 266
Hogan, P. J., 209n, 272, 276
Holder, Geoffrey, 74
Holiday, 45
Hollywood Homicide, 209
Holt, Tim, 52
homosexuality and bisexuality: *Alexander*, 229–30, 236–8; Cary Grant, 46; Dorothy Arzner, 46; gay icons, 46; George Cukor, 41, 46; *Gigli*, 212–14, 215; Howard Hughes, 46; Joan Crawford, 46; Katharine Hepburn, 46; *A Nightmare on Elm Street 2: Freddy's Revenge*, 180–1; *Philadelphia*, 237; *Synecdoche, New York*, 263; Wilson Cruz, 184; *see also* gender fluidity
The Honeymoon, 19
Hook, 272–3
Hooper, Tom, 283–4, 285–93
Hopkins, Anthony, 239
Horn, Alan, 257
horror, advent of, 29, 36; *see also Freaks*
horses: battle scenes, 232, 234, 235; carriage chase, 151; causing explosion, 115; chariot racing, 10, 62; falling off, 234; injuries and fatalities, 75n
Horsley, David S., 32
Howard, Leslie, 44
Howard, Noël, 59–61, 62, 65, 66
Hud, 135n
Hudson, Jennifer, 286
Hudson Hawk, 5, 125n
The Hudsucker Proxy, 131–40
Hughes, Howard, 43
Hula-Hoop montage, 133, 137–8
Hunt, Helen, 157
Hunt, Linda, 102
The Hunt for Red October, 186
Hunter, Ian, 136

Huntingdon-Whiteley, Rosie, 164
Hurd-Wood, Rachel, 209n
hurricane, wrecks set, 160; *see also* winds, damage sets
Hyams, John, 249
Hyams, Leila, 30
Hyams, Peter, 243, 245–50

I Was a Male War Bride, 47
ice cubes: perking up nipples, 22n; thrown at Bill Paxton, 156
Idle, Eric, 111, 115, 116–17, 177
In the Mix, 205
incomprehensibility: *Intolerance*, 13–14; *Rollerball* (2002), 188–9, 191–3; *Supernova* (2000), 179, 183–4
injuries, sickness and fatalities: cast and crew, 32, 88, 101, 148–9, 156–7 160, 234; horses, 75n
Intermedia, 232
Intolerance, 7, 8–15, 17, 19, 28
Iron Man, 251–2
Ishtar, 5, 112, 114n
It's All True (unfinished), 50, 53, 56
Ivano, Paul, 21

Jack the Giant Slayer, 280
Jackie Brown, 214
Jackman, Hugh, 220, 274, 275, 276, 278
Jackson, Peter, 232, 271, 280
Jackson, Samuel L., 193
Jacobs, Arthur P., 73, 74, 76–7, 95
Jagger, Mick, 96
Jaglom, Henry, 55
James Bond films, 178, 220–1
Jarrott, Charles, 95
Jaws, 81, 82, 161
Jersey Girl, 217
Jodorowsky, Alejandro, 95–6
Jodorowsky, Brontis, 96
Johansson, Scarlett, 278
John Carter, 280
Johnson, Duke, 262n
Jolie, Angelina, 191, 208n, 221, 229–30, 236
Jones, Freddie, 101
Jonze, Spike, 264–5
Journey into Fear, 51
Jovovich, Milla, 221

Judd, Cris, 210
The Jungle Book, 78
Jupiter Ascending, 258, 272
Jurassic Park, 186, 247
Justine, 44

Kahane, B. B., 43
Kamen, Michael, 185
Kassar, Mario, 143–5, 147–8, 149–50
Kaufman, Charlie, 261–70
Kazan, Lainie, 214
Keener, Catherine, 262, 263
Kennedy, Joseph P., 20, 22–3
Kidman, Nicole, 136, 176n, 222, 233
Kier, Udo, 96
Kilmer, Val, 229, 231
King Arthur: Legend of the Sword, 280
King-Smith, Dick, 164
The King's Speech, 286
Kingsley, Ben, 248–9
Kinski, Klaus, 89n
Klein, Chris, 189, 191, 192–3
Knowles, Harry, 190–1, 195
Koerner, Charles, 56
Kondell, Kate, 222
Korda, David, 113
Kravitz, Zoë, 227–8
Kristofferson, Kris, 86, 94
Kroeger, Wolf, 148
Kroll, Jack, 90
Krull, 105, 108
Kurnitz, Harry, 61, 62

Labyrinth, 108
Ladyhawke, 108
Laemmle, Carl, 18
Lamb, Irene, 113
Lambert, Gavin, 43
Lamprell, Mark, 164
Land of the Pharaohs, 59–67
Langella, Frank, 151
Langley, Donna, 283
Lara Croft: Tomb Raider series, 162, 221
Last Action Hero, 186, 194–5
Laurel Awards, 269–70
Lean, David, 95, 275–6
'Lee, Thomas' (pseudonym), 176
Legend, 108
The Lego Batman Movie, 227–8

Leigh, Jennifer Jason, 133, 135, 137, 262n, 263
Lemmons, Kasi, 266
Leonard, Franklin, 275n
Lerner, Alan Jay, 73, 74
Lerner, Michael, 132n
lesbian 'conversions,' 209n
Leto, Jared, 229, 236
Levin, Bob, 191
Levy, Peter, 148
lice, in costumes, 100
The Life of David Gale, 188n
lift, escape from, 267
The Lion King (2019), 296
lion, scalps cinematographer, 156
Litt, Paulie, 256
The Little Mermaid (2023), 296
Little Women, 41, 42
Liu, Lucy, 244n
LL Cool J, 189, 192–3
Lloyd Webber, Andrew, 283–5, 292
Loewe, Frederick, 73
London, Daniel, 264
The Lone Ranger, 280
The Long Kiss Goodnight, 151–2
Long, Walter, 8
Loos, Anita, 13
Lopez, Jennifer, 200, 207–8, 210–17
Lopez, Kristen, 36
Lord of the Rings trilogy, 232
Lorenz, Edward, 242
Lowery, David, 281
Loy, Myrna, 30
Lubezki, Emmanuel, 211
Lucas, George, 81–2, 84, 94, 97, 253
Lugosi, Bela, 29
Luhrmann, Baz, 233–4
Lynch, David, 94–5, 97–106, 167

McCarthy, Todd, 64, 133n, 138, 279
McCormack, Catherine, 247, 248
McCormick, Randall, 158
McCrae, Yves, 290–1
McDormand, Frances, 134
McGill, Everett, 99
McGovern, Tim, 246
McKee, Robert, 269
McKellen, Ian, 286
Mackenzie, Compton, 42

McKeown, Charles, 109, 110
MacLachlan, Kyle, 98–9, 104, 105–6
McLaglen, Victor, 28
McMillan, Kenneth, 101
Macqueen, Harry, 175n
McQueen, Steve, 85–6
McShane, Ian, 274
McTiernan, John, 185–95, 200
Mad Max series, 31, 88, 164, 172–3
Madsen, Virginia, 104
The Magnificent Ambersons, 49–57
make-up artists, lazy/careless, 111–12
Malahide, Patrick, 151
Malone, William, 177
Mancuso, Frank, 178, 182
Mankiewicz, Joseph L., 46, 71
Mara, Rooney, 276–7
Mars Needs Moms, 280
Marsh, Jean, 108
Marsh, Mae, 8
Marshall, Tully, 21
Marshall, Vanessa, 184
Marvel Cinematic Universe (MCU), 221, 228, 247, 251–2, 258, 271, 296; *see also* *Spider-Man* series
The Marvels, 296
Mary of Scotland, 45
Mary Poppins, 71
Masters, Tony, 99, 102
The Matrix trilogy, 252, 256, 258
May, Elaine, 5
Mayer, Louis B., 33
Medicine Man, 186
Meet Dave, 205
Meet Joe Black, 170, 211
merchandising and tie-ins: *Doctor Dolittle*, 77; *Dune*, 105; *A Sound of Thunder*, 246–7; *Speed Racer*, 257; *Star Wars*, 82
Merilees, Philip, 242
Merry-Go-Round, 19
The Merry Widow, 19
Meyers, Jonathan Rhys, 234
MGM Studios, 20, 28–9, 35, 44, 70, 93, 142, 178–9, 188; *see also* *Cutthroat Island*; *Freaks*; *Rollerball* (2002); *Supernova* (2000)
mice: excessive breeding, 165; played by children, 286
Midnight Express, 231
Milchan, Arnon, 109

Miller, George, 163–73, 297–8
Miller, Levi, 274, 276
Miller's Crossing, 132
Miracles for Sale, 35
Les Misérables, 285–6
Miss Congeniality 2: Armed and Fabulous, 155
Mission: Impossible series, 295
Mitchum, Robert, 86
Modine, Matthew, 146–7, 149, 150–1
Moffitt, John C., 34
Mohr, Jay, 204
Mona Lisa Smile, 209
Monster's Ball, 219–20, 228
Moore, Demi, 120, 123, 127, 130, 223n
Moore, Dennie, 41
Moorehead, Agnes, 52, 53, 56
Morning Glory, 42
Morris, Judy, 164
Mortal Engines, 280
Morton, Samantha, 264, 265, 266
Moss, Jack, 55
Murch, Walter, 50, 108
Murphy, Eddie, 105, 197, 198–9, 202, 203–4, 205
Murray, Bill, 130
musicals, 71–2, 73, 78–9, 292; *see also Cats*; *Doctor Dolittle*
My Fair Lady, 71, 73

Nadoolman, Deborah, 123
Naha, Ed, 98, 99, 101
The Name of the Rose, 109–10
Nathanson, Michael, 194
Nazism, 24–5
Neill, Sam, 183
Nemec, Joseph, 157
The NeverEnding Story, 108
Neville, John, 111
Newley, Anthony, 74, 76
Newman, Lionel, 78
Newman, Paul, 133, 135
Nichols, David, 148
Nicholson, Ivy, 63
night-vision effect, inexplicable, 192
A Nightmare on Elm Street 2: Freddy's Revenge, 180–1
Nina, 277
Nolan, Barry, 103
Nolan, Christopher, 193, 221, 227, 295

Noonan, Chris, 163, 164
Noonan, Tom, 262n, 264
Norbit, 205
Norman, Mark, 147
Nothing But Trouble, 119–24, 126–30
Noyce, Phillip, 176n
nudity: *The Adventures of Baron Munchausen*, 116; *Alexander*, 237; *Queen Kelly*, 20–1; *Rollerball* (2002), 191; *Supernova* (2000), 176, 183–4; *Swordfish*, 220; *Tarzan and His Mate*, 40; *see also* sex scenes

O'Bannon, Dan, 96
Offner, Mortimer, 41
One from the Heart, 4
Oppenheimer, Joshua, 245
orangutan, doleful, 167–8
origin stories, menace of, 272
Original Sin, 191
Oscars and nominations: *The Accidental Tourist*, 142; *Argo*, 217; *Babe*, 164; *Barton Fink*, 132; *Being John Malkovich*, 261; Best Actor, 28, 73, 211, 286n; Best Actress, 19, 24, 42, 219, 220, 220n, 228; Best Adapted Screenplay, 231; Best Art Direction, 132n; Best Costume Design, 132n; Best Director, 164, 286; Best Original Screenplay, 51, 61, 84n, 261, 268n; Best Original Song, 78; Best Picture, 29, 69, 77, 193, 217, 232, 286; Best Special Effects and Special Technical Achievement, 103; Best Supporting Actor, 132n, 164, 205; Best Supporting Actress, 277, 286, 286n; Best Visual Effects, 77, 164, 247; *Carol*, 277; *Citizen Kane*, 51; *Dances with Wolves*, 5; *The Danish Girl*, 286n; *Doctor Dolittle*, 77–8; *Dreamgirls*, 205; *The Elephant Man*, 97; *Eternal Sunshine of the Spotless Mind*, 268n; *The Fabelmans*, 69; *Gladiator*, 232; *Jurassic Park*, 247; *The King's Speech*, 286; *Les Misérables*, 286; *The Magnificent Ambersons*, 69; *Mary Poppins*, 71; *Midnight Express*, 231; *Monster's Ball*, 219, 220, 228; *My Fair Lady*, 71, 73; *Oppenheimer*, 193; *Scent of a Woman*, 211; *Shakespeare in Love*, 147; *The Sound of Music*, 71; *Star Wars*, 103; *West Side Story*, 69
The Other Side of Midnight, 82
Owen, Seena, 11, 19

Pacific Rim, 280n
Pacino, Al, 211, 212, 214
Palme d'Or awards, 132
Paltrow, Gwyneth, 226
Pan, 272, 273–7, 278–9, 280–1
Paramount Pictures, 19, 23, 45, 50, 63, 129, 161, 162, 171, 183, 276, 287, 297–8; *see also Sorcerer*
Parker, Alan, 188n
parrot, unhelpful, 76
Parsons, Louella, 34
Pascal, Amy, 265
Pastrone, Giovanni, 9
Paterson, Bill, 112, 113
Patric, Jason, 154, 159, 160, 162
Patriot Games, 187
Pattinson, Robert, 228
Patton, 79
Paxton, Bill, 156
Peary, Danny, 27
Pecorini, Nicola, 148
Pellicano, Anthony, 193–4
The People Under the Stairs, 120n
Perry, Matthew, 244
Pescucci, Gabriella, 110
Peter Pan, 209, 272, 276
Peter Pan & Wendy, 281
Petersen, Wolfgang, 232
Petri, Alexandra, 283
Pfeiffer, Michelle, 222
The Phantom of the Opera, 202, 284
Philadelphia, 237
The Philadelphia Story, 45
Phillips, Siân, 101
Picking, David, 113–14
Pink Floyd, 96
Pirates of the Caribbean series, 151, 152, 274
Pitof (Jean-Christophe Comar), 223–4, 226, 228
Pitt, Brad, 170, 211, 236, 297
Pixar, 171, 295
Plainview, Daniel, 275
Pockross, Adam, 90n
Poitier, Sidney, 74
Polley, Sarah, 111, 114–15, 116, 117
Polygram, 135, 139
Portman, Natalie, 255
portmanteau couple names, 210
Predator, 134, 185, 193

Price, Frank, 105
Pride & Prejudice, 273
Prince Charles Cinema, 293
private detective, 193–4
prosthetics, problematic, 180, 266
Puttnam, David, 113, 114n
Pye, Merrill, 33

Quaid, Randy, 202–3
Quality Street, 45
Queen Kelly, 19–24, 25

Rabal, Francisco 'Paco,' 84, 91
racism: *The Birth of a Nation*, 7–8; between crew in *The Adventures of Baron Munchausen*, 111; *Monster's Ball*, 220n; *see also* blackface
Raimi, Sam, 134, 137–8
Rain Man, 212, 214
Raise the Titanic, 161
Raising Arizona, 132, 134
Rambaldi, Carlo, 102
Randian, Prince, 32
Raspe, Rudolf Erich, 109
Redgrave, Vanessa, 72
Reed, Oliver, 110n, 115, 116, 149
Reeves, Keanu, 155, 157, 158, 159, 252, 280
Refn, Nicolas Winding, 84
René, Jacynthe, 203
Renoir, Jean, 18
Resident Evil, 221
Return of the Jedi, 97
Return to Oz, 108, 163
Revolution Studios, 208–9
Reynolds, Kevin, 141
Ricci, Christina, 256
Rickman, Alan, 187
rider, vegetable juice on, 148
Ringwood, Bob, 100, 102
Rio Bravo, 66
R.I.P.D., 280
Ritchie, Guy, 280
RKO Pictures, 42, 45, 51, 56, 69; *see also The Magnificent Ambersons*; *Sylvia Scarlett*
'roadshow' screenings, 70, 77, 79
Roar, 156
Robbie, Margot, 297
Robbins, Tim, 133, 135, 137, 146
Robbins, Tod, 28

The Robe, 60
Roberts, Julia, 208, 208n, 209
Roberts, Rachel, 76
Robin Hood: Prince of Thieves, 129, 141n
Robinov, Jeff, 237, 257
robots, randy, 202–3, 204
Roderick, Olga, 31
Rogers, John, 222–3
Rollerball (1975), 188, 189
Rollerball (2002), 185, 188–93, 194–5
Rollins, Henry, 252
Romeo and Juliet, 44
Romijn-Stamos, Rebecca, 191
Ronan, Saoirse, 273, 276
The Room, 293
Rooney, Mickey, 167, 168, 169
Ross, Stanley Ralph, 165
Rossitto, Angelo, 31
Roth, Joe, 208–9, 216
Rotten Tomatoes, zero per cent score, 244n
Rotundo, Giuseppe 'Peppino,' 110
Roven, Charles, 193–5
The Royal Tenenbaums, 52
Russell, David O., 297–8
Russell, Ken, 188n
Russell, Kurt, 244
Russell, Rosalind, 137
Russo, Rene, 188
Ryan, Jack, 187

Safran, Peter, 297
Sagovsky, Vladimir, 65
Salamon, Julie, 125
Salander, Lisbeth, 278
Saldaña, Zoë, 277
Salven, Dave, 88
Samaha, Elie, 243–6
Sammon, Paul M., 104
sand issues, 98–9
Sandell, William, 124
Sanford, Erskine, 52
Sara, Mia, 108n
Sarandon, Susan, 82n, 254
Scent of a Woman, 211
Schaefer, George, 51, 54–5, 56
Schaffner, Franklin J., 79
Schechter, Sarah, 275
Scheider, Roy, 83, 84
Schickel, Richard, 9, 12

Schühly, Thomas, 109–11, 112–13, 231–2
Schumacher, Joel, 221, 284
Schwarzenegger, Arnold, 144, 145, 186, 231
Scorsese, Martin, 43, 67, 84, 232
Scott, Ridley, 96–7, 108, 232, 277
seal, hat-wearing, 78
Second World War, 49, 53, 54, 56; *see also*
    Nazism
sets and props, extravagant: *The Adventures of
    Baron Munchausen*, 110; *Cutthroat Island*,
    148; *Dune*, 98–9, 102, 103; *The Hudsucker
    Proxy*, 135–6; *Intolerance*, 7, 9–12, 15;
    Land of the Pharaohs, 59, 65, 67; *Nothing
    But Trouble*, 120–1, 124, 126; *Sorcerer*,
    88–90; *Speed 2: Cruise Control*, 157, 160;
    Twister, 156; *The Wedding March*, 19
sets, 'cannibalised,' 136
sets, dangerous, 10–11, 32
sets, prematurely destroyed, 160, 165
sets, wind-damaged, 10, 160
sex-mad robots, 202–3, 204
sex scenes: *Alexander*, 236–7; *Event Horizon*,
    183; *Gigli*, 213–14; lesbian 'conversions,'
    213; *Monster's Ball*, 220n; orgies, 18, 183;
    Queen Kelly, 20; recycling and changing
    skin tone, 176; *Rollerball* (2002), 191;
    Supernova (2000), 175–6, 183–4; *The
    Wedding March*, 19; *see also* brothels, on
    screen
sexual assault on screen, 8
sexual harassment and assault, by cast/crew,
    18, 115–16, 149, 190
sexual references: *The Adventures of Pluto
    Nash*, 202–3, 204; *Freaks*, 37; *Gigli*, 212,
    214; *Nothing But Trouble*, 127; *Queen
    Kelly*, 19; *Supernova* (2000), 179; *Walking
    Down Broadway/Hello, Sister!* 24
Shankman, Adam, 200
Shearer, Norma, 44
sheep, urinating, 75
Sheldon, Willard, 32
Shelton, Ron, 209n
Sholder, Jack, 180–2
Showtime, 203
Sidney Kimmel Entertainment, 266
Silver, Casey, 169, 170
Silver, Joel, 134–5, 187, 252, 257
The Silver Chalice, 135
Silvestri, Alan, 185

Sin City, 253
Singer, Bryan, 220, 280
Singh, Tarsem, 200
Siskel, Gene, 172n
Skal, David, 32–3
skin tone darkening, 176, 277
Skiptrace, 152
Skouras, Spyros, 71
Sky Captain and the World of Tomorrow, 253
Sleepers, 159
Smith, Bud S., 83
Smith, Kevin, 213, 217
'Smithee, Alan' (pseudonym), 177
smuggling, 64
snail, giant model, 76, 77
So Ends Our Night, 25
Some Like It Hot, 47
Sonic the Hedgehog, 287
Sony, 156, 186, 191, 221, 222, 296; *see also*
    Gigli; *Synecdoche, New York*
Sorcerer, 81, 82–92
The Sound of Music, 71
A Sound of Thunder, 242–3, 245–50
Spacey, Kevin, 188n
Spader, James, 176, 178, 180, 181
Species and *Species II*, 178
Speed, 154, 155
Speed 2: Cruise Control, 153–5, 156,
    157–61, 162
Speed Racer, 251, 252–9
Sphere, 161
Spider-Man series, 136, 209, 221, 222, 227,
    258–9
Spielberg, Steven, 81, 84, 141, 161, 233–4,
    272–3, 280, 285
Splet, Alan, 102
squirrel, intoxicated, 75–6
Stage Door, 40, 44
Stallone, Sylvester, 143, 199, 245
Star! 73, 78, 79
A Star is Born, 41
Star Wars, 81–2, 83, 91, 94, 103, 105, 144
Star Wars prequels, 253
Steadman, Alison, 113
Steel, Dawn, 114, 193
Stein, Mary, 166
Stephens, John M., 88
Stevens, George, 42
Stewart, Patrick, 99

Sting, 99, 102
Stone, Emma, 277
Stone, Oliver, 143, 229–32, 233–9
Stone, Sharon, 67, 143, 223, 226–7
Stoppard, Tom, 285
streaming, straight to, 5, 258n, 281
Streisand, Barbra, 39, 46, 79
Stroheim, Erich von, 17–23, 24–5
stunts: *Cutthroat Island*, 149; *Dune*, 101;
    Intolerance, 11; *Sorcerer*, 88–90; *Speed*, 156;
    Speed 2: Cruise Control, 160; *Twister*, 157;
    see also explosions
Sunset Boulevard, 25
Supernova (2000), 172, 175–84
Supernova (2020), 175n
Swanson, Gloria, 19–24, 25, 96
Swift, Taylor, 292
Swordfish, 220
Sylvia Scarlett, 39, 40–4, 45–7
Synecdoche, New York, 261, 262–70
Szubanski, Magda, 166

talkies, advent of, 20, 24; 'synthetic sound,'
    23
Tally, Ted, 233
Tarantino, Quentin, 214
Tarkington, Booth, 42, 52, 53, 55, 56
Tarzan and His Mate, 40
Tatopoulos, Patrick, 183
Taylor, Elizabeth, 67, 70–1
Taylor, Russi, 166
Tears of the Sun, 209
Temple, Julien, 252
temporal anomalies, 160–1
Terminator series, 144, 186, 223, 232, 280n
Thalberg, Irving, 18–19, 23, 29
Thewlis, David, 262n
The Thomas Crown Affair (1999), 187–8
Thompson, Anne, 257
Thornton, Billy Bob, 220n
Thoroughly Modern Millie, 73
Three Thousand Years of Longing, 172, 297–8
Thurman, Uma, 115–16, 125
Time Bandits, 107
Titanic, 1, 4, 161
titles, off-putting, 207, 262, 268
To Have and Have Not, 61
Toll, John, 146n
Tomorrowland, 280

Too Much Johnson, 50
Toro, Guillermo del, 280n
Total Recall, 124n, 143, 201
Toto, 102
Touch of Evil, 50
Town and Country, 197
Tracy, Spencer, 45, 46
Trailer Voice Man, 180
trailers: cut scenes, 179; omission of
    lesbianism, 212; portentous, 83; ridiculous,
    179–80, 183, 224, 285, 286–7; spoilers,
    161, 180
Trauner, Alexandre, 61
Travolta, John, 193, 197, 244, 246
The Trespasser, 24
Troy, 232, 236
True-Frost, Jim, 133
Trump, Donald, 241n
Trust The Man, 266
Tucci, Stanley, 175n
Tunney, Robin, 175–6, 179, 180, 183–4
'turkey time' scene, 213–14
'twin film' phenomenon, 233n
Twister, 155, 156

UB40, 154, 161
uncanny valley, 287, 289
Underwood, Ron, 198–200, 205
Unger, Gladys, 41
The Unholy Three, 28–9
United Artists (UA), 19, 93, 182; *see also*
    Queen Kelly; *Supernova* (2000)
Universal Pictures, 3, 18–19, 29, 50, 73, 86,
    91, 107, 186, 271; *see also Babe: Pig in the
    City*; *Cats*; *Dune* (1984); *Sorcerer*
Universal Soldier franchise, 249
Usher, 205

Vajna, Andrew G., 144
Valerian and the City of a Thousand Planets,
    280
Verbinski, Gore, 280
Verhoeven, Paul, 143, 145
Victor, Henry, 33
Vidocq, 224
Vikander, Alicia, 286n
Village Roadshow, 258n
Villechaize, Hervé, 96
Villeneuve, Denis, 104

visual effects: 'digital backlot,' 253, 255, 279;
    headache-inducing, 254–5; laughable, 156,
    243, 246–8, 249, 287; poor treatment
    and scapegoating of teams, 288–9, 290–1;
    rushed, 288–91
volcano, trumps Steve McQueen, 85–6

Wachowskis, the (Lana and Lilly), 252–9,
    272
Walken, Christopher, 215
Walking Down Broadway, 24
Walsh, George, 11
Wanger, Walter, 67
Wapanatâhk, Alyssa, 281
wardrobe issues: fat suits, 266; lice, 100;
    overheating, 101; overly tight, 225;
    problem prosthetics, 180, 266
Warner Bros, 20, 71, 72, 159, 172, 182, 198,
    221–2, 244–5, 271–2, 291n, 297; *see also
    The Adventures of Pluto Nash*; *Alexander*;
    Catwoman; *The Hudsucker Proxy*; *Land of
    the Pharaohs*; *Nothing But Trouble*; *Pan*; *A
    Sound of Thunder*; *Speed Racer*
Warner, Jack, 59, 60, 65, 71n, 73
Wasserman, Lew, 86
Waters, Daniel, 222
Waterworld, 3, 141, 152
The Wedding March, 19
The Wedding Planner, 200
Weigert, Robin, 268
Weiss, Robert K., 121
Welles, Orson, 49–57, 69, 96
West, Mae, 40, 46
West Side Story, 69
Whale, James, 29
Whitener, Zane, 127n
whitewashing, 276–7
The Whole Nine Yards, 244
Wiest, Dianne, 264, 268–9
Wilder, Billy, 25
Williams, Andy, 76
Williams, Michelle, 264
Williams, Robin, 111
Willis, Bruce, 5, 125, 125n, 185–6, 209,
    244
Willow, 108
Wilson, David C., 179
Wilson, Lambert, 223
Wilson, Rebel, 286, 290

Wind, 146
winds, damage sets, 10, 160
windscreen, smashed by director, 113
wiretapping, 193–4
Wise, Robert, 53–4, 55, 71, 79
Wiseau, Tommy, 293
Wolf Creek, 188n
Wolfe, Tom, 125, 125n
The Woman in the Window, 5
A Woman Rebels, 45
The Women, 41
Wonder Woman, 228
Wong, Anna May, 276
Wood, Oliver, 148
World Wars *see* First World War; Second
    World War
Wrangell, Basil, 32
Wright, Frank Lloyd, 134n

Wright, Geoffrey, 178–9
Wright, Joe, 5, 273–7, 278–81
Wright, Steven, 167
Wryn, Molly, 104

X-Men series, 220, 221, 271

Yentl, 39, 46
Yost, Graham, 157
Young, Sean, 103
Yule, Andrew, 115–16

Zanuck, Darryl F., 72, 79
Zemeckis, Robert, 182
zero-gravity filming, 179
zero percent on Rotten Tomatoes, 244n
zero stars review, 292
Zhang Yimou, 277–8